אמת ואמונה

EMET VE'EMUNAH

STUDIES IN
CONSERVATIVE JEWISH THOUGHT

VOLUME II

UNDERSTANDING CONSERVATIVE
JUDAISM

BOOKS BY ROBERT GORDIS

The Biblical Text in the Making

The Wisdom of Ecclesiastes

Koheleth: The Man and His World

The Song of Songs and Lamentations

The Book of God and Man
A Study of Job

Poets, Prophets and Sages
Essays in Biblical Interpretation

The Book of Esther

The Word and the Book
Studies in Biblical Language and Literature

The Book of Job
Commentary, New Translation and Special Studies

The Jew Faces a New World

Conservative Judaism

Judaism for the Modern Age

The Root and the Branch
Judaism and the Free Society

Judaism in a Christian World

Leave a Little to God

Sex and the Family in Jewish Tradition

A Faith for Moderns

Love & Sex
A Modern Jewish Perspective

EDITED BY ROBERT GORDIS

Max L. Margolis
Scholar and Teacher

Jewish Life in America
(with Theodore Friedman)

Faith and Reason
(with Ruth Waxman)

Art in Judaism
(with Moshe Davidowitz)

UNDERSTANDING CONSERVATIVE JUDAISM

By ROBERT GORDIS

Edited by MAX GELB

THE RABBINICAL ASSEMBLY   New York 1978

Library of Congress Cataloging in Publication Data

Gordis, Robert,
    Understanding Conservative Judaism.

    (Emet ve'emunah—Studies in Conservative Jewish
thought ; v. 2)
    Bibliography: p.
    Includes indexes.
    1. Conservative Judaism—Addresses, essays, lectures.
2. Judaism—United States—Addresses, essays, lectures.
I. Gelb, Max. II. Title. III. Series: Studies in
Conservative Jewish thought ; v. 2.
BM197.5.G62   296.8'342   78-22010
ISBN 0-87068-680-1

Manufactured in the United States of America

CONTENTS

To our grandchildren

DEBORAH JOY

DANIEL HAYYIM

JOSHUA HAYYIM

ELIE

JONATHAN DAVID

LISA MICHELLE

ELANA BETH

In love and hope

בני בנים הרי הם כבנים

PREFACE

In the two final decades of the twentieth century, it has become clear that the single most important phenomenon in the history of American Judaism has been the emergence, growth, and persistence of Conservative Judaism.

This is not to gainsay the importance of such major developments as the influence of Zionism on American Jewry and the continuing and growing impact on Jewish consciousness of the two major events in world Jewish history during our time. The first is the Holocaust, the full impact of which is only now beginning to be experienced and evaluated by large numbers of American Jews both young and old, though still a minority. The second is the birth and progress of the State of Israel, which has had a vivifying effect on all aspects of American Jewish life. For a small but significant group, the State of Israel presents an option that did not exist in the past. *Aliyah* offers the possibility of participating in a full and "natural" Jewish life-style, however that be understood, in an all-Jewish environment. For the vast majority of American Jewry, physical contact with the Land of Israel is limited to short visits or longer periods of sojourn, or, particularly in the case of youth, a year or more of extended study in the Jewish homeland. Yet even for those whose relationship to Israel appears minimal, the existence of the state has powerfully stimulated their Jewish consciousness and imbued them with a new pride and solidarity. One observer, at least, has, with pardonable exaggeration, described loyalty to the State of Israel as "the religion of the American Jew."

Latterly, American society as a whole has witnessed an upsurge of evangelical Christianity, the strength, persistence, and content of which are still not easy to evaluate. The Jewish counterpart of this development has been the emergence of fundamentalist Judaism, expressed in a wide spectrum of Orthodox groups manifesting an ever-increasing sense of self-confidence and militancy in opposing all other interpretations of Judaism. In part, this trend has gained strength from the immigration to these shores of the survivors of the Nazi Holocaust, a substantial core of whom were among the most perfervid and passionate defenders of right-wing traditionalism. Contemporary Orthodoxy has displayed an outstanding capacity for utilizing the American techniques of public relations, publicity, and political pressure, in addition to fund-raising and organizational skills. As a result, sociologists who, a few decades ago, explained the progress of Conservative Judaism as representing a transitory phase in the upward mobility of American Jewry on the road to total assimilation, now prophesy the imminent demise of Conservative Judaism before the trimphant march of Orthodoxy. One is reminded that at the beginning of the century, Reform Judaism seemed so firmly established that one writer could, in all honesty, entitle a book describing the movement simply "American Judaism."

Nevertheless, throughout these kaleidoscopic changes and developments, Conservative Judaism has remained a major and constant factor on the Jewish horizon. All objective studies of American Jewry, whether they be surveys of the religious preference of Jewish servicemen in the American armed forces or more sophisticated polls by opinion-gathering agencies, demonstrate that Conservative Judaism continues to command the loyalty of the largest number of Americans who accept Judaism as their religion.

Meanwhile, ideological opponents of Conservative Judaism are often able to perform the extraordinary feat of simultaneously attacking the movement and pretending it does not exist. In addition, they often quietly appropriate some of its insights and practices. Thus, it is a common phenomenon, when a roundup of Jewish opinion on a given issue is solicited by the general press, that spokesmen from the movements on the left and on the right will be cited, while the existence of Conservative Judaism is all but ignored. This situation is facilitated by the fact that, from its inception, the Conservative movement sought to avoid creating a new alignment within Judaism. Indeed, some of its spokesmen still believe it best to avoid defining its content or demarcating its limits.

It is undeniable that the movement continues to be confronted by major problems. Perhaps a measure of comfort may be extracted from the fact that this characterizes every living organism. For nearly a decade I have been serving as editor of the journal *Judaism,* published by the American Jewish Congress and the World Jewish Congress, an independent, nonpartisan quarterly dedicated to all aspects of Jewish religion, philosophy, and ethics and their relevance to contemporary life. Since the Jewish Theological Seminary was founded in 1887, the Summer 1977 issue of the journal was dedicated to a broad-based symposium, "Conservative Judaism On Its Ninetieth Birthday." Eighteen writers representing all wings of Judaism—Orthodoxy, Conservatism, Reform, and Reconstructionism—evaluated frankly the plusses and minuses of the movement. The leaders and thinkers affiliated with Conservative Judaism were outspoken in dealing with the "unfinished businesss" of the movement.

Basically there are two principal items on the agenda of Conservative Judaism, distinct but interrelated. The first is the necessity for crystallizing and articulating a philosophy of Jewish faith and practice for the movement. The philosophy must allow for the diversity that has always characterized it and which, indeed, is a hallmark of the Jewish tradition during the most creative and significant phases of its history in the past. The second is the building of a committed laity, who will conscientiously strive to embody in their own personal lives the ideals, insights, and practices to which the movement is dedicated and which they have accepted as normative for themselves.

The present work, as indicated below, represents many years of activity in this area, and is a modest effort to contribute to the vitality of Conservative Judaism, which, I profoundly believe, will help determine the character and destiny of Judaism as a whole in the years ahead.

The first section of the book, "By Way of Introduction: A Sheaf of Letters," contains four brief letters that appeared recently in the Jewish periodical press within a short time of each other. Each offers a brief explication of a fundamental aspect of Conservative Judaism: the true meaning of traditional Judaism, the role of history, the issue of the ordination of women, and the Jewish prayer book.

The second section, "Foundations of Conservative Judaism," deals with some basic theological concepts. These include the survival of Judaism in the modern world, the basic characteristics of the Jewish tradition, the growth and development of Halakhah, the meaning of revelation, and a rationale for the observance of Jewish ritual practices.

The third section, "Aspects of Contemporary Jewish Life," treats of the relationship of Israel and the Diaspora, the place of Conservative Judaism in the State of Israel, the need for a Conservative alignment in the Zionist movement, the principles underlying the prayer book in Conservative Judaism, the philosophy of the Conservative day school, and the role of the rabbinate, past, present, and future.

The fourth section, "A Vital Judaism for Our Day," pleads for a recognition that the amateur spirit has been the secret of Jewish vitality through the ages, and urges a rebirth of love for Judaism among young and old as indispensable to its vitality. It closes with a brief statement of the fundamental principles of the movement.

It should be noted that by and large the volume is concerned with the specific characteristics of Conservative Judaism. Hence many theological issues that are common to high religion in general and to Judaism in particular are not treated in the present work. For such themes as the nature of religion, the relationship of religion and science, the existence of God, the role of the divine in history, the problem of evil, the nature of man, the foundations of morality, the faith in immortality, and the function of prayer and ritual, the reader is referred to my book *A Faith for Moderns* (revised and augmented ed., New York: Bloch, 1971).

I am grateful that I have been privileged to play some part in the growth of Conservative Judaism and in the articulation of its philosophy. This activity has been one of the three principal facets of my career, along with my lifelong dedication to biblical research and the exploration of the content of religion and its bearing upon the life of our times. These three areas of interest are, to be sure, disparate, but they are not unrelated to one another. I have sought to further them all through the written and the spoken word, by research and writing, in teaching and public activity.

The fruits of my research and thought in the first two areas, the Bible and the meaning of religion, are embodied today in about a dozen volumes that are generally available. On the other hand, the papers and addresses concerned primarily with Conservative

Judaism have remained scattered in various and often inaccessible publications.

Many of my friends and colleagues have suggested that assembling this material in a more permanent form would be a useful addition to the still too limited literature on Conservative Judaism. My honored colleagues Rabbi Stanley Rabinowitz, President of the Rabbinical Assembly, Rabbi Wolfe Kelman, its Executive Vice-President, and my classmate Rabbi Max J. Routtenberg, Chairman of its Publication Committee, warmly embraced the idea. That it came to fruition was due to the happy circumstance that my lifelong friend and colleague Rabbi Max Gelb, now Rabbi Emeritus of Temple Israel in White Plains, New York, and Dean of the Solomon Schechter School of Westchester County, volunteered to serve as editor of the projected volume. This was an offer I could not refuse. I proceeded to assemble and select the papers that seemed to be of more general and enduring interest, and to organize them into a reasonably coherent structure. Rabbi Gelb then read the material carefully, bringing to bear upon it his superb critical acumen, his personal commitment both to the theme of the book and to its author, and his years of experience and reflection as an active rabbi on the American scene. His role was not limited to suggestions on style. He also raised important issues that I had overlooked and challenged views I had espoused, frequently compelling me to think through afresh the problems of meaningful Jewish living in the modern world.

Simultaneously, I reread the material from my own vantage point and discovered that the task was more complicated and arduous than either of us had imagined. Some of the material had to be deleted, much of it needed to be updated, and all of it had to be revised to deal with the realities of American Jewish life in the last quarter of the twentieth century. Repetitions had to be eliminated, contradictions resolved, and stylistic changes introduced. Many papers were excluded as no longer relevant. Rabbi Max Gelb and I held periodic meetings every few weeks, and "what we had hammered out was again and again brought back to the anvil." Undoubtedly, telltale signs of the process remain, but we venture to hope that the volume is a reasonably coherent presentation of a philosophy for Conservative Judaism which, I profoundly believe, can be shared by most adherents of the movement.

The chapters of the present book contain material, substantially modified, that originally appeared in the *Proceedings of the Rabbinical Assembly,* the *Convention Reports of the United Synagogue,* and the periodicals *Conservative Judaism* and *United Synagogue Review.* The second section of the present work reproduces, in considerably revised form, material that was included in my book *Judaism for the Modern Age,* long out of print. The chapter "The Rabbinate: Its History, Functions, and Future," also updated, was first published in 1957 in *Two Generations in Perspective,* a *Festschrift* edited by Harry Schneiderman, honoring my beloved colleague Rabbi Israel Goldstein on his sixtieth birthday. The four letters which appear in the first section were originally published in *Midstream, Response, National Jewish Post and Opinion,* and *Jewish Spectator.* To the editors of all these publications, warm thanks are extended. My devoted secretary, Mrs. Trudy Kramberg, labored over the many revisions of the text with exemplary skill and dedication. My gifted and knowledgeable student, Elliot Gertel, undertook the important task of preparing the indices, that will considerably enhance the usefulness of this book, as students and readers will, I believe, readily agree. He played a major role in the preparation of the bibliography.

I venture to hope that this book will help advance an understanding of the fundamentals of Conservative Judaism, its ideals and goals. What is even more important, may it inspire the leadership and the laity, our youth and their elders, to intensify their loyalty to its cause, not for our own glory or that of our father's house, but for the glory of our Father who is in Heaven.

ROBERT GORDIS

Purim 5738
March 23, 1978

PART ONE

By Way of Introduction:
A Sheaf of Letters

1

THE MEANING OF TRADITIONAL JUDAISM

To the Editor of *Midstream:*

In the course of a letter on Conservative Judaism published in the August-September 1976 issue of *Midstream*, the well-known American-Jewish sociologist, Dr. Marshall Sklare, makes a reference to me in highly flattering terms: "Rabbi Gordis is blessed with a brilliant mind and consequently his colleagues have always looked to him for leadership. Gordis, for his part, has not hesitated to assume the ideological leadership of Conservative Judaism."

It is true that I have always maintained that it is important to grapple with fundamental issues and to articulate a forthright philosophy for the movement, allowing for natural diversity of views. During my career, I have sought to make my contribution to this creative and indispensable enterprise and to present my views clearly and without equivocation.

While it is a fact that I am now a past President of the Rabbinical Assembly and serve as Professor of Bible and the Philosophies of Religion at the Seminary, I hold no official position in the movement. Colleagues like Agus, Bokser, Greenberg, Kadushin, and Siegel, to cite only a few, have articulated other interpretations of Conservative Judaism, though there naturally is a basic body of agreement among us.

There are several fundamental substantive issues that are very important:

1. Dr. Sklare, who won a reputation as an authority on Conservative Judaism because of a sociological study of the movement that he published some years ago, exhibits a basic misunderstanding of the movement and its relationship both to Orthodoxy and to the Jewish tradition.

He writes, "The idea that Conservatism would supplant Orthodoxy—indeed that Conservative Judaism *is* twentieth-century Orthodoxy—has been expressed most strikingly during the past several decades by Rabbi Robert Gordis."

Conservative Judaism (*pace* Dr. Sklare) does not claim to be the heir of Orthodox Judaism, but of traditional Judaism, and he should know that the two are not synonymous.

For thousands of years, from the period of Ezra through the mishnaic and the talmudic eras, Jewish tradition exhibited extraordinary powers of development and growth, responding in various ways to cultural influences of the general environment, to new social and economic conditions, and to new, emerging ethical insights and attitudes. The process of growth and development continued, albeit with reduced momentum, during the Middle Ages. This period in Jewish history approached its close in the sixteenth and seventeenth centuries. This era was marked by the expulsion of the Jews from Spain (1492) and Portugal (1497), the Thirty Years War (1618–48), the Chmielnicki massacres (1648–49), and the Shabbatai Zevi debacle (1626–76).

In the face of this succession of calamities, the religious leadership of the time tried, and in large degree succeeded, to establish a uniform pattern of practice and belief, reflecting the situation of Jewish life roughly in the year 1700. The Halakhah, which has always been the hallmark of Jewish life, was codified in the *Shulḥan Arukh*. Whatever may have been the intention of its author, Rabbi Joseph Karo, or of its annotator, Rabbi Moses Isserles, the *Shulḥan Arukh* became the ultimate authority for Orthodox Judaism. The structure of Judaism as it existed in the late Middle Ages now became stabilized as "authentic." Henceforth, it came to be regarded as unchanged from the past, monolithic in the present, and unchangeable in the future.

The difference between traditional Judaism and Orthodoxy is crucial and should be clearly understood. *Traditional Judaism* is the product of the entire religious experience of the Jewish people from the days of Abraham to our own, including its mainstream, its secondary currents, and its cross-currents, all of which affected its progress and growth. *Orthodoxy* has adopted one stage in the history of Judaism, that of Eastern Europe about the year 1700, stereotyped it, and adopted it as the permanent and "authentic" pattern for Judaism for all time. To be sure, the recall is neither complete nor accurate, for one can never really turn the clock of time backward, but that remains the standard and the ideal of Orthodox Judaism.

It is possible to maintain this position only by denying or, far better, ignoring the history of the growth and development of Judaism throughout the biblical, rabbinic, and medieval periods, the evidence for which Jewish scholarship during the past two centuries has been revealing with ever greater clarity.

Conservative Judaism does not wish to supplant Orthodox Judaism, nor does it desire to see its demise. It regards itself as the heir, not of Orthodox Judaism, but of traditional Judaism, which survived through the ages because of its extraordinary capacity for growth—not abrogation but development.

This capacity for evolution, avoiding both revolution and stagnation, must be restored, if the Jewish tradition is to be a vital and meaningful factor in the lives of modern Jews, who, together with all their contemporaries, live in an age of rapid "future shock."

In other words, Orthodoxy and Conservatism represent two interpretations of the Jewish tradition, the first denying, and the second affirming, the reality and the necessity of growth for a living Judaism. Each movement naturally seeks to win the loyalty of contemporary Jews for its cause, and there are good men and women in both camps—and both are needed.

2. Dr. Sklare seems scandalized by my description of contemporary Orthodoxy as modern Sadduceeism. He cites a passage of mine:

> In spite of claims made in other quarters it is we [Conservative Jews] who are the authentic Jews of rabbinic Judaism. . . . Many of those who attack our movement as "deviationist"—a term totally repugnant to the authentic Jewish tradition—and who demand unswerving adherence to the written letter of the Law, are actually the Sadducees of the twentieth century. Had they lived in the days of Hillel, Rabbi Johanan ben Zakkai, Rabbi Akiba, Rabbi Meir or Rabbi Judah Hanasi, they would have condemned every creative contribution that the Sages made to the living Judaism of their age.

I was not using the term as a club or as an epithet, but as an accurate description of the realities. The ancient Sadducees were wedded to the letter of the Torah and opposed the Pharisaic reinterpretations of the biblical text, which led to the great development of rabbinic Judaism. Modern Orthodoxy, for the highest of motives, cleaves to the letter of the various rabbinic authorities and opposes every effort to extend the boundaries of the tradition.

That Conservative Judaism may legitimately regard itself as being in the mainstream of the Jewish tradition is no mere partisan claim. Let me cite the words of the greatest living Jewish historian, Dr. Salo W. Baron:

> Neo-Orthodoxy, equally with Reform, is a deviation from historical Judaism. No less than Reform, it abandoned Judaism's self-rejuvenating historical dynamism. For this reason we may say that . . . the "positive-historical" Judaism of Zacharias Frankel and Michael Sachs and the "Conservative" Judaism of America have been much truer to the spirit of traditional Judaism. By maintaining the general validity of Jewish law and combining with it freedom of personal interpretation of the Jewish past and creed, Frankel and his successors hoped to preserve historical continuity. . . . It is Conservative Judaism which seems to show the greatest similarities with the method and substance of teaching of the popular leaders during the declining Second Commonwealth, inasmuch as, clinging to the traditional mode of life, it nevertheless allows for the adaptation of basic theological concepts to the changing social and environmental needs.

3. Dr. Sklare, as an adherent of Orthodox Judaism, pleads with Rabbi Kelman to "strengthen the hands of Orthodox moderates" like Rabbi Emanuel Rackman. Rabbi Rackman is an old and honored friend, but as any observer of the Jewish scene or reader of some of his columns will recognize, Rabbi Rackman heads a faction in Orthodox Judaism of which he is virtually the only rabbinic member. All other groups in contemporary Orthodoxy vie with one another in the degree of their intransigence and their intolerance of other positions, at least in their public posture.

4. Perhaps it is his sociological training that leads Dr. Sklare to imagine that truth and value are determined by counting noses. He, therefore, gratuitously informs the reader that Temple Beth-El in Rockaway Park, of which I served as rabbi until 1968, is now

"encircled by Orthodox institutions." It is now ten years and more since I became Rabbi Emeritus of Temple Beth-El and moved away from the community. Dr. Sklare knows as little about the local situation as I do. He is probably referring to several Hasidic *shtiblach* which have been established with the influx of more affluent Hasidic Jews in the community. Even if Dr. Sklare's description of the community were true, what would it prove with regard to the validity of the various movements in contemporary Judaism? Precisely nothing!

Since this letter was originally published, I have been informed that all the *shtiblach,* except for one, no longer function in the community. Are we to infer from this change that Orthodoxy is in decline in America? I hardly think so.

5. The phenomenon of contemporary Judaism can be understood only against a broader background. Ours is an age of massive problems and catastrophes which have led men and women to a loss of confidence in their capacity to meet the challenges of the day and to overcome them through the exercise of rational means. As a result, the use of reason is decried and caricatured as "simplistic" and "naive." Instead, "gut reactions" are glorified and preferred over "intellectual responses." As happened during the breakdown of Greco-Roman society two millennia ago and the accompanying "loss of nerve," many people today are tempted to avert their gaze from the social and ethical issues of the day and to concentrate on their own personal "salvation." Many older folk have grown tired of thinking, while many younger people have been taught that it is heresy to apply the canons of rationality to the fundamental issues of life with which religion is concerned. No wonder that so many today are attracted by the promise of certainty, however weak and unsubstantial its foundation, offered by the plethora of contemporary sects and cults. Some operate within the religious Establishment, Jewish or Christian; some call themselves Oriental; and some are totally new American creations designed for the "spiritual" market.

6. It is astonishing that a sociologist of Dr. Sklare's reputation has chosen to ignore the fact that the resurgence of Orthodoxy in Judaism has its counterpart in the mass growth of evangelical Christianity. It is undeniable that fundamentalism, both in Judaism and Christianity, is in the ascendant today. How long these trends

will continue only time will tell. All that is certain is that the human penchant for what I call the "pendulum syndrome" will make itself felt sooner or later.

What the ultimate result of the interplay of these tendencies will be cannot now be foretold. If civilization is to survive, there must be a rebirth of faith in the human potential, in the capacity of men and women to confront and overcome the problems facing them, which are almost entirely of their own making. This new faith can draw its strength from the biblical view of mankind as fashioned in the image of God and endowed with a measure of God's creative power.

If the process of recovery is too long delayed, the results may prove calamitous for the human adventure on this planet. God may then turn elsewhere for the fulfillment of His inscrutable purposes in the universe. The future destiny of the various movements in contemporary Judaism would then pale into insignificance in the face of the debacle of civilization as a whole.

Since I am opposed to all monopolies, social, economic, political, and cultural as well as religious, and believe that the whole truth is only with God, I do not wish to see the extinction of Orthodox Judaism or, *horribile dictu,* even of Reform Judaism. I believe, on the basis of my study and observation of all three movements and the subgroups within them, that each has already made and is capable of making highly significant contributions to the greater and more vital Judaism of the future.

I do believe that Conservative Judaism offers the greatest hope for the meaningful survival of the Jewish people and the vital functioning of the Jewish tradition. To be sure, I cannot be certain, because I do not have a "hot line" to the Almighty. But neither, I venture timidly to suggest, do those who today loudly trumpet their claim in the marketplace.

2

HALAKHAH AND HISTORY

To the Editors of *Response:*

I read with considerable interest the interview with Rabbi Shlomo Riskin and the appended comments that appeared in *Response* No. 29. He is one of the most gifted and dedicated Orthodox rabbis in America today, and I esteem him greatly for his qualities of mind and heart.

There are several highly significant questions regarding the nature of Judaism and its future course that were not articulated either by the interviewers or the interviewee. Both Rabbi Riskin and his questioners begin with the unspoken assumption that the Halakhah is a fixed, self-contained, perfect, monolithic system, take it or leave it. From Rabbi Riskin's Orthodox standpoint, this is entirely comprehensible. What is striking is that the other participants, several of whom, at least, were educated in institutions committed to the historical method, operate pragmatically from the same basic approach. While Rabbi Riskin urges total adherence to the halakhic system, even if the process of achieving this level of observance by the individual takes a long while, they demur in greater or lesser degree. But they do not bring to bear the insights and implications of the nearly two hundred years of brilliant and dedicated research

9

that has illumined the true nature of Jewish tradition. For modern scholarship has demonstrated that the Halakhah is far from being uniform, complete, and unchangeable. The full record discloses that Jewish tradition includes within its corpus not merely minor divergences, but important currents, cross-currents, and even countercurrents, all of which enter into its present form.

Nor do his interlocutors challenge his entirely understandable, but indefensible, concept of a Halakhah arising and maintained in total isolation, ideologically—if not socially—from the world at large. Here, too, the evidence is abundant that in every age, the tradition of the past was influenced and modified by the needs and insights of the present. It was the result of this interaction in one generation that became the body of Halakhah in the next. This product in turn underwent a similar process of contact with the needs and attitudes of the new age and environment. Some of these influences came from beyond the confines of the Jewish community and official Jewish leadership. A large number of rabbinic principles, institutions, and dicta testify to the fact that the rabbis of the past were keenly aware of the world about them and responsive to it. *Obviously, there were elements in the surrounding culture that they rejected, but there was also much they accepted and even more that they modified and adapted for inclusion in the body of Jewish tradition and law.*

This process was preeminently true of the great creative periods in the history of Halakhah, notably the Mishnah and the Talmud. But it did not, by any means, cease even in the considerably more restricted atmosphere of the Middle Ages. One striking illustration must suffice. Note the fact that the prohibition of polygamy was adopted by Rabbi Gershom and his Synod in Christian Europe in the tenth century. On the other hand, no such enactment was adopted by Sephardic and Oriental rabbis living in Moslem countries, where polygamy was an acceptable and widely practiced marriage pattern.

Nor need we turn only to the past for evidence of the influence of the general world on Judaism. *Mutatis mutandis,* the current upsurge in Orthodox Judaism is parallel to the vast expansion of evangelical Christianity in America today. Obviously, there are important differences, but the parallels between the two movements are both striking and illuminating. This becomes clear from the description of contemporary Christian evangelicalism by Gary Wills in " 'Born Again' Politics," in the *New York Times Magazine*, August 1, 1976.

The history and development of Jewish law from its inception to the present has been traced in the researches of Frankel, Weiss, Ginzberg, Tchernowitz, and many other scholars during the last two centuries. Unfortunately, the implications for the future from their researches into the past have all too often been ignored. Their works can be disregarded, but they cannot be permanently obliterated.

To revert to the main point, the two alternatives envisaged in the interview do not exhaust the options available to the contemporary Jew, young or old, who is seeking to find his roots in the Jewish tradition. There is a third option, distinct both from rigorism and from anarchy. It requires neither the acceptance of a fixed and unchangeable pattern of practice and belief nor the adoption of an eclectic, "non-halakhic" stance, which, however well-meaning, is hardly designed to establish a sense of community in the present and continuity with the past for a widely dispersed people.

Like Rabbi Riskin, I believe that Halakhah is essential for Jewish survival. What I am pleading for is an understanding of the true nature of Halakhah as a living body of belief and practice, both ethical and ritual, growing in time and space. The widespread tendency today to denigrate history and to ignore its clear implications, both for understanding the nature of Halakhah and for plotting its future course, is intellectually disingenuous and pragmatically dangerous. It must lead to highly undesirable consequences, the petrifaction of Judaism, its loss of influence in the world, its isolation from the body politic of humankind, and the alienation of many of the most creative elements of Jewish youth and their elders. For Jews, whom Ludwig von Ranke described as the most historical of peoples, such a course is fraught with disaster. A man immobile on a raft may indulge himself in the illusion that, unlike the man in a rowboat using his oars, he is standing still. Actually, he is moving but has no control over his direction. What is more, when he encounters cross-currents, or a storm arises, he will be in trouble. That is precisely the condition of Judaism today.

History makes another fundamental contribution to our understanding of life. It reminds us of the truth that we do not understand any phenomenon if we conceive of it as a point; we must see it as a line. This is eminently true of the Halakhah. It is not enough to know where the law stands at any given moment, but what is its thrust and direction.

It is precisely in the area of women's liberation that we may find one of the abiding glories of the Jewish tradition. Allowing for eddies and minor currents, the mainstream of the Halakhah represents a constant movement in the direction of expanding women's rights and correspondingly limiting men's privileges and powers over them. The process, to be sure, has not reached its end, and there is unfinished business in this area; but this is true of general, secular society as well. When the trajectory of the struggle for equality of women in Jewish law is recognized and taken into account, we are not compelled to adopt the kind of unconvincing apologetics and tortured rationalizations with which many of the "defenders of the Law" seek to bolster indefensible positions with regard to women's rights.

I believe in the divine origin of the Torah and the eternity of Israel, whose function it is to keep Judaism alive and meaningful in God's world. For this task, we need not only piety and dedication, but also insight and compassion, uniting reverence for the achievements of the past with sensitivity to the problems and aspirations of the present.

A great Jewish thinker in our day, Professor Mordecai M. Kaplan, once pronounced a blessing for a grandchild: "May you know what you learn and understand what you know." This is a consummation devoutly to be wished for us all, whatever our background and outlook.

3

ON THE ORDINATION OF WOMEN

Editor, *Post and Opinion:*

Rabbi Leonard Gevirtz has every right to be opposed to the ordination of women. However, he should not categorically state that "Halakhah is opposed to women's ordination" and then cite a reference to the Talmud which would lead the inexpert reader to assume that the issue is cut-and-dried. The one talmudic reference he quotes is *Sotah* 20b. This tractate of the Talmud deals with the ordeal administered to a woman accused by her husband of adultery, the biblical source for which is Numbers, chapter 5.

In dealing with the subject, the Talmud quotes two opinions of mishnaic teachers: "On the basis of what has been said above, Ben Azzai says, 'A man is required to teach Torah to his daughter (so that if she should ever have occasion to undergo the ordeal of the accused wife she would know that any merit she possesses would create a suspension of punishment for her).' Rabbi Eliezer says, 'Whoever teaches his daughter the Torah is teaching her obscenity (because from the Torah she would learn how to circumvent the law and hide her immorality).' "

That is all the passage says. Evidently, Rabbi Gevirtz wishes us to infer from Rabbi Eliezer's statement that since it is forbidden to

13

teach Torah to a girl, she obviously cannot be ordained as a rabbi. Even this, however, is the opinion of one sage and is contradicted in the very same passage by the view of another. What is more, Rabbi Eliezer was one of the most conservative and strong-willed of the scholars who held highly individual views. Hence, the vast majority of his colleagues did not hesitate to overrule his judgment, as in the famous case of the "Stove of Achnai" in *Baba Metzia* 59b. So too, while virtually all his colleagues interpreted the famous phrase "an eye for an eye" in Exodus 21:24 to mean that monetary compensation is to be given for an injury, Rabbi Eliezer took the biblical phrase literally.

Undoubtedly, in the Middle Ages, the restrictive opinion of Rabbi Eliezer regarding the education of women was adopted by some later authorities. However, I would be interested to learn whether Rabbi Gevirtz would operate on the theory that the teaching of Torah to women is prohibited in the case of his own daughters and whether he forbids girls to be enrolled in his Hebrew school.

Similarly, the ordination of women will encounter objections in some quarters. Undoubtedly, its introduction will create new problems, but progress does not mean the solution of problems but rather the opportunity of facing new ones.

The truth is that the traditional Halakhah does not oppose the ordination of women any more than it favors it—it never contemplated the possibility. Some of us believe that in a time of acute shortage of personnel in Jewish life coupled with a new and widespread quest of Jewish values, it is shortsighted to exclude fifty percent or more of the Jewish people from service to Judaism on every level.

There is room for a legitimate difference of opinion on the ordination of women, and it is reflected within the faculty of the Jewish Theological Seminary and in the membership of the Rabbinical Assembly. But the question should be discussed on substantial, not on imaginary, trumped-up grounds.

4

THE LITURGY OF CONSERVATIVE JUDAISM

Editor, *Jewish Spectator:*

It was my privilege to serve as Chairman of the Joint Prayer Book Commission of the Rabbinical Assembly and the United Synagogue, which in 1946 issued the *Sabbath and Festival Prayer Book*, the first official prayerbook of the Conservative movement. I, therefore, read Dr. Eric L. Friedland's article, "Conservative Prayerbooks" (*Jewish Spectator*, Winter 1976), with considerable interest.

Anyone concerned with the present and future status of the Jewish religion in America will appreciate his comprehensive and fair-minded review of the liturgical publications issued by Conservative Judaism. Dr. Friedland's principal concern has apparently been the character of the English translations in these various prayer books, their accuracy, clarity, and esthetic appeal. He also devotes considerable attention to the changing temper of the times and the shifting winds of theological doctrine reflected in these works and noticeable in all branches of modern Judaism. To be sure, he has the advantage of hindsight that the editors of the various *Siddurim* and *Mahzorim* did not have at the time.

These preoccupations may explain why Dr. Friedland omits any discussion of the one factor which gives historical importance to the

Sabbath and Festival Prayer Book of 1946, which is still widely used throughout the movement. Translations may be better or worse and theological emphases have their ups and downs, and I would be the last to deny the importance of either. But what is basic in Jewish tradition is the Hebrew text of the liturgy. I submit the following paragraphs as an addendum to Dr. Friedland's excellent article.

Until the publication of the *Sabbath and Festival Prayer Book,* the Conservative movement had continued to use Orthodox rituals. This, in spite of the fact that while most of the accepted and familiar text was entirely satisfactory, there were several significant respects where it did not express the outlook and aspirations of the movement.

The changes introduced into the *Sabbath and Festival Prayer Book* underscored the legitimacy of the principle of change in the text, so as to reflect the insights, attitudes, and concerns of each generation. The evidence is clear that the prayer book, as a product of Jewish religious experience through nearly three millennia, has undergone countless accretions, deletions, and modifications through time. Nor need one turn to the record of history for the evidence. One has only to leaf through the different *nusha'ot,* or versions, in use today, the Spanish-Portuguese, the Ashkenazic, *Nusah Sepharad,* and *Nusah Ha'ari,* to see the varieties of Jewish religious experience in action.

The Conservative *Sabbath and Festival Prayer Book,* for the first time, applied this principle to modern needs and aspirations, while maintaining the basic content and structure of the traditional prayer book intact. This principle of growth and development and its application are fundamental. Equally important is the nature of the specific changes introduced.

Most modern Jews do not yearn for the restoration of animal sacrifices in a rebuilt Temple in Jerusalem, but this is precisely the basic theme of the Musaf Service. Yet there are other aspects of the Musaf worthy of retention. The *Sabbath and Festival Prayer Book* sought to make the Musaf Service relevant by changing the tense of a few verbs from the future to the past. As a result, the text no longer voices a plea for the restoration of animal offerings. It now serves as a reminiscence of the glories of the ancient Temple, the visible center of our faith, and the symbol of the devotion of our ancestors to God and His Torah. In praying for the reestablishment of the center of Judaism in the holy city of Jerusalem, we say what we mean and we mean what we say.

The *Yekum Purkan* prayer, which originated during the heyday of the talmudic academies in ancient Babylonia, was preserved—and rightly—for many reasons that transcend the merely rational. But a prayer for the well-being of "the scholars and teachers in the Land of Israel and in Babylonia" hardly does justice to the Diaspora in the twentieth century. All that is needed was to add the phrase *ubhekhol 'arat galvatana*—"and in all the lands of the Dispersion."

The plea *Sim Shalom*, "Grant peace to Israel," in the *Amidah* is given a universal meaning by the addition of one word, *ba'olam,* "in the world," following a text by Rabbi Saadia Gaon, so that it now reads: "Grant peace, well-being and blessing unto the world, with grace, loving-kindness and mercy for us and for all Israel, Thy people."

Of particular interest today, with the growing movement for women's equality, is the rephrasing of three of the Preliminary Blessings in the Morning Service. In the Orthodox prayer book, they are phrased in the negative: "Blessed are You, O Lord our God, King of the universe, who has not made me a Gentile, a slave, a woman." These benedictions have long been a subject of discomfort and concern for obvious reasons.

Since the third blessing can obviously not be recited by females, a substitute benediction is set forth to be recited by women, "who has made me according to His will." What is more important, the negative formulation did not do full justice to the sense of joy experienced by the Jew in contemplating his destiny and role in the world.

These Preliminary Blessings are accordingly rephrased in the positive and emerge as significant in substance and felicitous in form. The first blessing now reads: "Blessed are You, O Lord our God, King of the universe, who has made me in His image," a blessing that women as well as men can recite with genuine *kavvanah* as expressing their equality and their human state. The other two blessings appear as: "who has made me free, who has made me a Jew." All three blessings, it may be added, have a basis in the tradition and are obviously far more appropriate for most men and women in our age than the older formulations.

In espousing the principle of legitimacy of change in the liturgy, and by introducing such modifications as those we have described, the *Sabbath and Festival Prayerbook* gives tangible expression to the true spirit of Conservative Judaism, which is dedicated to utilizing the resources of the past to the utmost, while speaking to and for each generation in the present.

PART TWO

Foundations of Conservative Judaism

5

THE SURVIVAL OF JUDAISM IN THE MODERN WORLD

I

World War II and its cheerless aftermath mark a crisis in the life of Western man. For nearly two centuries he has participated in the slow or precipitate decline of religious values, confident that he could retain their distilled essence in secular form. Now he has discovered that the ethical fruits of the religious life shrivel up and die when no longer nourished by its roots. The system of morality which Western man took for granted as "natural" and "self-evident" has been shown, by modern totalitarian tyrannies of all colors, to be neither innate in human nature nor demonstrable by abstract logic. The faith in human progress as inevitable, which characterized the modern age, has been rudely jolted, if not destroyed forever. Long before atomic destruction became an ever-present peril, our generation began to realize that there was more than a little possibility that its hopes and aspirations might turn to ashes and that its ideals might dissolve like smoke in an unfeeling universe and a mechanized society.

This recognition lies at the base of the agonized search by modern men and women for a soil in which to root a viable system of values. This quest is a major factor, though not the only one to be sure, in the widespread interest in religion that characterizes our times and has penetrated even into the circles of the intellectuals, who were hitherto impervious to such influences. With something of a time lag, to be sure, the Jew is manifesting an increased desire to explore the insights of religion as a possible basis for faith and meaning in life. Beyond the anxiety of modern man in general, which he shares with his contemporaries, he suffers from a special complaint, the unease of the modern Jew. Seeking a new and enduring basis for Jewish identification, he recognizes that the fight against anti-Semitism or the support of Jewish philanthropies is not enough. Even Zionism cannot suffice of itself, for dedication to the welfare and progress of the State of Israel is the fruit of loyalty to Judaism and not its root.

Hence, from many different quarters the cry is heard, "Back to Tradition!" This quest, or at least this yearning for an anchorage in Jewish tradition, is evident today among a growing section of youth on college campuses and elsewhere, among sensitive men and women in all walks of life, and in progressive and intellectual groups. It is also encountered among some of the Jewish masses who have surrendered the Jewish way of life through a process of slow attrition and largely unconscious alienation.

But what is implied in this *teshubah,* or return? On this matter there is little clarity and no unanimity. Does a return to tradition mean a complete rejection of the insights and attitudes that emanate from modern science and philosophy, as we are being exhorted in certain circles, and the enunciation of a "postmodern" theology, which explains its similarity to contemporary Christian evangelicalism? Is a commitment to Jewish tradition impossible without a total acceptance of the old world-view of Judaism as it existed before the challenge of modernism made itself felt? In other words, is tradition a static concept, unchanged and unchangeable, or does it have a history and a dynamic of its own? In order to appraise the role of Judaism in the world of today and of tomorrow, one must decide whether Jewish tradition reveals a trend and a direction, or whether it comprises a completely articulated system of beliefs and actions which can be accepted or rejected only *in toto.*

II

These and other related issues constitute, to borrow the terms devised by Ahad Ha'am, "the problem of Judaism," as distinct from "the problem of the Jews." They are modern in more than a chronological sense, though they have surfaced principally within the last century and a half, as a result of the Emancipation and the Enlightenment. Both movements, which arose in the eighteenth century in Central and Western Europe, were organically related to each other. With many hesitations and evasions, the Emancipation admitted Jews into modern society as citizens. Being recognized as individuals, they surrendered the closely knit, compulsory, and autonomous character of the Jewish community. *Pari passu* with the process of Emancipation came the Enlightenment. As the Jews emerged from their all-Jewish environment, they discovered that the new ideas which they encountered in the outside world clashed, or seemed to clash, with traditional concepts. In sum, for many, if not for most modern Jews, the Enlightenment undermined the validity of the Jewish religion, while the Emancipation dissolved the authority of the Jewish community.

Thus, both the Jewish people and the Jewish religion were faced with a far-reaching challenge, the problem of finding some adjustment between tradition and the modern world. Various patterns of behavior and of thought now emerged. Only those who preferred to desert Judaism completely, by means of conversion to Christianity or through intermarriage, "escaped" the challenge and were exempt from the problem of Judaism. That they were exposed to other grave moral, psychological, and cultural liabilities is true, but this does not concern us here. That their grandchildren were punished by the Nazis for the sins of their grandparents is a bitter and ironic footnote to history.

Among those who were unwilling to sever the bond between themselves and Judaism and sought a bridge between their present and the Jewish past, there arose the movement which came to be called Reform Judaism. Besides being the first group to recognize the issues posed by the new position of the Jews in society, Reform made many positive contributions to Jewish life. But its weaknesses, the penalty of any pioneering effort, cannot be overlooked. Its characteristic mark was that it began by accepting the modern outlook completely, with all its limitations and blind spots. Quite naturally, only very little of traditional Judaism could be retained within such a framework. To be sure, the all-pervasive way of life enjoined upon Jews by Jewish tradition offered tremendous difficulties in a predominantly non-Jewish milieu. The observance of the weekly Sabbath rest, the celebration of the Jewish festivals, the practice of daily prayer, the use of the Hebrew language, the intensive study of Torah, and the maintenance of the Jewish dietary laws—these and other important features of traditional Judaism were not easy to preserve. But instead of seeking to evaluate the various elements in the Jewish way of life and to defend those possessing significance, Reform Judaism used the rationalistic critique of religion to justify the dictates of convenience. It countenanced, even when it did not stimulate, the abandonment of most of the distinctive practices of Jewish life.

Contemporary Reform Jewish leaders cannot be too highly praised for their intellectual courage and honesty in recognizing the errors of the movement in the past. They are attempting to restore more and more elements of Jewish observance and are seeking to intensify religious education at every age level. They have reaffirmed Jewish peoplehood and have espoused the Zionist ideal. But it remains to be seen how far this retreat from "classical" Reform will succeed with the laity, particularly in the area of personal piety.

The extreme action of early Reform vis-à-vis Jewish tradition led to an equally violent reaction. Faced by the wholesale dissolution of Jewish life in Western Europe, a new party arose which called itself the Orthodox. The "Frankfort School" in Germany, and its ideological allies in Hungarian Orthodoxy and Polish Hasidism, met the challenge of the new world by accepting some modern externals and patterns of behavior, while deliberately rejecting most of the values and assumptions of contemporary thought. Judaism was divine and hence fixed, unchanged and unchangeable throughout time. Loyalty to Judaism meant punctilious and undeviating loyalty to tradition, as received from the past and as codified for all time in the *Shulḥan Arukh.*

As is so often the case, extremes met. Classical Reform and Neo-Orthodoxy were basically at one in their conception of tradition, a word derived from the Latin and meaning "that which is handed over." In practice, both schools of thought treated tradition as a ready-made, neatly wrapped package, all complete, and they looked upon loyalty to tradition as a purely passive process of preserving the package and transferring it unchanged from one generation to the next. Since Reform Judaism regarded this body of doctrine and ritual as unacceptable and impractical in the modern world, it urged its abrogation. Orthodoxy, on the contrary, declared that all the sacrifices which were required to transmit it unimpaired were justified. Any modification of, or divergence from, the accepted norm would mean tampering with Divine perfection and destroying it.

Actually, both friend and foe misunderstood the nature of Jewish tradition. If tradition has ceased to be a living force in the life of so many modern Jews, many factors have played their part. But not the least among them has been this static conception, which is neither historically true nor life-giving.

What makes this situation difficult to understand is the fact that the evidence on the subject has been assembled and is readily available in the works of countless scholars. The researches of Leopold Zunz, Nachman Krochmal, Samuel Judah Lob Rapoport, Zacharias Frankel, Abraham Geiger, Samuel David Luzzatto, Heinrich Graetz, Isaac Hirsch Weiss, Joseph Z. Lauterbach, Solomon Schechter, Louis Ginzberg, and Harry A. Wolfson, together with their fellows and successors in our own day, have supplied abundant evidence that the law of growth and development, which is universal throughout nature and society, applies to Judaism as well.

Tradition is a dynamic concept, in which each generation has played an active role, contributing its share to the treasury of Jewish thought. The maintenance of tradition is a creative, not a passive, process, lasting as long as the life of the tradition itself. Jewish customs and ceremonies, Jewish laws and religious ideas, all have grown with time, exactly as a youth develops from a child, and as a man grows out of a youth.

The past century and a half of Jewish experience, marked by the wholesale disintegration of the Jewish way of life, has shown that to ignore or deny this process is not only a distortion of the past but also a disservice to the future. Because we stand on the shoulders of the giants of the past, we can and should see further than they. We honor them most truly not by standing immobile at the point that they have reached, but by moving forward on the trail they have blazed before us.

6

THE BASIC CHARACTERISTICS OF
JEWISH TRADITION

I

The principle of development in all areas of culture and society is a
fundamental element of the modern outlook. It is all the more
noteworthy that the Talmud, completed nearly fifteen hundred years
ago, clearly recognized the vast extent to which rabbinic Judaism
had grown beyond the Bible, as well as the organic character of this
process of growth. According to a talmudic legend, at once naive
and profound (*Menahot* 29b), Moses found God adding decorative
crowns to the letters of the Torah. When he asked the reason for this,
the lawgiver was told: "In a future generation, a man named Akiba
son of Joseph is destined to arise, who will derive multitudes of laws
from each of these marks." Deeply interested, Moses asked to be
permitted to see him in action, and he was admitted to the rear of the
schoolhouse where Akiba was lecturing. To Moses' deep distress,
however, he found that he could not understand what the scholars
were saying, and his spirit grew faint within him. As the session drew
to a close, Akiba concluded: "This ordinance which we are discuss-
ing is a law derived from Moses on Sinai." When Moses heard this,
his spirit revived!

The implications of this profound legend are far-reaching. For the
Talmud, tradition is not static—nor does this dynamic quality
contravene either its *divine origin* or its *organic continuity*. These
attributes of the Torah will be discussed below. Our concern here

26

is with the historical fact, intuitively grasped by the Talmud, that *tradition grows*. Hence the sages could say: "Things not revealed to Moses were revealed to Rabbi Akiba and his colleagues" (Midrash, *Bemidbar Rabbah* 19:6). It is significant that the same verb "revealed" is used both for the giver of the Law and for its interpreters a millennium and a half later.

In order to understand the dynamic nature of Jewish tradition, it is of fundamental importance to analyze both the causes and the techniques of its development. Various factors played their part. In many instances, the changes were induced by advancing religious ideas and ethical conceptions. Almost equally far-reaching in their effect were changes in the political, social, and economic conditions of Jewish life. These, in turn, frequently led to modifications in outlook. Another group of changes was the result of the feeling that practices hallowed in the past were inconvenient or out of harmony with new environmental conditions. In still other instances, the motivation eludes the historian, who can merely note the emergence or the decline of rites and observances, the presence or the absence of "survival value."

Equally varied are the modes of development. As the word "growth" itself indicates, it is, in the largest measure, a process of *accretion*, of addition to the corpus of Jewish tradition. This occurred in one of two ways. In countless instances, *new values, institutions, and laws were created* as a result of new experiences and new-felt needs. The entire development of postbiblical civil and criminal law and the elaborate laws and customs connected with the Sabbath, the festivals, and Kashrut occupy over twenty of the largest tractates of the Talmud, yet they rest on scriptural foundations of a few verses each. That important segments of rabbinic law have little basis in the biblical text was clearly recognized by the Mishnah, which speaks of many matters as being "mountains hanging by a hair" (*Ḥagigah* 1:8).

This process of growth did not end even with the completion of the Talmud, although the tempo was considerably reduced or slowed down after this great creative epoch was over. Nonetheless, post-talmudic Judaism is to be credited with such contributions as the crystallization of the Simḥat Torah festival, the Bar Mitzvah rite, Kaddish, Yizkor, and Yahrzeit, the prohibition of polygamy among the Occidental Jews, and the elaborate development of the traditional prayer book.

The second way in which growth took place is the method of *reinterpretation*. By means of this approach, older material was preserved intact, yet was made to reflect new religious and ethical insights. A case in point is the attitude toward capital punishment. Biblical law posits the death penalty for many crimes against persons, as well as for ritual offenses. The rabbis naturally did not abrogate the law of the Torah, but they virtually abolished capital punishment by insisting that there must be no doubt of the willful character of the crime. Here they were preserving the spirit of the Torah, which declares life to be holy and demands justice, by reinterpreting the letter of the law! Rabbinic law permitted the execution of the accused only if there were two witnesses to the crime, who could testify that before it was committed the offender had been explicitly warned of the sin and of its penalty (*hathra'ah*). Circumstantial evidence, it need scarcely be added, was never admitted in cases involving the death penalty. The motivation behind this development is clear from the statements in the Mishnah that a court which executed one murderer in seven (or even seventy) years was called "murderous," and that such distinguished sages as Rabbi Tarphon and Rabbi Akiba declared that if they had sat in the Sanhedrin, no accused person would ever have been subjected to the death penalty (*Makkoth* 1:10).

Another far-reaching area in which reinterpretation operated to transform the older law is that of women's rights. The Bible, like all ancient custom, gave to the father almost unlimited power over his daughter, whom he could sell into marriage or into slavery without her consent. Once married, she could be divorced by her husband at his will, while the woman had no initiative or voice in the matter (Deuteronomy 24:1 ff.). As part of their growing recognition of the personality and the rights of the woman, the rabbis took varied measures for her protection. On the one hand they gave the woman, in cases of manifest hardship or of incompatibility, the right to invoke the aid of the court in securing a divorce. On the other hand, they made it more difficult for the husband to divorce his wife in a moment of pique or anger, by ordaining that in case of a divorce he give her a substantial cash payment. This provision was incorporated into the *Ketubbah*, or marriage agreement.

As for the power of the father, which is explicitly laid down in biblical law, they curtailed it by means of a simple expedient. They restricted the biblical word *na'arah*, "girl," to the period between the ages of twelve and twelve and a half. Thus the *patria potestas* applied only during this six-month interval. Before that age she was a *ketannah*, or "minor," when the father was morally enjoined not to marry her off at all. Above that age she was *bogeret*, or "mature," and hence legally free from her father's authority.

Less far-reaching but perhaps more familiar examples of reinterpretation may be cited from the field of ritual. Thus it is customary at the Passover Seder to pour or spill out a drop of wine from the goblet as each of the Ten Plagues is mentioned. The basis for the custom undoubtedly lies in the desire to ward off evil, and the act has many parallels in primitive cultures. But this lowly origin has been transformed by Jewish thought into a symbol of deep humanity and universalism. The wine goblet at the Seder represents the cup of Israel's salvation. However, since the redemption of Israel from bondage was achieved at the cost of the suffering of the Egyptians, the cup of joy cannot be full for the Jew as he recalls the misery of his ancient oppressor. Hence, he pours out a drop of wine for each of the Ten Plagues. He is thus imitating the ways of God Himself, for according to Jewish legend, the Redeemer of Israel refused to let the angels praise Him when the Egyptian pursuers were perishing in the Red Sea, saying, "My creatures are drowning and you want to sing praises to Me!"

Another folk custom which was reinterpreted and which became a symbol of national loyalty is the practice of having the bridegroom break a small glass at his wedding, at the very end of the marriage ceremony. The origin of this practice, too, was undoubtedly the desire to drive off evil and malignant spirits, which were felt to be especially potent in so significant and critical an hour. In modern Judaism, however, the breaking of the glass has become a reminder of the destruction of the Temple and of the breakdown of the national life of Israel, a poignant reaffirmation of the psalmist's oath: "If I forget thee, O Jerusalem, may my right hand wither; may my tongue cleave to my palate, if I remember thee not, if I do not raise thee up above my chief joy" (Psalms 137:5–6).

II

These instances of accretion and of reinterpretation, which could be increased almost indefinitely, constitute the major modes of development in Jewish tradition. What has been much less generally noted is that the growth of tradition also includes, in fewer cases to be sure, the *surrender of ideas and practices* once widely cherished, or, at least, the *reduction of their importance*. Here, too, the various causes for growth enumerated above brought about the various changes.

Advancing religious attitudes led to the elimination in Jewish traditional thought today of the belief in Satan and the angels. This, in spite of the references to them in the pages of the Bible. Professor Louis Ginzberg believed that Rabbi Judah the Prince, in compiling the authoritative corpus of the Mishnah, consciously omitted any reference to these beings. Nonetheless, belief in them persisted throughout the talmudic and medieval periods, as the later literature abundantly attests. Yet in modern traditional Judaism, these ideas have ceased to play any part and have left few traces behind.

A far-reaching growth in ethical sensitivity is reflected in the accepted rabbinic interpretation of the *lex talionis,* the so-called law of retaliation, the law of "an eye for an eye, a tooth for a tooth" (Exodus 21:24). The history of ancient society demonstrates that this law itself is an advance over the more primitive doctrine that any injury could be avenged without limit. Even the taking of life for a hurt to a limb, or the massacre of an entire clan for a single life, was countenanced. The biblical law, on the other hand, restricts the punishment to the dimensions of the crime, as the Talmud clearly recognized when it commented, " 'An eye for an eye' and not 'a life and an eye for an eye' " (*Ketubbot* 38a).

Nonetheless, Rabbinic Judaism went beyond the biblical law by interpreting the phrase "an eye for an eye" as meaning "money," that is to say, equivalent financial restitution or compensation for the damage caused (*Baba Kamma* 84a). This thoroughgoing modification of the biblical law goes back at least to the second century, if not earlier, but its existence is frequently ignored both within the Jewish community and without, either out of ignorance or malice, or both.

As has already been noted, the ancient world gave to the father the power of life and death over his children. This authority is already restricted by biblical law (Deuteronomy 21:18 ff.), according to which a "stubborn and rebellious son" could be executed only if a duly constituted court found him guilty of filial disobedience. But in rabbinic times, even this law was felt to be too severe. Accordingly, it was declared to be inoperative by the rabbis, who said that the biblical ordinance regarding the "stubborn and rebellious son," like that ordaining the total destruction of the "idolatrous city" (Deuteronomy 13:13 ff.), "never was and was never destined to be," but was placed in the Torah merely to stimulate the hermeneutical skill of the sages and as a warning to possible sinners (*Sanhedrin* 71a).

Advancing religious and ethical ideals were inner processes, often imperceptible except after the passage of centuries. On the other hand, changed external conditions frequently led to the dramatic surrender of fundamental elements of Jewish tradition and ultimately to a shift in ideas. Such an event was the destruction of the Second Temple, which compelled the elimination of animal sacrifices, although up to that time they had been the heart and the essence of Jewish worship, as they were in all ancient religion. As though to fulfill the rabbinic dictum that "God sends healing before the plague," normative Judaism, even before the blow descended, had called a new and more modest institution into being, the synagogue, by the side of the resplendent sanctuary in Jerusalem. When the Second Temple was destroyed and the priestly caste was deprived of its functions, the new institution stepped into the breach, being equipped with the democratic leadership of the sages, which was based solely on character and learning, instead of on a hereditary priesthood.

In place of the animal offerings the synagogue created prayer— "the service of the heart," as the rabbis put it. To be sure, the daily prayers were named after the defunct sacrifices, and petitions for the restoration of the ancient Temple cult were included in the order of prayer. Nonetheless, the fact that for nearly nineteen centuries traditional Judaism has functioned without animal offerings has transformed the Jewish outlook on the subject. Today, some religious leaders in Jerusalem have taken steps to revive the knowledge of the laws of sacrifice, in anticipation of the rebuilding of the Temple. Such a restoration would prove gravely embarrassing to most traditional Jews, who have been weaned away from sacrifices as a mode of worship.

Fortunately for them, the possibility is extremely slight. For, as Professor Ginzberg pointed out, from the standpoint of the Halakhah, sacrifice may not be offered except upon the exact site of the ancient altar under penalty of death, and that only by lineal descendants of Aaron. Since the exact spot is unknown, and since the descent of the present-day *kohanim* (priests) is not beyond doubt, neither the site nor the functionaries would be available except through a new, miraculous revelation from on high.

The hue and cry raised in some circles against any modification of the traditional prayer book which seeks to remove the plea for the restoration of sacrifices is the result of a failure to comprehend the trend of tradition. As a matter of fact, Moses Maimonides, in his *Guide to the Perplexed* (bk. III, chap. 32), propounded the theory, nearly eight centuries ago, that animal sacrifices were ordained in the Torah as a concession to the religious immaturity of the ancient Israelites. They would have insisted upon imitating the customs of their neighbors, all of whom were wont to offer up animals to gods and demons. Nor does this view represent an aberration from traditional Judaism. Maimonides was anticipated in this theory by the Midrash (*Leviticus Rabbah* 22:8). The surrender of sacrifices began as a tragic necessity in Jewish life; it has become for large numbers of traditional Jews an accepted attitude.

A very recent instance of this process may be studied in the prayer book. In the closing prayer of the Daily Service, the *Alenu,* the governmental censors in Europe usually compelled the elimination of a line from the Ashkenazic ritual which refers to the pagans of the earth and is based on Isaiah 45:20. The passage in the liturgy read: "For they bow down before vanity and nothingness, and pray to a god who cannot help." Nonetheless, Jewish worshippers in Eastern Europe long continued to interpolate the passage from memory. Yet time has marched on. Today, in Western Europe and in the United States, no censorship exists. Nonetheless, no Orthodox synagogue which follows the Ashkenazic rite has taken steps to restore the deleted passage, which had originally been omitted under duress. The reason is obvious: the line is no longer felt to be in harmony with the Jewish outlook.

III

Changes in Jewish tradition were not limited to circumstances which rendered maintenance of the Law impossible; often it sufficed to note that the Law worked hardship or caused great stress. A fundamental postulate of talmudic law declared that "one may not enact an ordinance which the majority of the community cannot observe" (*Baba Batra* 60b). When new conditions made it difficult, even if not impossible, to observe the accepted law, the recognized leadership adopted new enactments, both positive and negative (*takkanot* and *gezerot*), which reckoned with the objective conditions of life and with the subjective attitudes of the people.

One of the earliest of such enactments, which illustrates the dynamics of change in Jewish tradition, is the *prosbul* of Hillel. As a part of its program of social justice, the Torah established the law of the year of release, according to which all debts were cancelled in the seventh year (Deuteronomy 15:1 ff.). In a predominantly agricultural society, where all lending was a form of charity and practically all borrowing was due to distress, this law was designed to prevent the concentration of capital in the hands of a few.

In a later period, however, as there developed in Israel a more advanced economy, largely urban and mercantile in character, this law was no longer a social advantage but a hindrance to the free flow of commercial credit. Moreover, it made it difficult for the needy borrower to secure a loan. The great sage Hillel (1st cent. B.C.E.) curtailed the operation of the biblical law by means of a legal fiction. The biblical text (Deuteronomy 15:2) forbade the lender to demand payment of the debt in the seventh year. According to Hillel's ordinance, the creditor transferred the debt "to the court" (Greek: *prosboule*), which was free to collect the debt (Mishnah *Shebiith*, chap. 10).

It is clear that as a *technique,* the rabbinic ordinance, which made possible the collection of an unpaid debt in the seventh year, nullified the biblical law, which forbade such payments. What is significant is that *the spirit and the objective remained constant in both cases*—to make it possible for the needy to secure the economic help they required.

Another illustration from the important area of economic life may be cited. According to biblical and rabbinic law, a Jew is forbidden to take interest from a fellow-Jew on loans of money. This proviso, both workable and justifiable in a simpler society, proved inapplicable to a more sophisticated economy in which the availability of credit was essential. Medieval Jewish authorities accordingly established the legal fiction of *heter 'iska,* which ostensibly transformed the lender-borrower relationship into one of partnership, and thus made the payment of interest legally permissible. Nevertheless, few Jews, even of the most traditional cast, utilize this legal fiction today. The taking of interest is virtually universal.

The life of modern Jews of Orthodox persuasion offers many illustrations of elements in traditional Jewish practice which were generally observed in the past but are now largely disregarded, because they are felt to be out of harmony with the ideas and practices of the environment. Thus the rabbinic requirement that married women must not display their hair in public and the post-talmudic objections to being photographed are rarely obeyed in Israel, in Western Europe, and in the United States, except in very right-wing Orthodox circles. Few synagogues today, even those of the most traditional character, would forbid women worshippers to sing at religious services, in spite of the clear-cut talmudic utterance on the subject (*Berakhot* 24a, *Kiddushin* 70a).

In ancient times, the Jews shared the ancient Semitic attitude that "the glory of the face is the beard" (*Shabbat* 152a). However, as the Jews came into contact with the clean-shaven Greeks and Romans, their attitude was transformed. The Pentateuchal provision forbidding the removal of the beard was restricted by the rabbis to shaving with a razor (*Makkot* 3:5). As a result, chemical depilatories, pumice stones, and electric razors are used among the most traditionally observant. Since beards were a rarity in Christian countries, the Jews, too, largely dispensed with them. Abraham Ibn Ezra quotes the view that the biblical prohibition against shaving in Leviticus (21:5) applies only to its use as a mourning rite, as indeed seems clear from the context. The famous Orthodox scholar Samuel David Luzzatto (1800–1865), who also lived in Western Europe, held that the biblical prohibition, which occurs in the Book of Leviticus, the "Priestly Law," applied only to priests. Whatever the historical background, it is clear that the widespread custom of wearing a beard largely disappeared.

In recent years, the growing number of dress styles characteristic of contemporary society has led to a revival of the wearing of the beard, particularly among the young. Modern Orthodoxy has utilized this new fashion to encourage the wearing of the beard, but it is by no means universal among Orthodox Jews even today.

In another respect as well, the latest fashions in male attire have had a direct effect upon the spread of Orthodox observance, paradoxical as it may seem at first blush. As a result of the "hippie" movement and other factors, the trend, particularly in the United States, has been in the direction of ever-greater informality in dress, with a premium on the bizarre and the unfamiliar. As a result, the public wearing of the *kippah* (skullcap), often reduced to minuscule proportions, is no longer felt to be out of keeping with the general environment. Increasingly, therefore, boys and young men of Orthodox persuasion have taken to the public wearing of the *yarmulke*, which comes in various sizes, colors, and shapes.

Feminine fashions have also undergone a striking metamorphosis. Early rabbinical authorities ordained that women, upon marriage, were to shave their hair and cover their heads with a scarf or other head-covering. In the seventeenth and eighteenth centuries the custom of wearing wigs, both by men and women, became prevalent in Western society. At the time, many Jewish women refrained from cutting their hair and insisted on following this trend, by donning a *sheitel*, or wig, instead. A distinguished rabbinic authority, Rabbi Jonathan Eybeschuetz, strongly castigated this practice as "an imitation of the Gentiles." It is ironic that this practice has now become the hallmark of Orthodoxy. As wigs have once again become fashionable, modern Orthodox women have not been slow to adopt the practice. Only in extreme right-wing Orthodox circles has the practice of wearing attractive wigs been attacked—and rightly—as defeating the spirit and intent of the original law.

The area of Jewish festivals reveals the same process of change. The festival of Ḥamishah Asar B'Ab was observed in Palestine during Second Temple days with great zest as a folk carnival. It has now disappeared from the calendar and remains merely an ancient historical memory.

On the other hand, Simḥath Beth Hasho 'ebah, the Festival of the Drawing of the Water, has had a happier fate. Observed during Sukkot in Second Temple days, it virtually disappeared during the nineteen centuries of the Dispersion. Today it has been revived in a completely reinterpreted form in Israel, where the opening of a well is an occasion for genuine thanksgiving.

The New Moon festival (Rosh Ḥodesh) was of preeminent importance in biblical days. It is still observed briefly in the ritual of the synagogue, but its significance in Jewish tradition has all but vanished. This reduction in its importance may very well have been induced by the desire of the rabbis in the mishnaic period to minimize the elements of folk-belief associated with the adoration of the moon. In recent decades the practice of *Kiddush Halebhanah,* the Sanctification of the Moon, has enjoyed new popularity in Hasidic and right-wing Orthodox circles.

The traditional prayer book offers illustrations of deletions and contractions in the ritual which are sometimes based, not on ideological considerations, but rather on the human impulse to shorten prayers. These instances are particularly interesting today, when it is argued, with more heat than light, that any deviation from the accepted ritual is a dangerous break with "tradition." Thus there are several alphabetical acrostics, of which only a few letters remain today. In the morning prayer *Tithbarakh,* only five letters have survived (*'ahuvim, berurim, gibborim, 'osim,* and *pothekhim*). In the deeply moving alphabetical "Selikhah" known as the *Adonai Elohei Yisrael,* only a handful of the poetical stichs are still intact (those beginning with Zayin, Heth, Teth, and Yod, and perhaps also He, Vav, and Kaph). The rest is now lost or changed beyond our power to restore.

In sum, the prayer book, like all the other aspects of the traditions of Judaism, testifies to the process of growth as the mark of a living tradition, which adds, reinterprets, and subtracts in accordance with new experiences and felt needs.

In exceptional cases Rabbinic Judaism had recourse to *legislation* through *takkanot* and *gezerot,* positive and negative enactments. However, the dominant characteristic method was that of *interpretation,* which generally proved adequate to the new conditions and new insights of each age. Only during the past few centuries did traditional Jewish law lose its flexibility and power of growth, due to the influence of historical conditions in Eastern Europe, where the bulk of world Jewry was concentrated. The *Aharonim,* or late decisors, who were their recognized legal authorities, were led to adopt an ever more passive attitude toward the Halakhah, generally avoiding any bold creative activity and relying on the principle, "When in doubt, the severer opinion is to prevail." This was emphatically not the case in the earlier periods which produced the Mishnah, the Gemara, and the great Codes of the *Rishonim,* the early authorities.

IV

Historically, the growth of Jewish law through interpretation, which was in vogue in the period of the Sopherim and the Tannaim (ca. 400

B.C.E.–200 C.E.), proceeded through two methods. The first, which many scholars regard as the older, was the method of Midrash, "the searching of Scripture." It consisted of the analysis by scholars of the text of the Torah, both literally and through special canons of interpretation, in order to deduce the laws from it. This *deductive* method, however, was limited by the extent of the biblical text, and its results were relatively circumscribed. Hence it was not generally utilized after the second century C.E. The Tannaitic Midrashim of the schools of Rabbi Ishmael and Rabbi Akiba, several of which have reached us in whole or in part, are the literary monuments of this technique.

Instead, an *inductive* method called Halakhah or Mishnah proved far more fruitful. This approach derived its impetus not from the text of Scripture, but from the context of a life-situation, be it a lawsuit or a more general problem in society. By and large, the process would begin with a felt need among the people, of which the scholars became conscious. The spiritual leaders would then determine for themselves whether the particular need or aspiration was ethically desirable and religiously valuable. If not, they would oppose it or seek to suppress and minimize it, as was the case with the absence of angelology and Satan in the Mishnah, already noted.

If the scholars concluded that the expressed need or idea was worthwhile, they would seek to bring it into the mainstream of Jewish tradition by finding a basis for it in the text of Scripture through a process of interpretation. To do this they would utilize the "Seven Norms" developed by Hillel, the expanded "Thirteen Principles" of Rabbi Ishmael, or the still more elaborate "Thirty-two Rules" of Rabbi Eliezer, son of Rabbi Jose the Galilean. Thus two scholars representing contrary points of view could both validate their positions by finding a biblical support. While at times the biblical text itself was the ground for the divergence, by and large the variety of outlook arose from the fact that the authorities differed as to what was desirable and necessary, and was therefore in accordance with the spirit of the Torah.

In the majority of instances recorded in the Talmud, this motivation is implicit, but often enough it is explicit. One or two examples may be cited. In arguing with Rabbi Akiba regarding the punishment of the daughter of a priest who has yielded to immorality, Rabbi Ishmael calls out to his colleague: "Because you press the meaning of the letter Vav in the word *ubhath* (in Leviticus 21:9), shall this girl be punished by burning?" (*Sanhedrin* 51b). Or again, the complicated and severe laws of ritual impurity were consciously set aside by the sages, as far as the soil of the Land of Israel was concerned, out of regard for the sanctity of the land and the national interest. Thus the statement of the Talmud on the subject *(Ketubbot* 20b, *Nazir* 65b) is explained by Rashi: "The sages discovered an excuse and grasped it, in order to lean upon it and declare the Land of Israel free from ritual impurity" *(ad locum)*. The city of Jerusalem was also exempted from these disabilities on similar grounds.

Even when this motivation is not specifically set forth, the process developed along these lines. It has its parallel in the American system of judicial review, in which laws enacted by the states or by the Congress may, upon appeal, be brought before the Supreme Court, which then seeks to relate them to the Constitution.

While no analogy is ever complete, this American parallel applies in all essentials even to the doctrine of the immutability of the Law, the impossibility of formally abolishing any enactment of the Torah. Technically, the Constitution of the United States, which lays no claim to divine origin, may be amended. Yet after nearly two centuries of eventful history in the life of a great nation, no more than some fifteen amendments have been added to the original Bill of Rights. On the other hand, hundreds of thousands of laws have been passed by the municipal, state, and national legislatures, all of which are, potentially or actually, brought into relationship with the existent Constitution through the process of judicial review and interpretation.

Undoubtedly, there are instances in which the Supreme Court justices reach their decision on the basis of an obvious infringement of the letter of the Constitution. Here no difference of opinion is possible. But more often than not, this is not the underlying motivation, as is indicated by the frequent bifurcation of the bench into "liberals" and "conservatives," and by the court's change of viewpoint with the passing of time, as in the "separate but equal" issue affecting the right of black Americans to be free from segregation. The judges begin by deciding in their own minds whether the given law is calculated to advance the goals laid down in the Preamble to the Constitution, "to form a more perfect union, insure domestic tranquility, provide for the common defense, promote the general welfare, and secure the blessings of liberty." If they are persuaded that such is the case, the law is "constitutional," that is to say, it is in the spirit of the Constitution. Like the lawyers who have defended the given statute, the court then proceeds to validate it by finding a basis for it in the text of the fundamental law. Thus the ultimate sanction is the social utility or the ethical validity of the law.

That this technique of *discovering* the law is indistinguishable from *creating* the law, students of legal philosophy like Professor Morris Raphael Cohen have pointed out. In human affairs, he says, inventing and finding are not antithetical, so that "the process of law-making is called finding the law." A judicial decision "decides not so much what the words of a statute ordinarily mean but *what the public, taking all the circumstances of the case into account, should act on.*" He argues forcibly against regarding this process as "spurious interpretation," pointing out that supplementary legislation by judges is not only inevitable but justifiable, because "*to make a detailed description of specific human actions forbidden or allowed and their consequences would be an endless and impossible task*" (italics his). He insists also that while judges do and must make law, it would be absurd to maintain that "they are in no wise bound and can make any law they please" (*Law and the Social Order*, pp. 121, 131, 133, 146). In sum, interpretation is not only a life-giving activity, but an inevitable process in any system of law that wishes to survive.

If tradition means development and change—and the evidence is impressive and undeniable—how can we speak of the continuity or the spirit of Jewish tradition? An analogy may help supply the answer. Biologists have discovered that in any living organism, cells are constantly dying and being replaced by new ones. It has been estimated that within a period of approximately seven years, every cell in a human body has been replaced by another. If that be true, why is a person the same individual after the passage of eight years? The answer is twofold. In the first instance, the process of change is gradual. A man does not awake one morning to find all his cells changed and himself completely transformed. The variation each day is imperceptible. In the second instance, the growth follows the laws of his being. At no point do the changes violate the basic personality pattern. The organic character and unity of the personality reside in this continuity of the individual and in the development of the physical and spiritual traits inherent in him, which persist in spite of the modifications introduced by time.

This recognition of the organic character of growth highlights the importance of maintaining the method by which Jewish tradition, in all its great creative stages, biblical, talmudic, and medieval, continued to develop. This the researches of Jewish scholars from the days of Zacharias Frankel and Isaac Hirsch Weiss to those of Chaim Tchernowitz and Louis Ginzberg have revealed.

To understand Jewish law truly, it must be recognized not as a point but as a line, not as a one-time event but as an ongoing process. Hence, to decide what Jewish law today requires on any given issue means not merely marking a point, but plotting a line on a graph on which tradition is one coordinate, and contemporary life the other. To disregard either spells death to Judaism. In other words, it is important to know not merely where the Halakhah stands, but in what direction it is moving.

V

The changes in Jewish law which have thus far engaged our attention may perhaps be described as "vertical, in time," the result of changing eras and conditions. In another significant and fruitful sense, however, Jewish law is not monolithic; it exhibits varieties that may be called "horizontal," that is to say, at any given period there are categories of greater and lesser severity within the structure of Jewish law.

Like every living legal system, Rabbinic Judaism recognizes that there are gradations in acts, both positive and negative. The warning of Rabbi Judah Hanasi, "Be as careful with a light commandment as with a weightier one, for you do not know the relative reward of the commandments" (*Abot* 2:1), is designed to stimulate the observance of the lesser commandments, the existence of which is obviously conceded.

Similarly, all violations are not of the same severity. This is self-evident from the various types of punishment imposed in rabbinic law, such as the four modes of judicial execution, which themselves vary in severity, as well as *karet*, flagellation, and the various fines (*kenas*). To be sure, we are not likely today to reintroduce these penalties; rabbinic law, with its insistence upon *hathra'ah*, "warning to the malefactor," and other safeguards against unmerited punishment, has seen to that. But the gradation of acts which exists in rabbinic law, both with regard to forbidden and to meritorious deeds, constitutes a suggestive concept which should be utilized by the modern halakhist in deciding contemporary issues.

The highest level of permissibility and of favor consists of acts which go beyond the requirements of religious and moral duty. These deeds Jewish tradition honors as *Kiddush ha-Shem*, "the hallowing of God's name," when they involve martyrdom or another major sacrifice for the preservation of fundamental religious values and the collective honor of Israel. Such actions are called *lifnim mishurat ha-din*, "a higher standard than is required by the letter of the law," when they relate to the individual in his civil relations to his fellow men. On the other hand, adherence to a higher standard of piety than the law requires with regard to ritual commandments (*mitzvot ben 'adam la-Makom*) is described in rabbinic literature by the phrase, "Keep thyself holy even in matters permitted to thee" (*Yebamot* 20a). From the medieval age onward, Jewish life knew also of those who chose to be *mahmirin le'atzman*, "more stringent for themselves than the law requires." Though acts of this type may differ in temper, motivation, and value, they are all performed in obedience to a categorical imperative: the desire to maintain the loftiest standard possible of adherence to God's will, free from the fear of punishment or the desire of reward.

The next level of permissibility consists of the prescribed *mitzvot*, the performance of which is regarded as praiseworthy. As has already been noted, these too are not all of equal importance or significance in Jewish law.

It is worth noting that acts which we might be disposed to regard as religiously or ethically "neutral" do not develop a special term in traditional Judaism. This is no accident, but flows directly out of the life-affirming character of the Jewish religion. For Jewish tradition regards the satisfaction of one's bodily needs, the enjoyment of life's pleasures, the cultivation of one's skills, and preparation for a useful career not as neutral acts, but as positive *mitzvot*, which are obligatory for man, because they are calculated to testify to the glory of God and enhance it. Hence Judaism ordains that they are virtually all to be sanctified by special benedictions.

Within the *'abherot*, or religious offenses, a similar hierarchy is to be found. The severest transgressions are those within the competence of human courts to punish, either by capital or physical punishment or by financial penalty.

Another widespread category in Jewish law consists of acts which the Codes describe as "acts which in advance are forbidden, but which, once committed, are not punishable." Even in so sacred an area as that of the family, the Talmud recognizes that certain marriages which violate negative commandments, while forbidden in advance, are nonetheless valid.

Rabbinic courts recognized that certain transgressions were beyond the competence of human justice. Offenses such as these they describe variously as *karet*, "worthy of extermination by God," or as "unpunishable by human agency but punishable by the laws of Heaven." This is explained in greater detail in the Tosefta (*Shebhuot*, chap. 3): "Legally he is not obligated to make restitution, but Heaven does not forgive him until he does."

It is a commonplace that the most difficult decisions facing us in life do not involve a clear-cut choice between right and wrong, but rather a conflict between two ideals, which special circumstances place in opposition to one another. Here the decision must necessarily be painful, for one value will need to be sacrificed in order to preserve the other. What is more, different individuals will decide in varying fashion, depending upon their scale of values, their temperament, and other subjective factors.

It is in areas such as this that freedom of the religious conscience operates. That a conflict of ideals or practices may arise in special cases would not justify a legal system in denying the validity of either ideal. Now the rabbis were well aware of instances in which the individual might be faced by such a conflict and thus be compelled to violate the law. Rabbinic law showed its keen insight into human nature, as well as its solicitude for the maintenance of the entire structure, through designating several such categories. Such is the category of *patur 'abhal 'asur*, "unpunishable but forbidden," which is applied by the Mishnah, for example, in the familiar Sabbath law: "He who extinguishes a lamp on the Sabbath because he is afraid of robbers or of an evil spirit, or to enable a sick person to sleep, is unpunished; if his object is to save the lamp, the oil, or the wick, he is punishable" (*Shabbat* 2:15).

Two such inner conflicts characteristic of modern life, one in ethics and the other in ritual, may be cited. With the scourge of cancer widespread today, a man may find himself confronted by an agonizing ethical dilemma. On the one hand, we are commanded to tell the truth by the Torah in the injunction, "You shall not lie" (Leviticus 19:11). On the other hand, we are solemnly adjured by the Decalogue, "Honor thy father and thy mother" (Exodus 20:12, Deuteronomy 5:10), to show concern and love for our parents. Should a child, therefore, tell his mother that her condition is hopeless, or should he, out of love for her, sustain her illusions? This question in medical ethics is frequently debated, with advocates on both sides. Necessarily the child must ultimately make his agonizing decision, which will necessarily be far less than satisfactory, indeed be fraught with great pain for him. Yet his choice of one ideal at the expense of the other does not mean that either has lost its validity, its power to command the human conscience.

Another such dilemma, which is the subject of continuing controversy, may be cited from the area of ritual. Particularly in the smaller cities of the country, but also in the suburbs of the great metropolitan centers, American Jews are increasingly finding their homes at a considerable distance from the synagogue with which they are affiliated. Only in the rarest of cases are they in a position to live within walking distance. The present writer strongly believes that the blessing of Sabbath rest, described in the prayer book as *menuhah shelemah*, "total rest," requires total abstention from travel with its many sources of tension and fatigue. On the other hand, observing the law strictly will preclude a family from attending Jewish services on every Sabbath and festival. Where there are small children, they would be unable to witness or participate in Jewish communal worship with all the values it enshrines. The dilemma is real and painful. No matter which alternative a family adopts, it will not be free from major disadvantages. The decision is one which only the individual involved can make for himself, but the validity of both principles is not thereby impuned.

In a not inconsiderable number of instances, the rabbis were confronted with practices which they could not favor, but about which they felt that nothing would be achieved by active opposition. Often the practice was deeply rooted in the life of the people, or the motives underlying the action were praiseworthy, or at least understandable. In other instances there was little likelihood of any change at that juncture by reason of prevailing conditions. In such cases, the Talmud tells us, "the sages did not protest publicly against the practice." These affected such varied aspects of life as the liturgy, agricultural laws, marriage laws, relationships with the Gentile community, and the prerogatives of royalty (cf. Mishnah *Pesahim* 4:8, *Ketubbot* 1:5, *Gittin* 5:8, *Sanhedrin* 2:4, *Menahot* 10:8; Tosefta *Shekalim* 1:12; Jerusalem Talmud, *Sukkoth* II, 52d; Babylonian Talmud, *Ketubbot* 3b).

In sum, there are vast resources within the Halakhah for its continued creative unfoldment and its contribution to the ennobling of life, especially when traditional law is illumined by the insights of modern scholarship. Our leadership must be imbued with genuine reverence and faith in God, coupled with a sensitivity to the problems, fears, and aspirations of modern man and the courage to act upon our convictions.

Jewish law is a perpetual tension between the two elements within it, the divine and the human, between its unchanging Source, which is God, and the finite vessel into which its living waters flow, which is man. If we, the human partners in this cosmic encounter, do our part, God will grant us the strength and wisdom to confront the perils and perplexities of our time and help save Israel and the world.

7

JEWISH LAW: ITS GROWTH AND DEVELOPMENT

I

The battle which raged around Jewish tradition in nineteenth-century Germany and later in other lands of the West generated light as well as heat. To be sure, even the liberal protagonists of traditional Judaism, like the staunch defenders of unswerving fundamentalism, were more concerned with establishing dikes against the floodwaters of dissolution than with digging channels for the stream of tradition. The basic concern of the "positive-historical" school was with preservation rather than with growth. Nonetheless, the historical method to which all the representatives of this group were committed by training and conviction had within it the resources needed for a theory of development in Judaism.

This is particularly true of the thought of the American-Jewish scholar and leader, Solomon Schechter, who carried further the ideas of the "positive-historical" school. He sought a basis in traditional Judaism both for conservation and for progress, which became the hallmark of Conservative Judaism. This he found in his now famous doctrine of "Catholic Israel," the theory that the community of the Jewish people is the ultimate authority for Jewish values and practices. "Judaism has distinct precepts and usages and customs, consecrated by the consent of Catholic Israel through thousands of years."[1]

Only through adequate learning, said Schechter, would it be possible for Jews, and particularly for the rabbis, to "know what is vital to Judaism and what may be changed with impunity." He disapproved of the continual dropping of various ceremonies which he regarded as essential to religion, as well as the unceasing innovations which must in the end, he insisted, "touch the very vital organism of Judaism."

Schechter had notably deepened the concept of authority in Judaism, but even in his formulation, which was usually parenthetical and incidental to another theme, the will predominates over the intellect. For he was primarily concerned with a working formula rather than with a logically perfect definition. He too had his gaze fixed on Reform, against the inundating tide of which he sought to erect a dam. Yet the fact must not be overlooked that this general outlook was sufficiently grounded in reality to serve as the basis for the rapid progress of Conservative Judaism in the United States, and even in Germany before World War I, where Frankel's trend became the dominant one.

Neverthless, for all its pragmatic value, Schechter's theory of Catholic Israel suffers from self-evident weakness. It has the virtue of recognizing the historical and evolving character of Judaism, but then it arbitrarily declares that what traditional Judaism has created until now must henceforth be maintained virtually unchanged. To cite Professor Ginzberg, the norm, according to Frankel, was the talmudic position that whatever observances are spread throughout the whole community must not be abrogated by any authority.[2] It thus creates a dichotomy in Jewish experience between the creative and committed past and the confused and unconcerned present. Moreover, had the same doctrine been invoked in past centuries, the development of Judaism, and perhaps also its very life, would have been halted.

Finally and most important, the practical application of the doctrine offers insuperable obstacles. If by Catholic Israel whose practice determines what is binding in Judaism we mean the majority of modern Jews, then we might as well eliminate the Sabbath, the festivals, and the dietary laws, since they are violated by most Jews today. If, on the contrary, we subsume under the category of Catholic Israel the observant Jews only, then the doctrine means a retention of the status quo, for, by definition, an observant Jew is one who observes the law as it stands.

For these reasons, in spite of the essential soundness of Frankel's and Schechter's theory in emphasizing the evolving nature of Judaism, the binding character of Jewish law, and the centrality of Catholic Israel in that development, the concept of "Catholic Israel" proves to be unworkable unless we rethink its implications.

II

The past half-century has, therefore, witnessed the emergence of a new approach to Judaism known as Reconstructionism. During this period the Reconstructionist movement has sought to implement its attitude toward ritual by the publication of a *New Haggadah*, the *Reconstructionist Prayer Books,* and a special pamphlet entitled *Toward a Guide for Jewish Ritual Usage.* Reconstructionism attempts to grapple with the problems of Jewish observance in the twentieth century. It deserves careful analysis, especially since its basic approach is shared by many modern Jews who are not official adherents of the movement and may, in fact, be unaware of its philosophy.

The position which is adopted in the Reconstructionist *Guide* may be summarized as follows: The traditional Jewish code of observance can no longer be maintained in its entirety. For practical and ideological reasons many, if not most, modern Jews are not prepared to preserve it. The anarchy of Reform Judaism, the supernaturalism and inflexible character of Orthodoxy, and the lack of clarity characteristic of Conservatism, render them all inadequate for modern needs. Therefore, a new rationale is needed. Every ceremony and rite must be judged in terms of its value as "a method of group survival and as a means to the personal self-fulfillment and salvation of the individual Jew."[3] We must reckon with the fact that a common pattern of observance is no longer possible. Jews living in different lands or varying in their social and educational levels will differ in their evaluation of specific rituals. All that may be expected today is a unity of ends; the means will vary sharply among groups and individuals.

Nor does "a stigma attach to those who permit themselves a wide latitude in their departure from traditional norms." For Jewish ritual is no longer to be regarded as law, but as folkways, if only because there can be no law without sanctions, and we possess no agencies for enforcing Jewish observance or for punishing any infraction of the Codes. In fact, Professor Mordecai M. Kaplan had urged the substitution of the term *minhagim*, or "folkways," for "the commandments between man and God," in order to make it clear that "they lack the connotation of being . . . imperative."[4]

The *Guide* then set up criteria for judging the value of specific rituals, in terms of the meaningfulness of their form, of their content, or of both. It then considered in some detail synagogal worship, the Sabbath, and the "dietary usages," retaining or modifying elements of the traditional Codes in the light of the criteria previously developed.

When this *Guide* was published, it naturally aroused heated discussion in Conservative Jewish circles and violent denunciation in the Orthodox camp. The Reconstructionist *Guide* raised fundamental issues with regard to the rationale of Jewish observance that are still pertinent today. We believe that it is important to indicate why we believe that basic elements in the *Guide* are unacceptable on theoretical or on practical grounds.

It is not true, for example, that Conservative Judaism makes the survival of the Jewish people the justification of Jewish observances, or that Orthodox Jews observe the dietary laws "out of the fear of God" rather than "the love of God." The motive obviously depends on the individual in question.

Moreover, it is grossly insufficient to build the future of Judaism on unity of purpose coupled with a variety of means. As John Dewey clearly pointed out, the means we always have with us, while the end belongs to an uncertain future. Given enough variety of means, no unity remains at all.

It is undoubtedly true that traditional Judaism deprecated the effort to explain the meaning of the *mitzvot*.[5] But this attitude prevailed only during the earlier stages of the Jewish religion, before the impact of other cultures became pronounced. When Judaism met Greek thought, whether directly, as in Philo, or through the medium of Arab civilization, as in medieval days, the search for the *ta'ame hamitzvot* became a central feature of Jewish religious thought and the subject of a considerable literature.[6]

Thus the great pioneer of Jewish philosophy, Saadia, in the tenth century, already classifies the commandments under two headings: the *'akliyyat*, which are those commandments the reason for which is clearly evident, and the *samiyyat*, which are those commandments which demand obedience although their meaning is not clear. By reinterpreting these categories in modern terms, we arrive at a sound classification of the *mitzvot:* (a) the rational commands, consisting largely of the ethical imperatives wherein Judaism is basically at one with all great religions; and (b) the uniquely traditional forms, the product of historical factors in Judaism. That the instruments of daily prayer are phylacteries and not a prayer carpet cannot—and need not—be justified on rational grounds, but is the consequence of a specific Jewish development. Nor need the justification of specific rituals be sought in the area of logic. Every personality, whether that of an individual or of a group, includes rational elements wherein it will resemble others. But the essence of personality resides not in them alone, but also, if not preeminently, in the nonrational elements, which alone are unique and distinctive. To attempt to build the human spirit purely from rational elements means to create an automaton, not a living organism.

III

The cardinal weakness of the Reconstructionist approach, however, consists in its denial of the concept of Jewish law. Dr. Kaplan emphatically insists that ritual observances are not law but folkways, and he cites Vinogradoff to prove that law implies sanctions, the employment of force against the recalcitrant individual. Unless, therefore, we are prepared to reinstitute flagellation and the other rabbinic punishments for violations of the ritual commandments, Jewish ritual observances must be regarded by us not as law, but merely as folkways.

To deal with the practical implications of this attitude before considering its theoretical basis, it seems obvious to us that *to declare Jewish observance merely a matter of folkways sounds the death knell of Judaism as a normative religion.* Nowhere is there a deeper appreciation of the beauty of Jewish "folkways" than among Labor Zionists, for example. One of the best books on the Jewish festivals emanates from a member of their circle. But a sympathetic attitude toward these customs, even an emotional relationship, is powerless to effect their observance. Undoubtedly, the observance of a Third Seder by the Labor Zionists or the Workmen's Circle is preferable to the Yom Kippur balls of the anarchists fifty years ago, but what about the First and Second Seders?

If we abandon the concept of Jewish law, we have unwittingly adopted the principles of Paulinian Christianity. For it must be remembered that Paul was by no means uncompromisingly antinomian at the beginning of his career. On the contrary, his early attitude was one of toleration and even of commendation. In I Corinthians 7:19 he declares: "Circumcision is nothing, and uncircumcision is nothing, but the keeping of the commandments of God." In Romans 2:25 he goes further and admits: "For circumcision verily profiteth, if thou keep the law." Yet though Paul began at that standpoint, he was led by a series of easy transitions to the complete repudiation of Jewish ritual law and the retention only of the ethical commandments. Ultimately, Paul could insist that keeping the law was a mark of sin.

So much for the practical consequences of this negation of the concept of Jewish law. That is not all. We find the theory of the Reconstructionist approach also unacceptable. To define law in terms of sanctions means to put the cart before the horse. Not sanctions create law, but law creates sanctions. To be sure, Vinogradoff does declare: "Every legal rule falls into two parts: first, a *command* stating the legal requirement; second, a *sanction* providing that, if the command is not obeyed, force will be employed against the recalcitrant person." But he is speaking of legal rules regulating *human* relations, and here sanctions are a central feature, for the obvious reason that legal codes which are concerned with the protection of the individual in society must interpose speedy and effective safeguards against aggression from other individuals. Protection and redress must be *immediate* in order to be effective, since the victim, being human, does not live forever! Hence laws "between man and his neighbor" which do not impose human sanctions are dead letters.

But for the religious spirit, the compulsion in law resides far elsewhere than in the police power of the state. For believers in God, every wrong act has its tragic consequences reflected in the universe and retribution is cosmic: "The shop is open, and the owner gives credit; the ledger is open, and the hand writes. Whoever wishes to borrow may come and borrow, but the collectors go about continually every day, exacting payment from a man whether he knows it or not; and they have proof upon which they can rely, and the judgment is a judgment of truth, and everything is prepared for the feast" (*Abot* 3:20).

That is the essence of the religious outlook, which regards the world as governed by the divine law of justice, which is binding even when no human penalties exist or can be enforced. Therein lies the significant contribution which religion makes to morality: its capacity to penetrate to areas beyond the reach of the law. The state punishes me if I hurt my neighbor, but hating him is no less a violation of law although the courts are powerless to act. Beating one's old father is punishable by sanctions imposed by the police court; but respect toward a parent is not enforceable by human agency, yet it is nonetheless obligatory. These and countless other ethical imperatives are law, not customs, practices, or folkways, yet no human, external penalty attaches to their violation.

These *a priori* considerations are reinforced by recalling the legal categories of the Talmud. No one will deny that to the rabbis the *mitzvot* were law, of binding power, yet as we have seen, every page of the Talmud refers to such concepts as "free from penalty but forbidden"; "unpunished in human law, but guilty by divine law"; and *karet,* "death at the hand of God." Recently a modern student of talmudic jurisprudence has called attention to the phenomenon in rabbinic law whereby legal rules, possessing human sanctions, tend to be transferred in the Talmud to the realm of ethics, with no external sanctions.[7] In fine, human sanctions cannot serve as the mark of religious law.

But, it will be argued, Rabbinic Judaism regards every enactment of the ritual as well as of the ethical code as literally divine, and violations of either are believed to entail divine punishment. For us today, however, revelation, which is rooted in the divine, as is all life, is a never-ending process, with institutions and ordinances created by men in whom the divine spirit works. Can we believe that the ritual code is enforceable by means of penalties? We submit that even in terms of our modern outlook, it remains true for us that the violation of Jewish ritual law is indeed attended by divine sanctions, as life demonstrates on every hand. We declare that the observance of the Sabbath brings deep and abiding rewards to the Jew, that it recreates his spirit as it regenerates his physical and nervous system, that it brings him into communion with God, links him with the profoundest aspirations of Israel, and draws him into the orbit of Torah. It follows inescapably that failure to observe the Sabbath brings its penalty in the impoverishment of the spirit, in the denudation of Jewish values, and in the alienation of the violator from the Jewish community; literally "that soul is cut off from its kinsmen."

However our outlook on life has changed under the influence of modern science, we reaffirm with our ancestors that God functions in human life and divine judgment operates in the world. For modern traditional Judaism, murder and the infraction of the Sabbath law are not on a par—incidentally, they never were.[8] Yet they are both violations of Jewish law, differing from each other just as crimes, felonies, and misdemeanors differ in American law, and therefore entail penalties of varying severity.

However—and this is significant for the outlook of modern traditional Judaism, which is based on the historical approach—the content of these categories will differ as changes take place in religious and ethical conceptions and in social and economic conditions. The commandment "Thou shalt not kill" was not, at the time of its promulgation, regarded as prohibiting clan vengeance, but as time went on this was subsumed under the category. First, the Torah restricted the activity of the kinsman, or "blood redeemer," in the case of an unpremeditated killing, and established cities of refuge. By the time of the Second Temple, tribal divisions had disappeared and clan vengeance, under any circumstances, would have been regarded as murder pure and simple, had it ever been attempted. The same process of development at work may be observed in the changed attitude toward lynching as a crime. Once widely practiced, even in the twentieth century, it is today universally outlawed as the epitome of cowardice and murder. Some day—it cannot come too soon—the mass murder of war will be recognized as falling under the same divine prohibition.

At present, kidnapping and terrorism practiced against civilians, even women and children, are defended, or at least condoned, in some quarters as legitimate weapons in the cause of "freedom." If civilized society is to survive, it will need to recognize these acts as acts of cruelty and cowardice, to be condemned and punished as major crimes. Not only crimes, but misdemeanors, change with time, but these modifications do not invalidate their status as law. It is well known that the content of our secular law codes change with time and circumstance, yet they remain obligatory for the citizen. Similarly, the recognition of the fact that the Halakhah is the product of growth and development does not impugn its binding power upon the religious conscience of the Jew.

IV

Wherein does the authority for growth and development in Jewish law reside, if revelation did not end at Sinai, or with the Mishnah or in the *Shulḥan Arukh?* The answer is to be found in the doctrine of Catholic Israel enunciated in general terms by Frankel and Schechter. In spite of its weaknesses, set forth above, we believe that if its implications be explored in terms of current trends and insights, it can serve as a basis for a living approach to Jewish tradition.

The conception of Catholic Israel is basically democratic. It declares that Jewish life is determined by no synod, conference, or executive board, but that it reflects the aspirations and the attitudes of the Jewish people as a whole. Now, theoretically, democracy is, in Lincoln's classic definition—which, incidentally, had been enunciated centuries earlier in the preface to John Wyclif's Bible— "government of the people, by the people, for the people."

In practice, however, no democratic government expresses the will of the entire people, but only of those persons who are sufficiently interested in it to exercise the franchise and to obey the laws. Indifferent citizens who do not exercise the franchise, and criminals convicted of an offense who forfeit their citizenship, constitute two classes which have no voice in the conduct of the government. At the opposite pole from the criminals are certain extreme idealistic groups, who voluntarily relinquish their rights in the state. Henry D. Thoreau, the great New England naturalist, was a philosophical anarchist who wrote on "The Duty of Civil Disobedience." He remains a great American, but he was not consulted in the town meetings at Concord. Similarly, pacifists in times of national crises are honored for their devotion to principle and they are not read out of the American people, but they are not asked to decide the military and diplomatic policies of the government.

In posse, democracy is the government of all the people; *in esse,* it is government by all elements of the people who recognize the authority of the law and actively express their interest, at least by going to the ballot-box. There are times when nearly all eligible voters exercise their right of franchise. Generally, the percentage is only a fraction, sometimes less than fifty percent, of the whole. Our government, however, remains a democracy because potentially every American has a voice in the conduct of its affairs.

If we apply this analysis to our problem, it will become clear that

Catholic Israel must be conceived of differently from Schechter's original formulation. On the one hand, it is not coextensive with the Jewish people; nor, on the other hand, is it restricted to those who observe the Law unchanged.

Catholic Israel is the body of men and women within the Jewish people who accept the authority of Jewish law and are concerned with Jewish observance as a genuine issue. It therefore includes all who observe the Law, whatever their formal affiliation. The character of their observance may be rigorous and may extend to minutiae, or it may include modifications in detail. Catholic Israel embraces also all those who observe Jewish law in general, although they may violate one or another segment in particular, as well as those who are sensitive to the problem of their nonobservance because they wish to respect the authority of Jewish law.

Moreover, Catholic Israel is vertical as well as horizontal, that is to say, it includes the generations gone before, whose lives and activities have determined the character of the tradition transmitted to us. Their practice cannot permanently bar the way to growth, but it must necessarily exert a very significant influence upon our decisions regarding changes from accepted tradition. They may not have a veto, but they do have a vote.

That past generations should play an important role in determining the content of tradition for the present is not astonishing. Any "best-seller" enjoys a current sale thousands of times greater than that of Shakespeare's *Hamlet*, but the perennial appeal of the latter is more significant for life, literature and culture than the sensational qualities of the former. Catholic Israel is universal in time as well as in space.

In spite of widespread impressions to the contrary, Catholic Israel, consisting of all those within the pale of normative Judaism, was never a monolithic unity, a homogeneous body. The divergences between the Hillelites and the Shammaites, between Palestinian and Babylonian customs, and among the rationalists, mystics, and traditionalists in the Middle Ages, down to the Hasidim and the Mitnaggedim in modern times, were often far-reaching both in theory and in practice. Only the passing of time has blurred the lines and softened the acerbities of controversy.

The character and limits of these differences may be illustrated by means of two historical instances. Talmudic Judaism had its strict constructionists as well as its liberal interpreters, who greatly extended the scope of the biblical text by means of their interpretations of the Hebrew particles *'eth, 'akh, gam,* and *rak* in the Scripture. The more liberal exegesis of Akiba generally prevailed over the stricter methods of Ishmael, yet the latter scholar had a considerable influence upon Jewish law. When, however, centuries later, the Karaites arose, a group of strict constructionists *who denied the entire validity of talmudic law,* they forfeited their right to determine the development of rabbinic law.

Variations within Catholic Israel always existed. For obvious reasons, they are more marked today than they were in the past. Catholic Israel is no single, homogeneous group. It has its conservatives and its liberals, as has the American electorate. It is, however, restricted to those who accept the authority of Jewish law.

It need hardly be emphasized that this conception does not read any Jew out of the Jewish fold. It merely declares what should be self-evident: that only those who recognize the authority of Jewish law should have a voice in determining its character. Many Jews will continue to select, on a purely personal basis, certain customs from the pattern of Jewish living which appeal to them, but since they deny the authority of Jewish law they naturally cannot expect to be consulted on its development. It is true that in recent years Reform and secularist groups have approved a growing number of Jewish practices, a tendency which is to be warmly welcomed. They should certainly be encouraged to an ever deeper participation in Jewish observance. But the judgment of the sages has particular relevance to our problem: "Greater is he who is commanded and fulfills the commandment than one who is not commanded and fulfills it" (*Kiddushin* 31a).

The conception of Catholic Israel here proposed sheds light on the process of change and development in Jewish law, as well as upon the technique by means of which these changes are to be legitimized.

Changes in Jewish observance can become part and parcel of Jewish law only if they emanate from Catholic Israel, from those who accept the authority of Jewish law, and not from those who for whatever reasons have broken with it. Thus the Prohibition Amendment was repealed, not as a result of the activities of the Al Capones and the "Dutch" Schultzes in the 1920s, but through the activities and behavior of law-abiding American citizens who opposed Prohibition. At the beginning, a small group of dissidents may object to a given law and slowly they persuade others to adopt their opinion. When they increase in number, the enactment becomes a dead letter and ultimately it disappears from the statute books. The growing trend today to decriminalize the possession of small quantities of marijuana is a current illustration of this process.

This process of change and development in Jewish law is to be traced not only during the great creative periods of the Bible and the Talmud, as modern Jewish scholarship has revealed, but even in the abnormal and chaotic history of the modern period. Before our very eyes, far-reaching changes are taking place in Jewish observance among those who live by Jewish law, as we have noted above. Recent inventions continue to create new problems and corresponding reactions on the part of Sabbath observers. The telephone tends to be used on the Sabbath by many Sabbath observers, as are electric lights, while the radio and television have added new elements to the problem! All these and similar modifications have occurred thus far without guidance or even a conscious principle, but the process is real. It is Catholic Israel at work, of whom the Talmud declared that if they are not prophets, they are at least the descendants of prophets (*Pesaḥim* 66b).

This recognition of Jewish law as the collective expression of Catholic Israel explains the fact that what was forbidden at one time—and properly so—may become permitted at another time with equal justice. For new conditions and new attitudes impinge on the lives of men and women and accordingly modify the outlook and practices of Catholic Israel. When pious East European Jews a century or more ago, who used to be clad in long coats, objected to the shorter "German" coats of the Maskilim, the adherents of the Enlightenment, it was not mere obscurantism, but a recognition of the fact that the surrender of the traditional Jewish garb in an all-Jewish environment was a symbol of a break with Jewish *minhag*, or custom. However, as time went on, the new mode penetrated into traditional circles as well, and it was now innocuous. The same process applies to the wearing of beards, the prohibition of photography, and other elements of what was once traditional practice.

For centuries, there prevailed the custom of "doing penance" on the eve of Yom Kippur by swinging a chicken around the head and thus symbolically transferring the sin and the punishment from the penitent to the fowl *(shlogen kapores)*. The *Shulḥan Arukh* stigmatized the practice as *minhag shtut,* "a practice of folly," but the custom persisted in the face of rabbinic authority. Today the rite has all but disappeared, and a contribution is made to charity instead.

The process of growth in the Halakhah is slow; it has its stresses and its conflicts. By its very nature, every general law will work hardships in exceptional cases which require amelioration. But it remains law, because we believe that it is binding and that its observance or violation entails consequences of good or evil.

V

Having redefined Catholic Israel as those elements of the Jewish people that recognize the authority of Jewish law and are sensitive to the problem, we cannot overlook the ominous change which has taken place in modern times in the ratio which Catholic Israel bears to the Jewish people as a whole. That Catholic Israel could be identified by Frankel and Schechter with virtually the entire Jewish people was due to the fact that until recently the two groups were largely coextensive. Today, however, Catholic Israel, as we have defined it, represents only a minority of American Jewry and, with the Nazi destruction of the European center of Jewry, also of world Jewry. A democracy in which only a fraction of the electorate is interested in the government is in grave danger, and the present status of Jewish religious life in the United States is equally intolerable.

In fact, a theoretical question may be raised as to the right of a minority to arrogate to itself the title of "Catholic Israel" and then to undertake to "legislate" for the majority. If the final authority is vested in the Jewish people, and if Jews do not observe the requirements of Jewish ritual, does not their practice or their lack of practice become the modern standard of the Jews? Practically and theoretically, then, the concept of Catholic Israel as consisting of a minority is subject to challenge.

The answer lies in the conviction—and in the will behind that conviction—that the present status of Jewish observance is, or must be made, only temporary. To borrow an analogy from American experience, we are still at the frontier stage of Jewish life in the

United States. Every American is familiar with the frontier towns which sprang up all over America, particularly in the wake of the Gold Rush and similar mass movements. In these mushroom towns, the basic moral practices of American society were observed by a small and often impotent minority. Drunkenness, murder, gambling, and sexual license were widespread. Had the social behavior of the majority of the early residents of these western towns been perpetuated, it would have meant the collapse of the accepted moral code of the United States.

Instead, a contrary process took place. The minority gradually was able to institute law and order, and its standards ultimately became dominant. Where did the minority draw the power to enforce its standards upon the majority? It derived such authority from the knowledge of the fact that its attitudes had the sanction of the entire American people, of whom it constituted an outpost. The weight of that authority ultimately prevailed, even though it was temporarily embodied in a minority on the local scene.

As Lincoln pointed out in his attack on the concept of "popular sovereignty" as expounded by Stephen A. Douglas, Americans would never have admitted the right of Mormons to practice polygamy in the territory which they occupied as a majority. It is of course undeniable that the frontier spirit, as Professor Frederick J. Turner has stressed, exerted an abiding influence upon the American character and institutions, but the pressure of American life as a whole proved decisive for the frontier towns.

The analogy with the present status of Jewish life and Jewish ritual observance in the United States is striking. The biblical phrase "each man doing what is right in his own eyes" is just as valid a description of our age as it is of the days of the Judges. Pretending that the present chaos in Jewish life and observance is "the American way" and seeking to justify it, or at least to acquiesce in it, under some high-sounding formula, constitutes sheer self-deception.

To modify traditional Jewish law in order to bring it into conformity with the way of life of American Jews today is tantamount to amending the Constitution of the United States so as to harmonize it with the viewpoint of an anarchist, however high-minded he may be. Such efforts, be they ever so well intentioned, can succeed only in undermining Jewish law for those sections of the Jewish people who still reverence it and seek to live by it, without gaining those who have strayed from the Jewish way of life. On the contrary, the task of winning back the erring and the estranged, heartrendingly difficult as it is, is more often successfully achieved by traditional religion than by its nontraditional substitutes. The phenomenal growth today in numbers and self-confidence of fundamentalist groups in Judaism and in Christianity demonstrates the truth of this conclusion.

When the Talmud said, "Go, see how the people conduct themselves" (*Berakhot* 45a, *Erubin* 14a), it referred to a period when virtually all Jews qualified by this test. Had there been a large number of heretics like Elisha ben Abuyah or of general Sabbath violators in their day, the rabbis would not have consulted them as to the proper manner of Sabbath observance.

Undoubtedly, current American Jewish practice will influence our future code of observances in many ways and must therefore be seriously taken into account. But it is undeniable that there is need for reviving the great body of traditional Jewish rituals and observances by interpreting them in the light of our modern attitudes and by ceaselessly campaigning on behalf of their observance by American Jewry. By and large, Jews and not Judaism need reforming.

Therein lies the fundamental challenge of the current crisis to modern Jewish spiritual leadership, one which has been unconscionably neglected. The first duty of the rabbinate is that of carrying on an energetic and broad-based campaign for Jewish observance, in which the values that inhere in Jewish ritual are effectively brought home to the people. We cannot overemphasize the fact that, *by and large, the regimen of traditional observance, in spite of changed conditions, is viable and meaningful for the individual, besides being indispensable for the Jewish people.* In the vast majority of instances, what is needed is the renewal of the Jewish way of life, not its surrender.

The second task facing the scholars lies in recognizing those areas where change is required, because of new conditions or because of advancing ethical attitudes. In some instances the surrender of a part may be essential in order to salvage the rest of Jewish law. In exercising their function properly, the spiritual leaders would be literally leading the people to finer Jewish living.

Thirdly, the rabbinate must be able to appraise the current scene realistically. When it finds a change generally acceptable and irreversible, and in addition judges it to be religiously or ethically desirable, the rabbinate, through its agencies, like the Rabbinical Assembly or its Commission on Jewish Law and Standards, must create the halakhic basis for bringing the change into the mainstream of Jewish tradition.

The technique for carrying out this last-mentioned function was evolved by the sages of the Talmud, who utilized the process of interpretation rather than that of nullification in keeping pace with the times.

It is frequently maintained that this method is impossible for us today. Rabbi Akiba, it is argued, could draw from the biblical text finespun deductions which were actually developments beyond it, because he believed it to be literally the Word of God. The Torah was therefore eternal in its application and significant in every letter, syllable, word, and phrase. Since, however, for us revelation is a communication to man through man, a continuous process and not a single act, and since we possess the modern sense of history, a similar procedure of interpretation is ruled out today.

This line of reasoning is, however, far from conclusive. The Constitution of the United States, to which we have already alluded, is not regarded as the literal Word of God even by its most perfervid admirers, and no one believes that its authors foresaw all the problems and conditions of our day. Yet the learned justices of the United States Supreme Court find it a perfectly sensible procedure to declare laws regarding minorities, trade unions, the media, or public utilities "constitutional" or "unconstitutional." By means of a process of interpretation of the letter of the Constitution, they seek to discover its underlying spirit and then make it relevant to contemporary needs.

The process in talmudic law was, as we have seen, entirely similar to this method of judicial interpretation. When the sages differed on a given issue, the biblical verses which they cited were generally not the reason for their respective positions, but only a formal justification. First came a felt need, which the sages recognized or found already embodied in popular practice. Then came the process of interpretation of the Scriptures to give it continuity with tradition.

There is nothing in our modern concept of revelation that makes this process either impossible or outmoded today. The survival of democracy in the modern world depends upon avoiding the Scylla of reaction and the Charybdis of revolution. So, too, the Jewish way of life depends upon our success in avoiding unbending adherence to the status quo on the one hand and wholesale nullification on the other. Our platform must be loyalty to Jewish law, as embodied in the practice and thought of Catholic Israel, subject to the changes adopted by Catholic Israel.

While this democratic concept vests the full authority in the people, it gives the scholars a significant role to play in the process. As in all systems of living law, changes may emanate from two sources: the practice of the people, which the legislature then places upon the statute books; and the insights of the accredited leaders, who pass a law and thus make it binding upon the people. When a change has already become part of the practice of Catholic Israel and is ethically and socially desirable, the Rabbi of today, like his predecessors, has the duty of aiding its legitimization by using the accepted principles of interpretation of the traditional Halakhah. When he finds changes needful, even though the people have not yet recognized the necessity, he must urge their acceptance and then must find room for them in Jewish tradition. He must make Judaism possible to live by and worth living for. In the present as in the past, the truth is clear: growth is the law of life, and law is the life of Judaism.

8

A MODERN VIEW OF REVELATION

I

A century and a half have elapsed since Abraham Geiger, the protagonist of Reform, Samson Raphael Hirsch, the defender of Orthodoxy, and Zacharias Frankel, the advocate of the "positive-historical" school of Judaism, or Conservatism, debated the nature of Judaism. In the interval, it has become increasingly clear that there is need for dealing with both facets of Jewish law; its binding power on the one hand, and its capacity for progress on the other. This recognition is reflected in the work and thought of many scholars and thinkers, who formally belong to various schools. The responsa of such earlier figures as the late Rabbi Chaim Hirschensohn, author of *Malki Bakodesh,* the activities of Rabbi Abraham Isaac Kook, the papers of the late Professor Jacob Z. Lauterbach of the Hebrew Union College, many of the decisions of the Law Committee of the Rabbinical Council of America, based in large measure on the guidance of Rabbi J. B. Soloveitchik, the brilliant theoretician of the Halakhah, the writings of Dr. Simon Federbush on Jewish law and ethics, some of the interpretations and ordinances issued by the Chief Rabbinate of Israel, the pattern of life evolving in the Poel Hamizrachi colonies, and the quest for vitalized ritual and ethical standards expressed in such Israeli publications as *Yavneh, Sinai, B'terem,* and *Ba'yot,* are far from uniform in character.

Programmatic differences and organizational cleavages divide these and similarly minded individuals and groups from one another. Nonetheless, they all share a conviction of the viability and inherent worth of Jewish law on the one hand, and on the other, a faith that it possesses the resources to meet the needs of modern life as effectively as it did those of the past.

Judaism is more than a system of laws designed to maintain the polity of the Jewish nationality, as was argued by Spinoza and Mendelssohn on the threshold of the modern age. This proposition is still maintained by secularists today, whether they be committed to Jewish survival, like Mendelssohn, or indifferent to it, like Spinoza. Beyond all else and subsuming all else, Judaism is a religion, an instrument for expressing man's relationship toward the world and its Creator.

So long as Judaism retains the fundamentals of its original character or any continuity with its past, the royal road for expressing man's relationship to his Maker will be the Halakhah. Ethics is central in Judaism, and the personal commitment of faith surely has its place within the Jewish scheme of things. Yet no disembodied ethicism or rarefied mysticism can replace adherence to the traditional Jewish way of life.

Can a man who is modern in more than a chronological sense, and who has integrated the results of modern science and thought into his world-view, accept the Halakhah as authoritative for his life? We believe that an affirmative answer is entirely possible. Judaism does not make adherence to a specific creed the touchstone of loyalty to tradition, allowing considerable freedom of view, particularly in the area of "beliefs and opinions." The credo which we set forth is therefore like any other, not "official." It may, however, help others to clarify and formulate their thinking and thus find a spiritual home in modern Jewish religion.

Basically, the sanction of the Halakhah lies, for us, in its divine character. We regard the Law, both Written and Oral, as the revelation of God. What Moses, the prophets, the sages, and the rabbis taught, from Sinai to our day, is divinely inspired. That it has functioned so effectively, not merely for the preservation of Israel, but also, and more significantly, for the enhancement of human life, buttresses, but does not supplant, our faith that its source is God. Hence we accept as fundamental to vital Jewish religion the principle of *Torah min hashamayim,* "The Torah as a revelation of God."

Like our predecessors in talmudic, medieval, and modern times, each of us is free to give the term a greater or a lesser degree of definitiveness and literalness of meaning. The common core in all such views, however, and the irreducible minimum, is the belief that the Torah, which encompasses the ethical and ritual traditions of Israel, inaugurated at Sinai and carried forward through biblical, talmudic, and post-talmudic times to our own day, is an emanation of God, a revelation of divine truth.

This conception need not mean that the process of revelation consisted of the dictation of the Torah by God, and its passive acceptance by men. To be sure, this view, which is widely held by pious believers, is implied in some rabbinic references to the subject. Such is the explanation, already cited in the Talmud, for the presence of the last twelve verses in Deuteronomy, which describe Moses' death: "Until this closing section, God spoke, Moses repeating and writing it down. When this passage was reached, God spoke and Moses wrote in tears" (*Baba Batra* 15a). But that is not the only approach to revelation that is adumbrated in our sources and is open to us today. On the contrary, we may espouse a view that is at once more satisfying intellectually and religiously more profound.

II

There are three great moments in history when the divine decisively penetrates the world, in the acts of Creation, Revelation, and Redemption. Traditional Judaism found no derogation of the creative power of God in describing man as "the partner of the Holy One, blessed be He, in the work of creation." So too, Jewish teaching, as embodied in the prophets and the sages, believes that the Messianic era depends not only on the will of God, but on the acts of men. Redemption cannot come until "the generation is ready." Similarly, revelation is not impugned by viewing it as another aspect of this eternal partnership, or *cosmic symbiosis,* in which God, so to speak, depends upon men as truly as man depends upon God. Commenting on the passage in Isaiah 43:12, "Ye are My witnesses and I am God," the Midrash does not hesitate to say,

"When ye are My witnesses, I am God, and when ye are not, I am not God" *(Sifre, Berakhah)*.

Revelation means communication; it requires *two* active participants. It depends not merely upon its infinite and divine source, but also upon its finite and imperfect human instrument. God is unchanged eternally, but man is perpetually in flux, varying in his capacity to grasp the revelation of his Maker. Hence the idea of a continuous and growing revelation is not merely compatible with faith in its divine origin, but is the only view that reckons with the nature of the human participant in the process.

A Hasidic teacher was wont to say that God tempers His message in accordance with the understanding of the people to whom He addresses Himself, just as a loving father will use baby talk in speaking to his infant. We may suggest a more modern analogy, to be found in one of the wonders of our time, the electronic transmission of sound. Let us imagine a group of people assembled in a room, and a man addressing them in a normal voice. The auditors, if they possess average hearing, can grasp his words without difficulty. But the naked ears of the audience are incapable of catching the radio waves which fill the atmosphere in the room at the same time. Then a child brings an inexpensive portable radio into the room, and now it becomes possible for the group to hear the sounds emanating from the nearest and most powerful transmitting stations in the vicinity. Nevertheless, the sound waves of distant or weaker stations still remain inaudible until a finer instrument is introduced.

Now, whether the group in the room hears only the human voice of the speaker in their midst, or the powerful, nearby stations, or the fainter and more distant broadcasts, depends upon the instruments of reception available; all the varied sound waves themselves are within those four walls, whether people are equipped to hear them or not. The objective factor of the sources of sound is unchanged; only the subjective factor of the recipients varies.

That is not all. In no case will the human ear grasp exactly what emanates from the source. Some degree of distortion of the purity of the original sound is inevitable—the finer the instrument, the higher the fidelity, but always the receiving instrument affects the timbre and the tone to a greater or lesser extent.

The implications of this modern parable are clear. God is the source of revelation, but He works through men, whose capacity to grasp the divine truth depends on their personal insight and on the conditions of their age, whose children they inescapably are. Moreover, what men receive they refract through the medium of their own personality. It will always be the revelation of God, but never the full revelation; it will be approaching the divine "infinity," but never quite reaching it. Hence, the content of revelation vouchsafed to men constitutes a growing and evolving body of truth.

The classic sources of Judaism were written in ancient times, long before the modern recognition of the importance of historical and environmental factors. Yet the rabbis have more than an inkling of their role, when they speak of various saints who were denied the revelation to which they were fitted by personal qualifications on the ground that "the generation was not worthy." On the other hand, certain ages are marked by unique spiritual perceptiveness, as the rabbis recognize when they declare: "What an ordinary maid-servant saw at the crossing of the Sea in the days of Moses, was not seen by Isaiah, Ezekiel, and all the prophets" (*Mekilta, Shirata,* chap. 3).

Even more clearly traditional Judaism recognized the variable human factor in revelation. The Bible itself distinguishes between the immediacy of relationship possessed by Moses and that of the other prophets (Numbers 12:16 ff): "If there be a prophet among you, I the Lord do make Myself known unto him through a vision, I speak with him through a dream. Not so My servant Moses; he is an intimate in all My house; with him I speak mouth to mouth, even manifestly, and not in dark speeches; and the very image of the Lord does he behold."

This distinction the rabbis amplify in their parable of Moses as a stargazer with a clear telescope, unlike the other prophets, who had blurred instruments of vision (*Yebamot* 49b). Similarly, the Talmud compares the prophet Isaiah to a city-dweller who is familiar with the king and therefore takes him for granted, while Ezekiel is compared to a rustic coming to the capital, gazing in unfeigned astonishment at the unfamiliar spectacle of a royal procession (*Hagigah* 13b). The parable represents a distinction between the levels of inspiration of the two prophets, as well as a description of their work.

III

Not only does revelation differ in content and depth, varying with the individual, but it is not limited in time. In other words, it is not an event, but a process. After the period of the patriarchs, to whom God revealed Himself, Sinai marked the commencement, not the conclusion, of revelation. The theophany on Sinai may be conceived of literally, mystically, or philosophically, but it represents a basic historical fact without which all the subsequent history of Judaism and, indeed, of the Jewish people is inexplicable. In increasing measure, contemporary biblical scholarship is recognizing this truth and accepting the historicity of Moses, and the presence of an authentic Mosaic core in the Pentateuch.

But scholarly analyses aside, for the Jewish religious consciousness, the first and greatest single hour of revelation was at Sinai. However, as rabbinic literature recognized, there were revelations after Sinai as well (cf. Bernard Bamberger, "Revelations of Torah after Sinai," in *Hebrew Union College Annual*, 1941). The relationship between these stages and Sinai is expressed in an utterance of Rabbi Johanan: "God showed Moses the derivations in the Torah and the derivations of the scholars, and whatever the scholars were to originate in the future" (*Megillah* 19b). The verb *ḥiddesh*, "to create anew," used in this passage, makes it clear that the rabbis recognized that their function was active, not passive; creative, not repetitive.

The same view attains to classic expression in a well-known passage which has often been misinterpreted: "Whatever any gifted disciple was destined to teach before his master was already said to Moses on Sinai" (Jerusalem Talmud, *Ḥagigah* 1, 76d). What this statement expresses is the recognition that the entire development of Jewish law after Moses is implied in the giving of the Torah on Sinai, as an oak tree is implicit in the acorn, and that the organic unity binding it all together gives to it all divine sanction.

One of the basic characteristics of classical Judaism embodied in the Bible and the Talmud, in which it differs significantly from Christianity, is the absence of a body of dogmas, on the acceptance of which salvation depends. Perhaps the closest the ancient rabbis came to setting forth articles of belief is in the Mishnah *Sanhedrin* (10:1). After establishing the general principle that "All Israel has a share in the world to come," the Mishnah declares, "These have no share in the world to come, he who says 'there is no resurrection of the dead' (or, 'the doctrine cannot be derived from the Torah'), or 'the Torah is not from heaven' (i.e., is not a revelation from God), or an Epicurean." Thus divine revelation, as all the great Jewish philosophers recognized, is a fundamental belief of traditional Judaism. In modern Orthodox apologetics, another phrase, *Torah missinai,* "the Law from Sinai," has been introduced and is read as though it were synonymous with *Torah min hashamayim,* "Torah from Heaven." It is worth noting that the former term, *Torah missinai,* "Torah from Sinai," unlike the phrase *Torah min hashamayim,* "Torah from Heaven," does not occur in rabbinic literature except in one Mishnah (*Abot* 1:1), where the words are not a technical term or an article of faith. The Mishnah wishes to establish the authority of the Oral Law and so declares, "Moses received the Torah from Sinai and transmitted it to Joshua, etc." Undoubtedly, the sages of the Talmud believed that the entire Pentateuch came from Moses, since they antedated modern scholarship by many centuries. *But they did not establish the Mosaic authorship of the Pentateuch as a dogma in Judaism.*

Such a dogma would mean to pass judgment on a question which only historical and literary scholarship can legitimately decide, and which, contrary to the widespread impression, is of no real consequence for religious faith. For as a modern traditional Hebrew commentator on the Book of Isaiah said with regard to the theory of a Second Isaiah, "What difference does it make whether there was one great prophet or two?"

To build the sanctions of Judaism on the doctrine that the Five Books of Moses were completely written in their present form by the great Liberator is to prejudge a scientific question, and to court disaster should the verdict of scholarship demonstrate otherwise. The famous Reform scholar Kaufmann Kohler testified that he lost his faith in traditional Judaism, as expounded by his master Samson Raphael Hirsch, when his study of Semitic languages demonstrated that Hebrew was not the oldest and original language of mankind, as his teacher had insisted.

A more profound approach to tradition is to be found in the words that Franz Rosenzweig wrote to Jacob Rosenheim: "Where we differ is our reluctance to draw from our belief in the holiness or uniqueness of the Torah and in its character of revelation any conclusions as to its literary genesis and the philological value of the text as it has come down to us. If all of Wellhausen's theories were correct and the Samaritans really had the better text, our faith would not be shaken in the least." That the Torah is Mosaic in essence is increasingly being recognized among scholars, but the ultimate disposition of this issue does not affect the religious validity of the revelation which is the Torah's source.

On the basis of my study of the biblical text, archaeological data, and religious, historical and legal material from the ancient Orient, I believe that there are significant elements in the Pentateuch that go back to Moses, of whose historicity I am convinced. Other scholars will undoubtedly evaluate the evidence differently and come to different conclusions. But the question must be determined by the canons of scientific method and not by an antecedent dogma barring the way to free and untrammeled research. Whatever conclusions are reached on the scholarly question of date and authorship, the call of the Torah to the Jew "to hearken and obey" is inherent in the content and quality of its message.

Properly used, both phrases, *Torah min hashamayim* and *Torah missinai*, express a fundamental of Judaism, the belief that Jewish law in its entire history and unfoldment bears the same relationship to the revelation at Sinai as does a spreading oak tree to its original acorn, in which all its own attributes are contained.

That this concept does not commit us to a static concept of Halakhah is clear from the profound talmudic legend (*Menahot* 29b) that describes Moses as not understanding all that Akiba taught, but being reassured by Akiba's linking his teaching with Moses' law. The unity of the Halakhah goes hand in hand with its growing and evolving character.

To recapitulate, revelation is a never-ending process, suffering all the vicissitudes of human life because human beings, weak and imperfect and varying widely in their profundity and insight, are creative partners with God in the process. Moreover, the process does not end with the Mishnah or the Gemara, or with Saadia, Maimonides, Jacob ben Asher, Joseph Karo, Rabbi Isaac Elhanan Spector, or Rabbi Abraham Isaac Kook. It also follows that not every stage is equally creative and fruitful; some are richer and more significant than others. Revelation is not unilinear, moving steadily upward in a straight line. It is better conceived of as a spiral with undulating dips and crests, but tending generally to deeper insight into the will of God, since each stage has the benefit of those preceding it.

One may venture to hope that the varied efforts in this direction being made in our day may prove to be among the instruments of divine revelation, and that these contributions will ultimately enter the mainstream of living Jewish tradition.

IV

A corollary of this recognition of the divine character of the Torah is the faith in its capacity to meet all the problems of life, however radically conditions may become altered. This conviction, to be sure, cannot be demonstrated mathematically, yet it is supported by the history of Jewish tradition. For the Halakhah has proved capable of growth and development through all the shifting fortunes of the Jewish people. Both in Palestine during the periods of independence, autonomy, and subjugation, and in the Diaspora, whether in the Greco-Roman world or in the various Christian and Moslem societies, Jewish law did not stand still.

It is highly significant in this connection that frequently institutions develop new rationales under changed conditions. To cite a paradoxical example, it would not be difficult to argue that in the simple, largely sedentary life of Jewish householders in the Polish and Austrian villages of the nineteenth century, the traditional Sabbath, with its complete cessation of mobility and activity, was scarcely necessary! In those communities, moreover, Jewish worship and study, which we associate with the Sabbath day, found ample expression in the life of the people during the week. On the other hand, it is precisely in our harried and hurried age, which has all but lost the *locus standi* for the individual and the sense of unity in the family, that the *menuḥah shelemah*, the "complete and perfect rest," of the traditional Sabbath is most necessary for the physical and psychic health of the people.

Thus the difficulties which modern Judaism encounters in inculcating the observance of these time-honored prohibitions against workaday activities do not justify their surrender. On the contrary, the breaches in the fortress of the Sabbath testify all the more vividly to the burning need for the traditional Sabbath and to the vital role which it, and it alone, can play in modern life. For in rapidly growing degree the hazards of modern life consist not so much in the area of physical fatigue and exhaustion as in the field of mental and nervous disorders, as well as of other diseases of hypertension, such as high blood pressure, heart ailments, and stomach disorders, and perhaps even cancer. What modern man needs most is not physical rest, but nervous and mental relaxation. Considerations such as these do not categorically rule out any modification of the Sabbath laws, but they should guard us against a superficial approach to the problem.

The character of the Halakhah, creatively viewed, is paralleled by its universality of scope. Beginning with the Decalogue, the Book of the Covenant, and the Holiness Code, Jewish law has always concerned itself with man's entire life, individual and social, and has expressed itself in both ethical and ritual enactment.

While tradition considers both the ritual and the ethical elements of Jewish law as binding, it is a distortion to maintain that it regards them as of equal significance. The authoritative statement of Rab, "The commandments were given only in order to purify human nature" (*Genesis Rabbah* 44:1), clearly recognizes ritual as the means and the ethical life as the goal of religion.

This attitude is not limited to the Aggadah. No other "commandment between man and God" can rival the Sabbath in importance. Yet the Halakhah, which establishes the norm that "Saving a human life takes precedence over the Sabbath" (*Ketubbot* 5a; cf. *Yoma* 85a), insists that even life itself must be sacrificed rather than violate the basic religious and ethical commandments against idolatry, immorality, and murder. It is noteworthy that even of these three, Rabbi Ishmael permits the practice of idolatry under duress, except if it be publicly committed, where its impact upon the people as a whole would be disastrous. Thus, for him, only two commandments, and these both ethical, remain supreme under all circumstances (*Sanhedrin* 74a). The same hierarchy of values is implied in the familiar Mishnah: "For transgressions between man and God, the Day of Atonement makes atonement; for transgressions between man and man, the Day of Atonement cannot atone, until he appeases his fellow-man" (*Yoma* 8:9).

In sum, while both the ritual and the ethical elements of the Halakhah are binding, the latter are more important than the former.

Here, as so often, the classical position of Jewish tradition, when perfectly understood, is echoed by our own highest aspirations.

This is not to deny that in many fields Jewish law today is far from being in consonance with the conditions and ideals of contemporary life. The fault, however, lies with the bearers of tradition in our day, who have failed to maintain the momentum of interpretation and growth established by earlier and more creative spirits. Common sense would dictate a realistic approach to the contemporary problems of Jewish law by reviving the process first in those areas where the need is most acute and where the prospect for success is likeliest. After several centuries during which the entire field of Jewish law has lain fallow, it is obvious that all the broken fences cannot be mended at once.

Conditions in the State of Israel have already forced action in several fields, notably that of the marriage law, where the Halakhah is demonstrating its protean capacity to meet the issues of a new age. In the Diaspora, Jewish law is operative largely in two areas: family law and synagogue life. Without ruling out action elsewhere, it is both the duty and the opportunity of the rabbinate to deal courageously and reverently with such a fundamental problem as the disability of women in Jewish law, which still exists in the synagogue service, in marriage law, and in religious life generally. Family pews are becoming the norm in traditional American synagogues without recourse to the Halakhah. The various *agunah* proposals, which do have recourse to the Halakhah, are discussed elsewhere in this volume. They represent aspects of the basic issue of women's role in Judaism which require thought and action today. Other phases of the same problem are the calling up of women to the reading of the Torah, the Bat Mitzvah rite, and the counting of women in the *minyan*.

Jewish religious leadership must become actively aware of the problems of our time. It must evaluate the various solutions proposed, and relate the preferred conclusion to the body of Jewish law, through the interpretation of the existent Halakhah. It would be as unjust as it is impractical to dismiss this method as having failed; actually, it has not been tried.

The historic responsibility of American Jewry goes beyond the protection of Diaspora Jewry and the defense and buttressing of the State of Israel. It cannot evade its duty toward a spiritual renascence of Judaism, the indispensable elements of which are a quickened love for Jewish faith, thought, and practice, and a deep zeal for the maximum Jewish education of its youth and its elders. The nobility and wisdom of Judaism and the dedication of its devotees will avail nothing in the face of invincible ignorance. As Israel Zangwill pointed out, not differences in Israel but indifference is the mortal foe. "If you have acquired knowledge what can you lack? If you lack knowledge, what can you acquire?" (*Vayyikra Rabbah*, chap. 1).

9

A RATIONALE FOR RELIGIOUS PRACTICE

The revitalization of Judaism as a way of life requires the restoration of its capacity for growth and adjustment. Yet in the face of widespread calls for easing "the burdens of the law," it cannot be too strongly emphasized that the area of change will necessarily be small, relative to the large number of permanent values in Jewish ritual. We must not forget the wise words of Leopold Zunz: "Not Judaism, but Jews need to be reformed." In order to win Jews to Judaism, and to persuade them of the wisdom and beauty of their heritage, we must utilize every means at our disposal. We must create a rationale for Jewish living, producing modern counterparts for the medieval works on "the reasons for the commandments." We must guide the path of development in Jewish law by setting up criteria for religious observance, so that each specific element may be judged by those standards and by the people educated to adopt these practices in their lives. It seems increasingly clear that "Guides to Jewish Practice" must be created anew. The establishment of criteria for Jewish observance is no simple matter, as previous efforts in this direction have indicated, but the search must go on.

A fundamental principle, restated by as modernistic a thinker as Professor Kaplan, is that our attitude toward Jewish observance is

74

not neutral. We must be definitely "prejudiced" in favor of Jewish observance. We do not approach Jewish life with a *tabula rasa,* any more than in any other department of civilization. "The presumption should always be in favor of traditional procedure."

In order that this principle shall serve as a practical guide, we may suggest, with apologies to Maimonides, a theory of "negative attributes." Below we shall adduce several positive norms by which ritual is to be judged. Any Jewish practice *eo ipso* has a claim upon us, unless it can be proved that it does *not* perform any of these functions, and that it cannot be reinterpreted to do so.

The fundamental function of all the *mitzvot* is *Kedushat haḥayyim,* the hallowing of life. This is indicated in the opening phrase of most traditional benedictions: "Blessed are You, O Lord our God, who has sanctified us by Your commandments." Judaism, unlike some other religions, seeks to sanctify life not by suppressing the natural but by making every activity and impulse an avenue for the service of God. Such activities as eating, drinking, resting, sexual gratification, the enjoyment of fine clothes, or the pleasure of a beautiful sight are not concessions to man's "lower" nature. When properly conceived and related to the universe, they are revelations, nay more, experiences of the divine. Thus the physical and nervous rebuilding of a human organism through the Sabbath rest becomes part of the cosmic process.

The various rituals of Judaism constitute dramatic and vivid attempts to make every aspect of existence reflect its divine source and every human activity fulfill man's purpose on earth, which is the glory of God. As the prayer book puts it, "Blessed is our God, who has created us for His glory, separated us from those who go astray, given us the Torah of truth, and planted eternal life within us." In the fine Hasidic simile, the blessings of this world remind us of God, just as jewels remind a lover of his beloved.

From this fundamental goal of the hallowing of life and the deepening of our awareness of God, four criteria for Jewish practice may be derived, as follows:

1. *The Cosmic or Religious.* These are observances which bind us to the universe and lend a cosmic significance to the events of our ordinary life. One of the remarkable aspects of Jewish observance is its rich collection of special benedictions. The Jew is bidden to

pronounce a blessing not only before the performance of a ritual like the Waving of the Four Species, the *etrog,* the *lulav*, the *hadas,* and the *arabhah,* or the eating of matzah at the Passover Seder, or upon the occasion of entering into marriage. He is also enjoined to pronounce a blessing before partaking of food, like bread, wine, fruit, or water, or witnessing a great natural event, like lightning or thunder, or meeting a distinguished sage or scholar. Thus the benediction before partaking of bread is, "Blessed are You, O Lord our God, King of the universe, who brings forth bread from the earth." In this benediction, as in all others, the specific act is associated with God, who is the Creator and the Ruler of the cosmos. Ritual, when it is beautiful and meaningful, places such occasions as birth, puberty, marriage, and death against the background of a vital universe and its Creator. They no longer remain accidents of animal existence, but become part of the unending miracle of life, suffused with a sense of holiness. Ritual declares, with the unanswerable logic of beauty, that man counts in the universe, that he is not an atom of dust, but a spark of God.

2. *The Ethical or Social.* It is of the essence of ideals that they must be taught continually. Unlike the multiplication table, learning ethical principles by rote is insufficient, because life, which in the largest sense depends upon them, is always conspiring through a thousand petty devices to defeat man's aspirations for peace, understanding, and justice. As Albert Einstein declared in an address on education: "With the affairs of human beings, knowledge of truth alone does not suffice. On the contrary, this knowledge must continually be renewed by ceaseless effort, if it is not to be lost. It resembles a statue of marble which stands in the desert and is continuously threatened with burial by the shifting sand. The hands of service must ever be at work in order that the marble continue lastingly to shine in the sun."[1] To teach ideals perpetually and yet avoid monotony is the special function of ritual. Because ritual is symbolic in character, it lends itself to varying emphases and interpretations and thus avoids the perils of repetition. The Sukkah, the Shofar, and the Seder, like the sancta of all religions, are rituals symbolizing ideals which can be reinterpreted anew and differently at succeeding seasons and for different purposes.

By the constant evocation of God's presence in the blessings accompanying the ritual, we are given new strength to combat the ever-present temptation to violate the ethical commandments of Judaism, in public or in private. This basic function of ritual is beautifully exemplified in the two passages, one biblical and one rabbinic, which are customarily to be found engraved over the Holy Ark in the synagogue: "I have set God always before me," and "Know before whom you stand."

3. *The Esthetic or Play Function.* A principal reason for the fact that ritual observance, when reverently and meaningfully executed, avoids the pitfalls of monotony is its esthetic character. Rituals constitute a source of poetry in life and offer an avenue of play for adults, who increasingly in our modern civilization find amusement in mechanical, passive, and commercial forms of entertainment. A religious service offers the adult the opportunity to sing; the Passover Seder, a chance to reenact a great drama; a Havdalah service at the close of the Sabbath, a bit of pageantry which most grownups find nowhere else.

It is symptomatic of the atrophy of the play function today that adults who seek to reintroduce a religious ceremony into their practice after long disuse are often self-conscious and uncomfortable about it at the beginning. It is equally characteristic of the decay of vitality in many modern synagogues that the congregation is a passive and virtually inaudible group of spectators rather than active participants in a religious service. The esthetic, participating element in Jewish ritual is all the more essential for the psychic well-being of a people.

4. *National or Group-Associational Values.* Finally, we recall the function which so many men and women mistakenly regard as the sole *raison d'être* of Jewish observance. Jewish ritual has national or group-associational values, linking the individual Jew to his family, his people, and his God. While early, extreme Reform sought to abolish *milah* and decried it as a barbarous custom, the rite of circumcision possessed such strong survival value that it has remained the universal mark of God's covenant with Abraham and his descendants.

Even the dietary laws were never completely abolished by Reform Judaism. American Jewry reflects untold patterns of dietary observance, down to the Jew whose only rule is that he buys his non-kosher meat from a Jewish and not from a Gentile butcher!

Ludicrous as these variations are from the standpoint of traditional Halakhah, they represent the periphery of a circle at the center of which is the full code of Kashrut. But all the degrees of observance recognize that the dietary laws draw the Jew close to his people and make him conscious of his Jewish allegiance.

In stressing the national element in Jewish observances, along with the other values inherent in them, we are affirming that whatever strengthens the bond of Jewish loyalty is a good, because we believe that Jewish survival is a blessing to the world. If that is not our profound conviction, we have no business trying to preserve either Judaism or the Jewish identity.

It is obvious that the most valuable elements of Jewish traditional observance contribute to the hallowing of life by performing all these functions, the cosmic, the ethical, the esthetic, and the group-associational. At times, an observance may perform only one or two, but may do it to such a transcendent degree as to justify its retention.

By standards such as these the heritage of Jewish ritual must be evaluated. So vital is most of Jewish tradition that by and large it can be maintained, if it is properly interpreted. Some aspects require modification or reinterpretation or both, while others, no longer serving any of these purposes, may lose their hold and disapppear. One of the basic functions of the spiritual leader is to foster not merely the appreciation of Jewish ritual, but the maximum observance of Jewish *mitzvot* and thus mold the life and content of Catholic Israel.

The final authority, however, rests, as we have seen, with the Jewish people, although the formal retention, reinterpretation, or surrender of Jewish observances should come from accredited rabbinical leadership. So long as some heartbeat of vitality may be detected in a custom, its value should be discussed with an eye to its resuscitation. But death is an unanswerable argument; if it has died utterly and completely, Catholic Israel has spoken and there is no returning.

It is undeniable that such a liberal approach to Jewish tradition faces grave dangers. How can one be certain that the changes introduced or permitted will not, because of their nature and extent, distort the true character of Judaism and snap the link of continuity beyond recovery? The honest answer is that there is no guarantee except the sincerity, learning, and insight of Jewish leadership. Life is always dangerous; only death is free from peril.

Different observers will naturally evaluate a given situation differently. What will seem to some to be needed growth will appear as anarchy in the eyes of others. That is nothing new in the history of Judaism. The right of dissent has been one of the great contributions of Judaism to the world and the saving grace of our tradition. Priest differed with prophet, and Wisdom teacher with both. The entire Talmud is a monument to the freedom of the human mind and to the right of each man to defend the truth as he sees it before the court of opinion of his fellows.

There are those who glory in the fact that for them all issues are settled and all answers are set forth once and for all in the great rabbinic Codes, preeminently in the *Shulḥan Arukh*. They might well note that there was no such easy refuge available to the Jews in the most creative periods of Jewish tradition. In the days when the Hillelites differed with the Shammaites, Rabbi Joshua with Rabbi Eliezer, Rabbi Akiba with Rabbi Ishmael, Rab with Samuel, Raba with Abaye, or Rabbi Johanan with Resh Lakish, there was no rule of thumb to tell in advance which position was justified and which was to be surrendered. Later ages reechoed to the controversies of the Rabbanites with the Karaites, of the Maimonideans with the anti-Maimonideans, of the Kabbalists with the anti-Kabbalists, of the Hasidim with the Mitnaggedim. Life itself ultimately disclosed that some movements, like Pharisaism, were life-giving, while others, like Karaism, were sterile. But even those which were rejected by Catholic Israel made some contribution to the living stream of Jewish religion and culture, if only as a foil or a challenge.

The Talmud commented on the controversies of the schools of Hillel and Shammai that "both these and the others are the words of the Living God" (*Erubin* 13b), but that did not prevent its deciding whose views were to be normative on each issue.

It is obvious that the reinterpretation of the concepts of Catholic Israel and of the authority of Jewish law, as well as the suggested criteria for evaluating Jewish ritual observances here proposed, do not constitute a full solution to the issues of modern Jewish religious life. Many problems as to the growth of Jewish tradition still remain, such as the respective functions of the people and of its leadership in the process, the role of custom versus law, and the interplay of authority and freedom. But the basic pattern of development is clear: life creates law, and law in turn is embodied in life.

A philosophy of Jewish law such as has been outlined above seems to us to offer the means of meeting the challenge confronting Jewish ritual today. For it is essential to answer the questions that arise with regard to observance. Some come from those who are still loyal to Jewish observance but lack an integrating philosophy of Jewish law. Other objections emanate from those whose indifference and even hostility to Jewish values have led them to cast overboard the entire regimen of Jewish practice.

The latter group cannot be won back by means of an appeal to the authority of Jewish law; they must first be educated to the cosmic, ethical, esthetic, and national values contained in Jewish ritual. Through this voluntary approach, it may be possible to bring this group, which includes some of the most valuable elements in the Jewish people, at least to the edge of the camp of Catholic Israel. As for the former group, it does require a conception of Jewish law which will guide and organize its practice and give it continuity with the past, stability in the present, and the capacity of growth in the future.

Signs are multiplying that "there is a hunger in the land, not merely a hunger for bread and a thirst for water, but to hear the words of the Lord" (Amos 8:11). For all our unworthiness, we must summon up all our resources of wisdom and faith and be ready to answer the call.

If the leadership of American Jewry proves worthy in some measure of its predecessors, we may succeed in transforming—as has happened in the past—the anarchy and the ignorance which are characteristic of the pioneering stage into a rich, deeply-rooted pattern of Jewish life. The great battle waged by Ezra and Nehemiah against intermarriage and against the violation of the Sabbath in Judaea (Palestine) in the fifth century B.C.E.; Rab's achievement in Babylonia in the third century C.E., where he "found an open valley which he fenced in" (*Hullin* 110a); Moses ben Enoch, who helped lay the foundations of Jewish learning in Spain; Chaim of Volozhin, who lamented the ignorance of Russian Jewry and created his famous *yeshiva*—all these represent the rhythm of Jewish rebirth, which, *mutatis mutandis,* must be our guide in the United States as well. Granted that the problems are infinitely more complicated than ever before, it does not follow that our cause gains by inactivity or by surrender to the forces of dissolution.

The history of human culture, no less than that of Jewish experience, has shown that ages of indifference and of hostility to religion give way to periods of spiritual revival. The skeptical period of the eighteenth century, which itself conserved important religious ideals in secular form, gave way to the nineteenth century, which was, in many respects, an age of faith as well as of science. There are more than a few signs that men and women are seeking their way to God. Experience has shown again and again that it is easier, not harder, to win people for the traditional concept of the Living God as interpreted by our greatest teachers than for a reconstructed concept that denies His existential reality.

Judaism has no room for the anti-rational, for the *credo quia absurdum* attitude, but it does not exclude the emotional, the nonrational, the act of faith before the abyss of the unknown. A radical writer has declared: "Religion dissolved into ethicism is no longer religion. What is left to worship after dogmas and mystery have been taken away?"[2] For "dogmas" we may substitute *mitzvot*, the obligations of Jewish law, interpreted in the light of our learning and our ideals. Without them, Judaism as a way of life is doomed.

Religion is, in essence, the all-embracing attitude of man toward the universe. It must, therefore, reckon with the unknown and mysterious in the cosmos as well as with the rational and the known, but it dare not minimize or postpone the moral imperative to build a just society of just men. In order to achieve this purpose, it must unfurl the banner of the Living God. To keep that faith ever vivid and real, ritual is essential. The evidence of history and the needs of the hour unite in emphasizing that ritual is an important part of Jewish law.

Obviously, it is much easier to hold on to the old unchanged, at least in theory, or to cut loose from tradition altogether. It is far more difficult to evolve the principles and the techniques necessary for conserving and revitalizing a 3,500-year-old tradition. Nonetheless, the history and character of Jewish tradition offer assurance that it still has largely untapped resources for growth and that it can yet play a significant role in the humanizing of society and in the enhancement of human life. To make Jewish tradition live in the modern world is the deepest challenge facing American Jewry. It may well prove to be its greatest contribution to Israel and to the world of tomorrow.

PART THREE

Aspects of Contemporary Jewish Life

10

WOMEN'S RIGHTS IN JEWISH LIFE
AND LAW

In many quarters, the plea is being voiced for a fuller recognition of the rights of women in Jewish religious life. It should be recorded that it was Reform that first established the principle of equality for women in Judaism. But since Western society continued to be male-dominated, the principle remained largely formal and inoperative, with women playing only a minor role and exerting relatively little influence in the councils of the movement. Besides, since ritual observances in Reform are relatively few, the abolition of women's disabilities and their admission to all the religious prerogatives was not overly significant.

One major step was taken in the nineteenth century with the introduction of mixed seating in Reform synagogues, but it was probably due more to the example of Christian churches than to a drive for women's equality. Probably the single most dramatic step in the twentieth century has been the ordination of women as rabbis in Reform Judaism, a move which Reconstructionism has followed. It has not been accomplished without considerable resistance among the laity. The issue of women as rabbis is under intense discussion within the Conservative movement as well, and considerable heat has been generated on the subject. Nonetheless, it is safe to say that the equality of women, including their ordination, represents the wave of the future in Judaism.

85

To be sure, the Reform movement has not been confronted by the problem of making traditional law—Halakhah—function in the modern world. Conversely, this has been the major challenge for Conservative Judaism. It would be idle to claim that we have gained everything that is to be achieved in this area. As already indicated, fifty percent of our constituency is denied the opportunity to enter the rabbinate by reason of sex. Nevertheless, substantial progress has been registered by the Conservative movement in advancing women's rights. The entire record is worthy of examination.

One of the recurrent personal tragedies in Jewish life has been the plight of the *agunah,* the subject of a powerful novel of the same name by the contemporary Yiddish master Chaim Grade. For centuries, ever since talmudic days, rabbinic leadership has been troubled by the legal disabilities and human misery involved in the status of the *agunah,* the "chained wife," whose husband has disappeared with no witnesses to his death and who has no *get,* or Jewish divorce, that would permit her to remarry. Various ameliorative steps were taken by medieval and modern rabbis, but no comprehensive measure for dealing with the problem was implemented.

The problem of the *agunah* became aggravated in modern times. The old category of the "disappearing husband" who had abandoned his wife and children grew in numbers with the spread of Jewish communities from Europe to the other continents. The technological improvements in modern warfare created many instances of men blown to bits or lost at sea, with no remains of their bodies or witnesses to testify to their death. Finally, the massive increase in civil divorce produced many cases of a husband who had dissolved his marriage by a divorce in the civil courts but refused to issue a *get* to his wife out of malice or greed, or both.

In 1935 the Rabbinical Assembly adopted a plan proposed by the late Rabbi Louis M. Epstein for freeing such a woman from her shackles. The plan, though complicated in practice, was halakhically sound. Basically, it called for the appointment by a bridegroom, at the time of the marriage ceremony, of agents to execute a conditional divorce *(get 'al t'nai)* under certain circumstances. These would include the disappearance of the husband or his willful refusal to issue a Jewish divorce after having secured a civil divorce, or his being reported missing in military action.

To meet the practical problem of the last category, the Epstein Plan was implemented during the Second World War. In all essentials, it was also adopted by the Orthodox Rabbinical Council of America during that period.

Subjected to a barrage of misrepresentation and proving unwieldy in operation, the Epstein Plan, after being put into practice in many cases, fell into disuse. But the principle of an active concern for the *agunah* and a determination to act on her behalf persisted in Conservative Judaism. The Lieberman text reflects this concern.

The leadership of the movement was well aware that in traditional Halakhah there were several resources available for dealing with this problem. These procedures have now been put to practical use in Conservative Judaism. To meet this persistent, heartrending situation, several years ago the Committee on Law and Standards of the Rabbinical Assembly turned to the talmudic principle, *kol hammekaddesh 'ada'ata derabbanan mekaddesh,* "Whoever contracts a Jewish marriage does so under the authority of the rabbis" (Babylonian Talmud, *Ketubbot* 3a). This is not merely an abstract principle. It is applied in the Talmud itself and by post-talmudic authorities to annul a marriage when circumstances require it. In the words of the Talmud, "The rabbis retroactively break *('afke'inho)* the husband's marital contract *(kiddushin)."* Even if children have been born to the couple, this does not prevent the application of the principle, since their legitimate status in Judaism is not impugned by the annulment.

In implementing this procedure, the *beth din* (Jewish court of law) of the Rabbinical Assembly has followed the clear precedents to be found in these talmudic and post-talmudic law formulations. When a marriage has been civilly dissolved and all pleas and warnings addressed to the husband requesting him to issue a *get* prove unavailing, the *beth din* proceeds to annul the marriage and thus sets the woman free from a lifelong "enchainment." Often, the husband's knowledge that a remedy is at hand impels him to adopt the right course of action, and he grants the *get.* When he does not respond, a solution is available that has already proven its worth. Thus, Jewish law makes it possible to fulfill the great injunction in the Torah, "You shall do what is just and right in the sight of God" (Deuteronomy 6:18).

Less important, perhaps, but affecting a far larger number of women, is the decision by the Rabbinical Assembly to permit (not to compel) individual rabbis and congregations to count women for the *minyan,* or quorum in prayer.

There is also the growing practice in Conservative congregations to extend to women various religious "honors," such as being called to the Torah. This last practice, it should be added, is expressly sanctioned by the *Shulḥan Arukh (Oraḥ Ḥayyim,* sec. 282, paragraph 3) and is based on a tannaitic statement in the Talmud *(B. Megillah* 23a) which is not later than the third century C.E. The *Shulḥan Arukh* ("Prepared Table") was written by Rabbi Joseph Karo, who codified the practice of Sephardic Jewry. Karo's work attained universal authority because Rabbi Moses Isserles, a great Polish scholar, added to it his *Mappah* ("Tablecloth"), a body of annotations incorporating the customs of Ashkenazic Jewry.

The text written by Rabbi Joseph Karo reads as follows: "All may go up (for the Torah reading) within the number of seven (*aliyot*), even a woman or a minor who knows to whom we offer our praises. But the sages have said, 'A woman shall not read publicly because of the honor of the community.' " Then follows the comment of Rabbi Moses Isserles: "These (the woman and the minor) may be joined to the number of men being called to the Torah, but they should not *all* be women or minors (so *RaN* and the *Ribash*)."

Not only is the permission for women to have *aliyot* clearly indicated, but the intent is equally evident. Rabbi Joseph Karo is concerned that if women are given the honors of the Torah, it would suggest that the men in the community are too ignorant to perform the *mitzvah.* Rabbi Moses Isserles adds that so long as *all* the honors are not given to women or minors, and a number of men are called up with them, the honor of the community is safeguarded. It should be remembered that originally each person called to the Torah read his section from the Scroll, so that a substantial amount of expertise was involved.

It is all the more noteworthy that both Rabbi Joseph Karo, the great Sephardic authority, and Rabbi Moses Isserles, the great exemplar of Ashkenazic Jewry, seriously contemplated the possibility of a woman or a minor's having sufficient Jewish knowledge to read from the Scroll of the Torah. As the current controversy on the subject demonstrates, the practice marks a significant advance in the religious enfranchisement of women in traditional Judaism, even though it remained in the realm of theory.

Those who oppose counting women to the *minyan* seek to justify their position by referring to the fact that traditional Halakhah exempted women from the obligation (*mitzvah*) of prayer. This exemption in turn is buttressed by the talmudic principle that women are free from commandments that must traditionally be performed at specific times (*mitzvot 'aseh shehazman grama*). However, even in talmudic and medieval times, the principle was not universally applied. Always there were exceptions, such as the kindling of Sabbath and festival lights, hearing the Shofar on Rosh Hashanah, and the blessing of the *lulav* (four species) on Sukkot, that were held to be obligatory for women. So, too, rabbinic law commanded women to hear the reading of the Megillah on Purim, like the menfolk, "since they, too, were involved in that miracle of salvation." It is therefore a reasonable conclusion that the principle that women were excused from the obligation to observe *mitzvot* having a specific time-frame is a generalization from a few specific instances and not a universally binding rule. Its application to women's prayer is, consequently, a rationalization rather than a reason, serving to maintain the inferior status of women.

The argument has even less justification today. In this age of labor-saving devices, a woman who is a homemaker and takes care of a family has at least as much free time as her husband who is a worker, businessman, or professional. And the woman who is gainfully employed outside the home is in exactly the same position as her male counterpart.

James Harvey Robinson, the American historian, once said, "Every event in history has a good reason and a real reason." In the case of the *mitzvah* of prayer for women and their exclusion from the *minyan*, the real reason is not good and the good reason is not real.

It is undeniable that there is a paucity of rituals to mark important occasions in the life of women. One advocate of women's rights has suggested that a special ceremony is needed to mark the onset of menstruation, but this hardly commends itself. However, puberty rites are to be found in all societies and religions. In Judaism we have a relatively recent rite for marking this period in a boy's life. The Bar Mitzvah ceremony is actually only a few centuries old. During the past two decades, it has become practically universal in Conservative synagogues to conduct a Bat Mitzvah service in order to highlight the same event in girls' lives. We should remember that the idea and the term originated with Professor Mordecai M. Kaplan. As the father of gifted daughters, he undoubtedly was sensitive to the need.

No ritual practice has yet become widespread to celebrate the birth of a girl, although several services of thanksgiving have been created by individuals, both rabbinic and lay. Obviously, the occasion deserves to be marked with the kind of solemnity and joy characteristic of the *brit* and *pidyon haben* ceremonies for boys.

As for woman's role in religious life, it is noteworthy that as long ago as 1946, the *Sabbath and Festival Prayer Book* issued by the Prayer Book Commission of the Rabbinical Assembly and the United Synagogue, on which I had the honor of serving as chairman, introduced a significant change in the *Siddur*. As is indicated in detail in the chapter on the prayerbook below, the Commission rephrased the three Preliminary Blessings in the Morning Service, which had long been the subject of discomfort and controversy. These three blessings read as follows: "Blessed are You, O Lord our God, King of the universe, who has not made me a Gentile, a slave, a woman." In the Conservative prayer book these three blessings are expressed in the positive: "Blessed are You, O Lord our God, King of the universe, who has created me in His image, has made me free, and made me an Israelite." Incidentally, there is warrant in rabbinic sources for these formulations, as an appendix in the *Sabbath and Festival Prayer Book* makes clear.

The modified text is not merely less objectionable per se. It expresses a fundamental religious and ethical insight of the Jewish tradition. As is clear from the first chapter of Genesis, every human being, male or female, is created "in the image of God" and possesses an innate worth and an inalienable dignity. The two succeeding benedictions articulate the joy of Jewish belonging and the privilege of human freedom.

The solution to the problem of the inequality of women in Judaism can be met only by an approach to Jewish tradition which is both sympathetic and reverent. At the same time, we must be aware of the millennial experience of the Jewish people and be sensitive to the conditions and ethical insights of the contemporary world. Traditional Jewish law arose in the ancient world and developed during the medieval period. During both eras, women occupied a position of inferiority everywhere in society, both in life and in law. The glory of traditional Halakhah is that, notwithstanding, it took giant steps to extend the range of women's rights and to circumscribe the originally unlimited powers of men.

That the process was not completed in the Halakhah in the past is not surprising. Even modern society still has a long way to go before the full equality of women is achieved. What is remarkable is not that women still suffer various disabilities in Jewish law today, but that so much progress has been registered. Jewish tradition possesses important resources for advancing the process, if we utilize the insights available to us from history, sociology, and psychology, as well as the inherent wisdom and humanity of Halakhah.

One would wish to see this progress initiated and carried forward by all or most halakhic authorities, preferably in association with all elements dedicated to making Jewish law viable in the modern world. A working union of Orthodox and Conservative leadership in this area would be a blessing for Judaism. Above all, we would welcome signs that the Torah is coming forth from Zion. But the likelihood of such a cooperative effort today is slight, in view of the growing intransigence of most Orthodox groups. So, too, the character of the Israeli rabbinate today shows few signs of awareness of the problems involving the status of Jewish women, particularly in the Diaspora.

Fortunately, those who cherish Jewish tradition and wish to see it on the highest level of wisdom and nobility need not lose hope. There are increasing signs of a vital concern for living Halakhah in Conservative Judaism, which may well encourage some Jews who are not officially within the movement to speak out with us. In any event, we must act on behalf of the more than half of the Jewish people who have yet to achieve full equality and justice.

11

ISRAEL AND THE DIASPORA

I

Datable events, even of the greatest magnitude, rarely produce far-reaching changes in society. They generally serve to mark the culmination of a process that has been a long time in the making. In a sense, no new revelation has come to light as a result of the Yom Kippur War and its aftermath, the latest chapter in the all-out campaign of the Arab states to destroy the State of Israel. Arab propaganda notwithstanding, it is clear that Israel won a major military victory in this conflict, the fruits of which Israel had to surrender under pressure from its most powerful friend. Nonetheless, there is a measure of truth in the observation that Israel "lost" the Yom Kippur War because it did not win it, and that the Arabs "won" the war because they did not lose it.

What has occurred as a result of this bloodiest of Arab-Israeli confrontations has been a change in the *perception* of the realities of the Jewish situation, as well as in the emotional timbre both of Israeli and Diaspora Jewry. An all-pervasive war-weariness has taken hold of the Israeli people, coupled with a growing cynicism and disillusionment with regard to the integrity and ability of its leadership, both in government and in society as a whole. The feeling has become general that the tragic succession of wars must cease and that a genuine peace must be achieved if Israel is to survive in any meaningful sense.

While the Yom Kippur War has led to no transformation in the underlying relationship between world Jewry and the State of Israel, the realities stand out more clearly than before. It has compelled Israeli Jewry to reassess its position and Diaspora Jewry to reexamine the validity of its own outlook.

The brief history of the State of Israel has been marked by an unending series of violent domestic controversies. Nor am I thinking of the rash of financial scandals that has irrupted in recent years. These distasteful episodes have demonstrated the truth of the old adage that Jews are like other people, only more so. Virtually all the recurring issues in Israel in recent years—the Brother Daniel Case, the agitation about amending the Law of Return, the "lightning conversion in one day" of Mrs. Seidman carried through by Rabbi Goren, the problem of *mamzerut,* the validity of civil divorce, the recognition of Conservative conversions and *gittin,* indeed the entire question of the status, or more accurately the *non*-status, of Conservative and Reform Judaism, the role of the state in enforcing a religious monopoly, as well as the influence of the "religious" factor in the Jewish settlement of the occupied territories—all are directly or indirectly related to a crucial question of theory: What is the nature of Judaism? In more concrete terms: What is a Jew?

Twenty-five centuries ago, Socrates declared that the first obligation of man is "Know thyself." The establishment of the nature and content of Jewish identity is the basic question for the modern Jew, whether he lives in Israel or outside its borders. The problem is peculiarly of modern vintage. In the vast expanse of talmudic Halakhah and medieval Jewish philosophy, the question never arises. For traditional Judaism (which, be it noted, is not identical with modern Orthodoxy) Saadia's statement was all-sufficient: "We are a people only by virtue of the Torah."

The birth of the Emancipation in the wake of the French Revolution, imperfect and half-hearted as it proved to be, and the impact of the Enlightenment, with all its blind-spots and prejudices, created a new species of Jew, of whom the biblical Joseph may have been a prototype. Living in two communities and cherishing two traditions in greater or lesser degree, the modern Jew was anxious to validate his right to political and civic equality and his claim to economic and cultural opportunities. The rise of anti-Semitism in the aftermath of Napoleon's defeat, punctuated by such dramatic events as the

Damascus Affair of 1840 and the Mortara Case of 1857, raised the question of the relationship of Jews in various countries to one another, as well as to their respective "fatherlands."

The nature of Jewish identity in the modern world was, and is, no mere exercise in semantics. It was, and has remained, of overriding practical importance. No wonder, therefore, that during the last two centuries persistent efforts have been made to propose definitions of the Jewish group. Since a definition is always an explanation of the new or unfamiliar in terms of the familiar, it is only natural that the attempt was made to subsume the Jewish community under already familiar sociological categories.

There is no need to rehearse in detail the history of these efforts. The first solution was to define Judaism as a "religion," paralleling Protestantism and Catholicism, and thus validating the claim of Western Jews to political citizenship and concomitant rights. The theory originated in Reform Jewish circles in Germany, but it was adopted in all essentials by the Neo-Orthodoxy of Samson Raphael Hirsch, who was equally anxious to validate Jewish rights to civic emancipation. There was a difference, to be sure. Reform maintained that Jews had been a nation until the Emancipation, but had now been transformed permanently into a religious denomination. Hirsch accepted this description, but added that Jews would again become a nation in the Messianic Age. With regard to the present, Reform and Orthodoxy were in agreement—*les extrêmes se touchent*—and both Reform and Orthodoxy were hostile to Jewish national aspirations.

The "positive-historical" school had come into being when Zacharias Frankel walked out of the Frankfort Rabbinical Conference of 1844 in protest against its downgrading of the Hebrew language in prayer. This school continued to stress the national motif in the pattern of Jewish group experiences, as in Graetz's great *History*. Nonetheless, the demand for civic equality and political rights was so strong that no effort was made by Frankel or his successors to think through the nature of Jewish identity and its implications. By and large, they were at one with Reform and Orthodoxy. Thus, Moritz Guedemann, the scholarly rabbi of Vienna, was one of the leading *Protestrabbiner* who opposed the planned meeting of the Zionist Congress in Vienna, which led to its transfer to Basel.

In our day, all three religious movements have long abandoned the conception of Jews as a "religious denomination," at least *kelapei p'nim*, with regard to inner Jewish life. The nationalist emphasis in Conservative Judaism has been, perhaps, its most obvious element ever since its inception. In the light of the hellish fires of Nazism, the other movements surrendered their original view, except for vestigial remains like the American Council for Judaism or the Satmar Hasidim. The Agudat Yisrael, which arose as the offspring of German Neo-Orthodoxy and East European right-wing Orthodoxy, is today a political party in the State of Israel. The Reform Jewish community in the United States and throughout the world is overwhelmingly committed to the State of Israel.

Long before the twentieth century, it was obvious that the "Jewish expression" had an overplus going beyond adherence to religious practice and belief. The most striking element was the sense of kinship and common descent, a feeling of being members of an enlarged "family." To describe this aspect of Jewishness, some other category was needed, and so the then newly fashionable term "race" was invoked, because it seemed to focus upon past descent rather than upon present commitment.

Its untenability is obvious. The theory that Jews represent a biologically "pure" group of descendants of original ancestors has little warrant, either in history or in tradition. The marriages of the Patriarchs, of Joseph, and of Moses, the "mixed multitude" from Egypt who participated in the Exodus, the intermingling of the Israelites and the Canaanite inhabitants after the "Conquest," are amply attested in our sources. For the later biblical period, the prophet Ezekiel, who described Jerusalem's parentage as "Your father an Amorite and your mother a Hittite" (Ezekiel 6:3, 43), and the Book of Ruth are eloquent testimony. In addition, there are the countless passages which refer to the accession of *gerim* both in the Torah and the Prophets.

For the rabbinic period we need note merely the rabbinic relaxation of the biblical prohibition against marriage with the Moabites and the Ammonites, an interdict they restricted to males: "The biblical prohibition applies to male Ammonites and Moabites, not to females" [like Ruth] (Jerusalem Talmud, *Yebamot* 8:3). A landmark in historical understanding is the statement of Rabbi Joshua: "Are the Ammonites and Moabites settled in their original lands? Sennacherib came and mixed all the racial stocks" (*Berakhot* 28a).

During the Hellenistic and Roman periods there was a tremendous infusion of Gentiles in the Jewish community through conversion. The process was ultimately reduced by the rise of Christianity, which carried on an aggressive missionary campaign of its own, and by Roman imperial edicts; but proselytism was never completely cut off. Through the Middle Ages the accession of non-Jews to Judaism continued in greater or lesser degree. The conversion of the king of the Khazar kingdom, and ultimately of all his people, in about 840, is of course the most dramatic example.

Actually, the term "Jewish race," for all its superficial attractiveness, is a tragic misnomer. The term "race," which is of unclear etymology, was popularized in 1853–55 by Count Joseph Arthur de Gobineau, who presented a pseudoscientific rationale for his doctrine of group superiority and inferiority in his *Essai sur l'inégalité des races humaines*. In it he adopted the totally indefensible procedure of transferring the linguistic term "Aryan" (later "Indo-European"), which encompassed a vast family of languages from India to Britain, to the ethnic area. He then added the notion of pure and impure races which, he claimed, were stamped with superiority or inferiority by biology. This arrant nonsense of the nineteenth century became the bloody horror of the twentieth, with the rise of Nazi nightmare. Mankind would be better served if the term "race" were totally expunged from the human vocabulary. The only legitimate use of the term is in referring to the human race in its totality.

A third term rarely applied to the Jewish group is "nationality," because its inapplicability is patent when it is understood in its proper sense as "political allegiance." Obviously, Jews are conscious of a bond uniting them the world over, but it is not that of a single political allegiance.

II

On the other hand, the most popular concept applied to the Jewish sense of community—and undoubtedly the most fruitful—has been that of Jewish nationalism. Nationalism is probably the single most dynamic force in modern history, affecting all races, cultures, and socio-economic systems. The nineteenth century saw the emergence of modern nationalism in the creation of the Balkan states after the Greek revolt, and later the unification of Italy and Germany.

Nationalism continued to march forward with seven-league boots in the twentieth century. After the First World War, a half-dozen new states, primarily in the Baltic region, emerged in Europe. Following World War II, scores of new nations from Asia and Africa have appeared in the councils of the United Nations.

Nineteenth-century European nationalism had a powerful impact on European Jewry, which was reeling under the unrelenting impact of one crisis after the other: the Damascus Affair of 1840, the Mortara Case in 1857, the Tiszaeszlar blood accusation trials in Hungary in 1882, the May Laws in tsarist Russia that same year, not to speak of the steady barrage of pogroms in Eastern Europe, and, finally, the Dreyfus Affair which began in 1894.

In direct response to the Dreyfus Case, Herzl created political Zionism. He proposed a simple and straightforward remedy for the "Jewish problem," with which he had long been concerned. Herzl indicates in his *Diaries* that he had flirted in his youth with the idea of solving the Jewish problem by a mass conversion of all Jews to Christianity. Instead of the furtive baptism of individual Jews, he contemplated the idea of a dignified march of all Jewish leaders to the baptismal font in St. Stephen's Cathedral in Vienna. Herzl was soon convinced of the inefficacy of this idea. After many years, during which his Jewish concerns lay dormant, he was galvanized into action by the brutal and unabashed anti-Semitism of the Dreyfus Case. After witnessing the humiliation of Dreyfus, Herzl wrote his *Judenstaat* in a feverish burst of energy, and political Zionism was born. Its great goal was the normalization of Jewish life through the establishment of "a politically secured, legally recognized home-land for the Jewish people in Palestine," to cite the formulation of the Basel Program. Thus there would emerge a new Jewish national-ity open to all Jews in the Diaspora who were willing to emigrate to a Jewish state in Palestine. Those Jews who continued to live in the Diaspora would assimilate and disappear. Thus the "Jewish prob-lem" and anti-Semitism would both be effectively disposed of.

Some Zionist thinkers, notably Ahad Ha'am, who were far more aware of the riches of Jewish culture and the complexities of Jewish existence, saw Herzl's political Zionism as naive and simplistic. They stigmatized it as unlikely to be fulfilled and, indeed, as undesirable if it were to be realized. On the most obvious level, the Land of Israel was too small and the Diaspora too large for so simple a solution. It is noteworthy that Ahad Ha'am was almost the only voice reminding Jews at the time that Palestine was not an empty land, but possessed a substantial indigenous population. He therefore set forth his vision of the Land of Israel as a *merkaz ruḥani*, a spiritual center, with world Jewry constituting the circumference of the circle. Ahad Ha'am anticipated that this periphery in the Diaspora would derive sufficient Jewish inspiration, vitality, and content from the center to preserve its Jewish character.

While Ahad Ha'am was not personally committed to Jewish religious life, his conception that the essence of Judaism lay in its spiritual and ethical values was highly congenial to all Jews who loved Jewish religious ideals and practices and sought to perpetuate them. Many in our movement saw in it a more realistic approach to the Jewish future than in simon-pure political Zionism. Witness Solomon Schechter's espousal of religious Zionism. Israel Friedlander, who served as Professor of Bible at the Seminary until he met a martyr's death after World War I, was an enthusiastic exponent of Ahad Ha'am's views. Professor Mordecai M. Kaplan, *lehavdil bein haḥayyim vehaḥayyim,* was also deeply influenced in the same direction. If a personal reference be permitted, in an early presentation of the philosophy of Conservative Judaism, I included Ahad Ha'am as one of the seminal thinkers affecting the movement. Reconstructionism programmed the relationship of the Land of Israel and the Diaspora through the form of a wheel with spokes leading out from the center to the circumference.

The basic merit of Ahad Ha'am's conception of spiritual Zionism was its removal of the death-sentence from Diaspora Judaism which was implicit, though often not explicated, in political Zionism. Spiritual or cultural Zionism made room for the survival of Diaspora Jewry; indeed, it looked forward to its vital and meaningful survival nourished by the spiritual center in Zion.

The major weakness of Ahad Ha'amism, which did not become apparent until much later, was its oversimplification of the process of spiritual influence. It conceived of the homeland as the active factor in the process and the Diaspora as the passive recipient. It failed to reckon with the fact that all human relationships are two-directional, that there can be, as the old psychological adage has it, "no impression without expression."

Ahad Ha'am regarded it as self-evident that the new culture

emerging from the spiritual center would be rooted in the totality of the past Jewish experience. Thus he wrote with equal enthusiasm of Maimonides and of Moses. He could not contemplate the possibility of a new *dor hamidbar* arising in the Land of Israel that would reject or ignore the *sebhel hayerushah,* the "burden of the inheritance."

Finally, he was a son of the most Jewishly educated community in history, bounded by a thousand ties, visible and invisible, to Jewish religious and ethical values. He thus took for granted the existence of this fountain of living waters and never felt constrained to explore the theological foundations of the Jewish ethical consciousness, or the relationship of Jewish religion to Jewish culture.

The Zionist movement, both in its philosophy and its practice, represented an uneasy marriage between Herzlian political Zionism and Ahad Ha'am's cultural Zionism. This relationship has persisted in the policy of the State of Israel. The *kibbutz galuyot,* the ingathering of the remnants of European Jewry after Hitler, of the Oriental communities from Islamic countries, and of the refugees from Soviet tyranny, constitutes a striking fulfillment of the basic goal of political Zionism. To be sure it is partial, but three million Jews in Israel are far more than could have been anticipated before the irruption of twentieth-century anti-Semitism, whether black or red, whether under the Cross or the Crescent.

All his life, David Ben-Gurion continued to expound the doctrine that only he is a true Zionist who settles in Israel. It is not difficult to understand why his views are echoed by many, if not most, of our Israeli brothers. They find in them an indispensable rationale for bearing the heavy burdens and facing the manifold perils confronting them each day.

They support the idea of *shelilat hagolah* by pointing to the inroads of assimilation on free Diaspora communities the world over. From this standpoint the Diaspora is important, but only temporarily. American Jewry needs to be cultivated for three reasons: its political clout, its financial support, and its human resources, from which *aliyah* is to be recruited.

To my knowledge, no Israeli leader or Zionist theoretician has spelled out the implications for Diaspora Jewry and the effect on Israeli Jewry if *aliyah* were to be elected by the majority of Jews living in the Diaspora, or even if the majority of Diaspora Jewish leadership were to settle permanently in Israel. Like Karl Marx's eschatological doctrine of the ultimate "withering away of the state" after the establishment of Communism, the inevitable conclusion of the "shriveling up of the Diaspora," which flows from the theory of political Zionism, remains *halakhah v'ein morim ken,* a situation rarely contemplated and never discussed.

The doctrine of cultural Zionism propagated by Ahad Ha'am has also registered extraordinary triumphs in the State of Israel. Its most striking achievement, without parallel in the history of any other people restored to national independence, has been the rebirth of the Hebrew language and its phenomenal progress as a means of expression and communication adequate for all areas of human concern. With the all-but-universal use of Hebrew in Israel has come an extraordinary cultural efflorescence in literature, the press, and the theater. Jewish creativity in the natural sciences, both theoretic and practical, has been phenomenal. The humanistic disciplines, such as history, law, anthropology, and sociology, have also achieved significant results in many areas, often expressing for the first time a Jewish concern within a broader universal context. The products of Israeli scholarship are beginning to make their mark on the world scene, particularly since Israeli scholars and scientists are energetic in bringing their work to the attention of the West through frequent academic visits, as well as copious publications and translations.

Most important of all, the creative achievements and heroic deeds of our Israeli brothers have been the single most important factor in revitalizing the Jewish loyalty of the Diaspora communities and their wish to live as Jews. In particular, no other aspect of Jewish experience is even remotely comparable to the impact of the people and the State of Israel in rekindling the "spark of the Jew" in the hearts of our youth the world over. In a world that has seemed to vow death and destruction for the Jewish people, Israel has given us a new gift of life.

Yet there is need for evaluation, not merely for self-congratulation. The fact is that most of the important Israeli scientists and scholars were born and trained in the Diaspora. In the field of Judaic studies, Israel has thus far produced several major works—Yehezkel Kaufmann's monumental *Toledot Ha'emunah Hayisra'elit,* the writings of Martin Buber, the corpus of Gershom Scholem's pioneering and revolutionary work in the field of Jewish mysticism, and Ephraim Urbach's *Ḥazal,* to mention only the most outstanding. Yet it should be noted that all these figures are Diaspora-born and Diaspora-educated. Moreover, much of contemporary Israeli scholarship in Judaism is eclectic in character, taking the form of various types of collections, anthologies, and encyclopedias, or studies of earlier scholars and thinkers. Undoubtedly, this material is highly useful, but the innovative and creative element in this work is relatively minor.

To be sure, the State of Israel is very young and the Yishuv as a whole not much older. But there are two factors in the spiritual physiognomy of Israel that must give us pause when we seek to gauge the present and future role of Israel as the spiritual center of modern Judaism. First is the wholesale importation of American, Canadian, and European scholars to teach Judaic studies in Israeli universities and other institutions of learning. It is undoubtedly a tribute to the quality and attainments of these scholars. Incidentally, it testifies to the high level of the Diaspora institutions in which they were trained. As I know out of my own experience, teaching Jewish religion, literature, and history in the Land of Israel is an unforgettable spiritual and intellectual experience for the participant. From the standpoint of the long-term productivity of Israel, however, it suggests that the country is not producing its own corpus of younger scholars for the next generation, at least not yet.

The second factor is the persistent and, indeed, the widening chasm between the *yeshivot* and the universities, between the devotees of traditional Jewish learning and the practitioners of modern Jewish scholarship. In the past, nearly all the giants of Jewish scholarship united the breadth of knowledge and depth of understanding of the traditional Torah scholar with the methodology, system, and critical analysis of modern scientific research. There is little, if any, evidence in Israel of any bridge between these two worlds.

In 1951 the late Professor Moshe David Cassuto told me in his home that he was hoping to create a rabbinical seminary in Israel, to train rabbis for spiritual leadership in the country, that would be traditional in character but cognizant of modern scholarship and responsive to contemporary conditions. I asked him whether there were not students coming from the *yeshivot* into the Hebrew University for a modern, secular education, a process which had gone on for virtually two centuries in Europe and America. Dr. Cassuto answered that the world of the *yeshivot* is hermetically sealed off from that of general Israeli life. In the quarter of a century since our conversation, the situation has not changed, if indeed it has not intensified. By and large, the great reservior of talmudic learning to be found in the *yeshivot* has offered little nourishment of the spirit to modern Israel.

The problem is not merely one of scholarship. Closely allied to this phenomenon is one fact that has not been noted. There has been little religious creativity in Israel, whether in theory or in practice, in theology or in law. Virtually the only example that comes to mind is the institution of the *Oneg Shabbat,* which was instituted by Bialik at the Ohel Shem in Tel Aviv long before the establishment of the State of Israel. The *adloyada* carnival on Purim and the *bikkurim* festival at Shavuot also come to mind as new practices, but there is little more. Let us set aside the unseemly politicking and quarreling of the Chief Rabbis in Israel. The high hopes that a sovereign Jewish community would develop a living Halakhah for world Israel were represented by Rabbi J. L. Maimon a generation ago, who pleaded for a renewal of the Sanhedrin, but they have not been realized. It is not merely that many of the problems confronting Jewish tradition in the Diaspora, such as the *agunah,* are not equally pressing in Israel, where the state can enforce rabbinical decisions. There is a deep-seated unwillingness to reckon with the problems, needs, and insights of the twentieth century, or even to invoke the available resources of Jewish tradition in meeting them.

Moreover, the prospects for the future are not encouraging. There has been a retreat toward ever-increasing severity in the application of the Halakhah by the religious Establishment in Israel. Most observers are agreed that the younger rabbis and *dayyanim* are even more intransigent than their elders. For the foreseeable future, living Torah is not likely to come out of Zion. On the contrary, it is the Diaspora that must continue to supply much of the manpower and the willpower even for the older traditional forms of Torah scholarship.

In sum, both the political Zionism fathered by Herzl and the cultural Zionism developed by Ahad Ha'am have incredible, indeed miraculous, achievements to their credit. Yet neither can lay claim to the total realization of its visions and goals, which is the usual lot of the human condition. As a result, Zionism has discovered for itself the failure of success, the tragedy of achieving one's goals. In the *Millon Olami L'ivrit Medubberet,* by Dan ben Amoz and Netivah ben Yehudah, which has gone through many printings in Israel, we read (p. 196) this definition of Zionism (*tzionut*): "Follies, high-flown words lacking in content, an epithet for a hortatory address raising up high ideals in a discussion by the use of empty phrases."

III

With the decline of the ideology of Zionism as Jewish nationalism, a surrogate has appeared—the concept of Israeli nationalism. Since the period of the birth of the State of Israel until the Yom Kippur War, a process has developed and gained in momentum to replace the concept of Jewish nationalism with Israeli nationalism. Perhaps Jews have a past, but only Israelis have a future. Its cardinal tenet states that one cannot be a Jew except in Israel, and to think otherwise is *tzionut*.

Several years ago, a furor was created by the emergence of a small group of intellectuals who called themselves "Canaanites" to underscore their affinity with the aboriginal inhabitants of the land. Since the Canaanites are long dead, that was hardly possible or necessary. Their purpose was to underscore their separation from Diaspora Jews, who are still very much alive, and to dismiss the nineteen hundred years of the Exile as a blank page, or worse.

The marks of this tendency are better sought in incidents of daily life than in public statements or published words. I recall two conversations at different times with two high Israeli officials. One explained, "I go to synagogue only in the Diaspora because the Jewish religion is an institution for the preservation of Jewish national consciousness. In Israel we no longer need this institution." The other explained that his daughter refuses to attend a synagogue in the Diaspora because, for her, "the God of Israel lives only in the Land of Israel." I was too polite to inquire how often she goes to synagogue in Israel.

At another time, my wife and I joined a group of Israeli teachers touring Jerusalem. They were being escorted through the YMCA building there with one of their own number as a guide. The group was shown a collection of plaster casts depicting in sequence two brothers living in peace, quarreling with one another, and then being reconciled. The Hebrew teacher serving as a guide dismissed it and said, *Zehu ra'ayon notzri,* "That's a Christian idea." I must confess I remonstrated with his interpretation. I tried to remind him that *slichah* and *mehilah,* "forgiveness," were good Jewish concepts, not to speak of *hava'at shalom bein 'adam lahavero,* "establishing peace between one man and his fellow."

On one of our visits to Athens, my wife and I saw a family of Israelis in the Forum looking at Hadrian's monument. I hazarded an observation on the irony and the glory of Jewish history. Hadrian's monument here, like the Arch of Titus in Rome, had been erected by enemies of Israel for their own glory. Now it served to commemorate a dead empire, while the Jewish people is still very much alive. To this remark, the father of the Israeli family responded curtly: *Keshe'anu 'ozvim 'et ha'aretz, anu shokhehim 'et kol zeh,* "When we leave the land we forget all this."

The Israeli actor who played the role of Tevye in the Hebrew version of *Fiddler on the Roof* declared in a published interview, "I have more in common with an Israeli Arab than I have with a *galut* Jew."

Some time ago a very well-intentioned series, "Israelis and Arabs," was shown on American public television. In one segment an Israeli delivered himself of the statement (which I cannot quote verbatim), "I don't believe in historic rights of Jews in the land. The fact is the Jews could not live in Europe and they had a right to take a part of the country for themselves. They saved themselves from the Holocaust, and without the state they would have died. The Palestinians should accept that half of their property has been taken by people who were starving." At this point I am not concerned with evaluating either the truth or the wisdom of this statement, which could hardly be improved upon from the standpoint of pro-Arab propaganda. It exhibits the trend of Israeli simon-pure nationalism deriving from the conception of Israel as a "normal" nation *kekhol hagoyim,* "like all the nations."

IV

I have devoted attention to this critique of Zionism and Israeli nationalism precisely because they are far closer to the realities of Jewish life than the concept of Jews as a "religious denomination" or a "race." The purpose is not academic but pragmatic. Zionism has unquestionably been the most vital movement in modern Jewish life, and its achievements are monumental and enduring. It is no diminution of its contribution to recognize that it is not an all-encompassing philosophy of Jewish life. It is unable to do justice to basic questions imperiously demanding an answer in our day. What is the relation of Israelis to Diaspora Jewry? What is the relation of an Israeli Jew to the Jewish historic past and its creations outside of Israel? What is the relation of an Israeli Jew to an Israeli Arab?

An adequate philosophy of Judaism should make it possible to approach these practical problems of today and tomorrow. These issues cannot be faced, let alone answered, until we establish properly the nature of Jewish identity and the character of the Jewish group.

The only viable basis for meeting these issues is to emphasize some fundamental truths which have been either overlooked or ignored, or have become so familiar as to be taken for granted. I firmly believe that our point of departure must be *the recognition of Jewish uniqueness*. Judaism has expressed this truth in its belief in God's election of Israel, but the doctrine of Israel as the Chosen People is not true because it is an article of faith; it is an article of faith because it is true. The singular character of the Jewish group is neither an expression of group conceit nor a figment of the historical imagination, nor a mere theological doctrine. It is an empirical fact, the logical consequence of thirty-five hundred years of a special history which mirrors an unparalleled experience unlike that of any other society. This is why none of the usual sociological categories are able to do justice to the reality. The Jewish group includes all that the terms "religion," "nationalism," and "race" seek to describe and more, for the whole is greater than the sum of its parts.

The only term which is sufficiently inclusive to describe the Jews—precisely because it has no technical meaning—is the old biblical word '*am*, meaning "people," from a Semitic root probably connoting "togetherness." In Buber's words, "Israel is not one species of the genus 'nation'; it is the only species of the genus 'Israel.' "

If, nevertheless, we insist upon a modern sociological term, the Jews may be described as a religio-cultural-ethnic group. Nor are these three elements mechanically superimposed upon one another; on the contrary, they are organically interrelated, mutually interdependent, and ultimately indivisible.

I remember a discussion of the subject one evening at a social gathering that included an anthropologist. The idea of the sociological uniqueness of the Jewish people offended his scientific penchant for categorization, and he insisted that there were other groups possessing this organic triad. When I asked him to name them, he thought quite a while and finally came up with an answer—the Parsees in India, who are a distinct ethnic group possessing their own religion and culture. I then pointed out that even if this small group be allowed, they constitute one tiny and remote instance within a world which now numbers nearly two billion souls. This would hardly affect the validity of the observation that the Jewish group is basically unique.

The special character of the Jewish people is both the cause and the consequence of its unique history. This weak, tiny people, which never built a great empire or an extended domain, created the Bible, the greatest work of the divine and the human spirit we possess. It is the source of the two great religions of the Western world, Christianity and Islam. It has fathered the great social and humanitarian ideals of the modern world. Its children have, in Heine's words, "fought and bled on every battlefield of human freedom." Its sons and daughters have continued to enrich every area of human culture.

But these are subjective evaluations. One aspect of this uniqueness is objective and incontrovertible. Other nations lost their independence for greater or lesser periods, but they remained on their native soil—the Irish, the Poles. Only the Jews were exposed to nineteen centuries of persecution, expulsion, and massacre—far removed from their homeland—and survived. This was possible because the uniqueness of the Jewish group endowed the Land of Israel with a special place in the hierarchy of Jewish values, unlike the relationship of other nations to their respective lands of origin.

Thus Jews in the Diaspora like ourselves do not look upon the State of Israel as the "old country" which they have left behind in order to avoid poverty, discrimination, or political tyranny. In fact, most American Jews have not yet been in Israel. It is not part of the receding past for them, as are Germany and Italy, Ireland and Russia, for the millions of first-generation, second-generation, and third-generation Americans whose families originated in those lands. Jews do not intend to forget Jerusalem or weaken their ties to Israel with the passing of time.

The Land of Israel is far more than a geographical locale or even a point of origin for the Jewish people. It is rather an integral component of every element of Jewish experience. Hence, the Diaspora has far more than a merely sentimental relationship to the land, be it historical, religious, or cultural; it has an existential bond.

To be sure, an Israeli Jew has much more at stake in the state, being literally on the firing line; but his primary role does not negate the lesser but still significant role of his Diaspora brother. Being less immediately concerned in the problems confronting the inhabitant of the state, the Diaspora Jew is morally bound to refrain from involvement in *lesser* Israeli issues. But being basically and ultimately concerned, Jews the world over have both the duty and the right to concern themselves with all the *major* problems facing the state and all the policies proposed for meeting them. The *decision* must remain with our brothers in the State of Israel, for they bear the brunt and pay the price. But the *discussion* is one in which all committed Jews have a part to play.

An analogy is available in the biblical law regarding the division of the spoils captured in war (Numbers 31:25, 27), which David actually put into practice (I Samuel 30:24). The custom may be referred to in Joshua 22:8, and has a partial analogue among the Arabs (Qoran 8:1, 48). The booty was divided into two halves, one half going to the small band who had borne the brunt of battle (*tofsei hamilḥamah hayotzim latzava*) and the other half being divided among the far larger number in the commonality (*ha'edah*) of all male members who had remained behind with the supplies (*hayoshev 'al hakeilim*).

It cannot be sufficiently stressed that the full recognition of the role of the Diaspora, far from weakening the sense of obligation of world Jewry to the political defense and economic support of the State of Israel, intensifies the obligation, since Israel and the Diaspora are the two elements of *'am 'olam,* an eternal world-people.

V

If we seek a graphic symbol of the ideal relationship of Israel and the Diaspora, we may turn to the concept of Shimon Rawidowicz. In his important work *Bavel Virushalayim,* he suggested a paradigm—not a center and a circumference, but an ellipse with two foci. If I may modify it slightly, I would suggest two gravitational fields, because each exerts tension upon the other.

Historically, the relationship of the homeland and the Diaspora was rarely co-equal. In virtually every era, one predominated and the other was secondary. But at no time after the destruction of the First Temple—and probably long before—was Jewish life concentrated in only one or the other. Always there was more than one center, with influence proceeding in both directions. In mishnaic times, Palestine was unquestionably dominant, but the center shifted to Babylonia in the Amoraic era. Yet Palestine was highly creative in the post-mishnaic era, as is evidenced by the Midrashim, the Palestinian Talmud, the creation of the calendar, the *Masorah*, and the early *piyyut*. In the Gaonic age, Saadia fought a vigorous battle for the supremacy of the Babylonian academies over Ben Meir and the schools of Palestine. The weight of influence seems to have remained in Babylonia until the eclipse of the Eastern center as a whole. During the Middle Ages, Spain, the Provence, and Italy were the major centers, with Palestine in the shadow. The destruction of Spanish Jewry brought about a new era of creativity in the Holy Land centered in Safed. In succeeding centuries, the quantitative and creative center of Jewish life was unquestionably to be found in the Diaspora of East and Central Europe, which produced both talmudic Judaism and Hasidism, the Gaon of Vilna and the Ba'al Shem Tov.

This creativity continued in the Emancipation era. The Emancipation cannot be written off as a blank or dismissed as sterile. In the face of new challenges, Diaspora Jewry, including preeminently its emancipated segments in Western Europe and America, was able to create all the modern movements in Jewish religious life—Reform, Orthodoxy, Conservatism, and Reconstructionism. It fathered the scientific study of the Jewish heritage known as *Jüdische Wissenschaft*, and thus laid the only sure foundation for Jewish self-understanding for the modern Jew. To this modern Jewish learning all Jews are indebted, including those who, in violation of the talmudic injunction, delight in throwing rocks into the well from which they have to drink. Diaspora Jewry brought about the rebirth of Hebrew and the efflorescence of Yiddish. It produced the Jewish labor and progressive movements and, last but by no means least, was the seedbed of Zionism and the State of Israel.

There is little to be gained in attempting to delimit in advance the precise nature of the partnership between Israel and the Diaspora and the future importance of each vis-à-vis the other. I am not suggesting that the Diaspora in the United States is a modern creative Babylonia, but neither is the Land of Israel today populated by Moseses, Isaiahs, Hillels, and Akibas. The influence each community will exert on the other will be decided by their respective contributions to the treasure-house of the Jewish spirit. What is basic is to recognize that both have enduring significance and that both are indispensable for the Jewish future.

The first-century Greek-Jewish philosopher Philo of Alexandria put it succinctly when he said: "We who live throughout the world all owe a debt of loyalty to our fatherland. But we also have a motherland which is the holy city of Jerusalem."

Therein lies the inner significance of the Yom Kippur War—it has set in bolder relief attitudes already widely held by thinking and committed Jews that they tended to soft-pedal because of the glamour of a triumphant state and the power, prestige, and publicity of great fund-raising agencies.

We do not love the Land of Israel any the less, nor are we lacking in pride in the State of Israel, if we resist the extreme statements being bandied about, either because of hysteria or as a propaganda device, that the destruction of the State of Israel—Heaven forbid—would mean the death of Judaism and the end of the Jewish people. With God's help, and our united efforts, the State of Israel will never be destroyed. Neither will Judaism nor the Jewish people, for the Guardian of Israel neither slumbers nor sleeps.

All the propaganda and self-delusion of the Arab leaders notwithstanding, Israel did not lose the Yom Kippur War. On the contrary, Israel registered an extraordinary military victory. But the equivocal character of the outcome, aggravated by the piratical assault of the Arabs on the Western world, has brought to our Israeli brothers a growing recognition that Israel is a minority people in the Middle East, surrounded by hostile neighbors.

We may conclude that in a profound theological sense Israel, now isolated among the nations of the world, is in *galut*. The reason inheres in its role as the people of God. Israel is the prototype of all mankind, which is in *galut*, alienated from God and exiled from the new Jerusalem, which is yet to be built.

In a very thoughtful paper ("Changes in Israel and the Diaspora," *Judaism,* vol. 23, Summer 1974) an Israeli thinker, Efraim Shmueli, seeks to establish qualitative distinctions between *galut* and Israel. That they exist is undoubtedly true, but the differences are less extreme than was originally believed before the Yom Kippur War. Seeking to do justice to the Diaspora, he evaluates it in these words: "The positive aspect of this Diaspora dimension is manifested in the astonishing achievements of Jewish talent in all fields of human endeavor. In a relatively very short time, emancipated Jews have not only absorbed, with great enthusiasm, the accumulation of ideas and techniques of Western civilization, they have also become pioneers of thought and skills in the technoscientific mastery of nature." But this judgment is equally applicable to Israeli achievements.

He defines *galut* as "ultimately meaning the possibility of a Holocaust. Basically, the inherent quality of the *galut* experience is habitual anxiety, a non-specific expectance of grave events." But one could hardly give a better description of the state of mind of contemporary Israel—or, for that matter, of mankind as a whole today.

Shmueli makes the valid point that in defending themselves the Israelis are not helpless. This is obviously clear even to the Arab enemy. However, this too is not an absolute difference from the *galut.* Diaspora Jews are not totally helpless either in protecting their rights, in seeking to defend the State of Israel, or in fighting the ravages of the Arab boycott, as is becoming increasingly clear.

He notes that the Arab hatred of Israel has been obsessive and irrational, like anti-Semitism, and is unlike the "normal" group antagonisms between nations and states. Thus, the old view that anti-Semitism is the burden of *galut* Jewry, from which Israel is free, has been destroyed by the harsh realities of the present. He concludes, "The Yom Kippur War has cast a shadow of *galut* over Israel's existence." Jews the world over are brothers not only in kinship, but also in destiny.

VI

Those who have not yet recognized the uniqueness of the Jewish people and its special role in history may well reflect on the human condition in our times. Three major challenges have been aimed at the ideals of the free world in the twentieth century—the onslaught of Fascism, brown and black, by Hitler and his allies, the attack of Soviet dictatorship on the values of human liberty, and the piracy of Arab feudal potentates and dictators directed against the resources of the West. In each of these earth-girding struggles, the final outcome is yet to be decided. But who stands as the symbol of resistance barring the road to the triumph of evil? Who is singled out by the tyrants and oppressors as the enemy, be he victim or martyr?

The world, not Israel alone, is in deep distress today. In the wise words of our sages: *kol tsarah sheyisra'el ve'umot ha'olam shutaphin bah tsarah vekhol tsarah shel yisra'el 'atzman 'einah tsarah.* "Every trouble in which both Israel and the nations of the world are involved is a real trouble. Every trouble in which only Israel is involved is not true trouble" *(Devarim Rabbah* 2:14).

There will be a greater willingness in the future than in the past to recognize the creative achievements of the Diaspora. When the world overcomes the chaos, conflict, and imminent catastrophe of the present, Israel will be on the road to solving its special problems and breaking down its present isolation. Differences will remain, to be sure, but one destiny for Israel and the Diaspora will unite us as one people.

It is not only in the world of practical affairs, of economic and political aid, that world Jewry can exert a salutary influence upon the State of Israel. In the aftermath of the Yom Kippur War, Israeli Jewry is more likely to welcome a genuine mutuality of relationship with the Diaspora, and the Diaspora will recognize increasingly the necessity of this higher task and the privilege awaiting it.

In the field of scholarship and thought also, the interaction of the Diaspora and Israel will prove a blessing. Being a branch of culture, learning naturally and legitimately reflects the society which gives rise to it. It is entirely natural, and salutary, that Israeli scholarship will tend to emphasize the distinctively Jewish elements in our common past and present. Diaspora scholarship, on the other hand, will have the equally significant task of helping to trace the historic interaction of the Jewish people and its neighbors through history. One of the most significant attributes of Judaism from the biblical era onwards has been the creative tension between particularism and universalism—a balance which must be the model for all men and nations if mankind is to survive. In the future, we may anticipate that Israeli scholarship will tend to highlight the particularism while Diaspora learning will underscore the universalism, both of which are essential to a living Jewish tradition.

Israeli and Diaspora Jewry are the two indispensable branches of the house of Israel. Their sense of mutual responsibility, exercised in reciprocal help and cooperation, criticism and encouragement, is the only sure foundation for the meaningful survival of the Jewish people.

12

CONSERVATIVE JUDAISM IN ISRAEL

Creative interaction between Israel and the Diaspora is essential for the survival of Jews and Judaism. In this process, Conservative Judaism has a special role to play.

It is sad that there is so widespread a sense of "inferiority" and uncertainty within our ranks with regard to the duty and destiny of Conservative Judaism. A lay leader in our movement, who came to Israel several years ago, declared, "Conservative Judaism is not for export to Israel." He must have been thinking of English responsive readings as the hallmark of Conservative Judaism! The truth is that, with the exception of extreme right-wing Orthodox groups, the majority of our brethren in Israel need—and many of them want—an interpretation of Jewish religious thought and practice that will retain continuity with the past and respond affirmatively to the present.

The time is long overdue for us to consider concrete plans designed to make our movement a living factor in the spiritual life of Israel. To be sure, much has been done in this direction. But more remains to be done with ever-greater zeal. It is clear that the greater openness to traditional Jewish values which has come in the wake of the Yom Kippur War has given us the greatest opportunity thus far for fruitful achievement.

1. Our synagogues in Israel should not be Anglo-Saxon enclaves. The Hebrew language should be the language of preaching and teaching as well as of prayer within their walls, so that they can reach out to Israeli men, women, and children, and not merely to Anglo-Saxons, whose needs should, of course, continue to be met.

2. We need to arrange for extended tours of duty by members of the Rabbinical Assembly in Israel, in the cities, the *kibbutzim,* and the schools, to lend support to our colleagues now serving in Israel. What is needed there is the physical presence of our most creative and dynamic members; in a word, increased personal participation in the life of Israel by those committed to the distinctive philosophy of Conservative Judaism.

3. This distinctiveness must be free from truculence on the one hand and obsequiousness on the other. The Seminary Student Center in Neve Schechter and the United Synagogue congregations in Jerusalem and elsewhere must not be pallid imitations of already existent paradigms. They must demonstrate in life that the Jewish tradition is not the monopoly of one segment of Jewry.

4. We have already embarked on a program of adult education through lectures and conferences, as well as a modest publication program. This program must be increased many-fold. It should include translations of important writings by our most creative spirits. A periodical such as a weekly or a monthly would also add a much-needed dimension of topicality and relevance, and stimulate interest in our movement.

5. We need to organize schools, both elementary and intermediate, in Israel for the education of Israeli children in the spirit of our philosophy of Judaism, demonstrating the viability of Jewish tradition in the contemporary world. With a high academic character and a generally enlightened spirit, these schools would surely appeal to many Israelis outside the Anglo-Saxon community. Summer camps for Israeli children would be as important as Ramah has proved for Conservative Judaism in America.

6. There is another direction our program in Israel should take which has been urged upon us for many years by Rabbi Morris Dembowitz. In extenuation of our failure to act thus far, we may offer the explanation that this goal was not within the realm of possibility until recently. He has urged the creation of at least one Conservative *kibbutz* in which the life-style of our movement, our

code of affirmative religious practice within an atmosphere of freedom, and our standards of ethical conduct would be manifest to all. The Ramah movement, the USY and LTF groups, as well as the student body at the Seminary in its various schools in New York, the University of Judaism in Los Angeles, and the Seminary Student Center in Jerusalem, are reservoirs rich in human resources. From them young people may be drawn who would wish to make *aliyah* to Israel and participate in the building of an ethically just and religiously vital society. Among the membership of our congregations there will be older men and women who might wish to join in such an undertaking. One *kibbutz* conducted in the spirit of the Conservative movement would prove more effective than any other activity we might undertake to bring together the Land of Israel that we love and the philosophy of Judaism we cherish.

Not the least of the benefits from the existence of such a *kibbutz* would be the fact that when hundreds of our youngsters come each summer to the State of Israel, they would no longer need to be given a choice only between "nonreligious" and "Orthodox" *kibbutzim*. Israel would then be truly their spiritual home, in which they would experience the joy of *havruta*, "the fellowship of community."

Now at last, a *moshav shutafi* settlement under Conservative auspices is taking shape.

7. Paralleling the project of a *kibbutz* would be the buildir of cooperative apartment houses under the auspices of our movement in Jerusalem and in other major urban and suburban areas. These would constitute living communities exhibiting the religious, intellectual, social, and ethical ideals that are precious to us. Families in the active years of life, as well as those who have retired, would welcome the sense of *havruta* that would permeate the atmosphere.

8. We have, at long last, begun to make our position felt with regard to proposed amendments to the Law of Return and the challenge it poses to the legitimacy of Conservative Judaism. The efforts in this direction must be maintained and intensified. We must demonstrate that one is not compelled to choose between authoritarianism and chaos, whether in religion or in government, or in society as a whole. By our presence and activity, we can help to teach the truth that while Jewish society and Jewish religion cannot be separated without grave injury to both, this is not identical with the union of the state and a religious Establishment. If Sephardim

and Ashkenazim in the Orthodox community do not recognize the authority of one Chief Rabbi, and the Agudat Yisrael has a third, there is no reason why we must plead for a few crumbs of recognition from the government, the press, the electronic media, or the Orthodox "religious" Establishment.

Several years ago, it was reported that the Minister of Religions had advised Reform Jews who pleaded for religious rights to declare that they were not adherents of Judaism but members of another religion, like Bahai, and then they would receive full and equal recognition.

The recent scandal with regard to the refusal of the Orthodox religious Establishment in Israel to permit a wedding to be solemnized in the Conservative synagogue in Ashkelon evokes a strong sense of déjà vu. Some years ago, Henry N. Rapaport, then President of the United Synagogue, invited me to go with him to see the Minister of Religions in Jerusalem. As President of the United Synagogue, Mr. Rapaport came to protest a recent incident, likewise affecting the young and struggling Conservative congregation in Ashkelon. At the time, the congregation had no building of its own and had rented the B'nai B'rith building for services. Strong pressures had been put upon the officers of B'nai B'rith, and they had announced the termination of this arrangement. Ultimately it was "solved satisfactorily" when the Conservative congregation threatened that they would conduct services in the street, and the pressures were relaxed.

At our meeting, Dr. Warhaftig said with a smile: "B'nai B'rith is a nondenominational organization. I would object equally if an Orthodox congregation wished to use its facilities for services." I replied: "Dr. Warhaftig, your remark recalls Anatole France's statement, 'The law with majestic impartiality forbids the rich and the poor alike to sleep under the bridges over the River Seine.'"

The struggle for religious freedom can and must be won if true mutuality between Israel and the Diaspora is to exist.

However, this battle cannot be won if we consistently avoid taking our place in the seats of power—the lesson which our Orthodox brethren learned decades ago. One of these foci of power is the World Zionist Executive, which makes many of the decisions that matter. We must be there to raise our voices and exert our influence, bringing to bear our philosophy of Judaism and our emphasis upon Jewish ethics regarding the practical issues that arise constantly. One act *lekhate'hilah* (in advance) is worth a hundred protests *le'ahar hama'aseh* (after the deed is done). The time has come to take our place with all other groups in world Jewry that recognize the unique and indispensable significance of the Land of Israel for the Jewish future, though these groups do differ with regard to their conception of this Jewish future. The hour is long overdue for Conservative Judaism to liquidate our massive locking-the-stable-after-the-horse-is-stolen department. We must break with our pattern of "too little and too late" or it will really be too late.

9. Energetic political activity and massive economic aid for Israel must go on and will remain a necessity for years to come. But they do not represent *all* our obligations toward Israel, and surely do not replace our priorities in America—the building of vital religion, meaningful education, and better human beings and Jews everywhere. What holds true for Israel holds true for us: survival is not enough. Both Israel and the Diaspora must survive significantly for our own sake, for world Jewry, and for mankind.

If I may be permitted an original *midrash*, I would wish to expound a verse in Koheleth (11:6): "*Baboker*, in the East, the land of the morning, sow your seed, and *ba'erebh*, in the West, where the sun sets, do not let your hands be idle, for you cannot tell which seed will prosper or whether both will prove equally fruitful."

We are told that in Chinese the word "crisis" is expressed by the ideograms for "danger" and "opportunity." In this hour of manifold danger, let us take hold of the opportunity for building genuine mutuality between our brothers in the State of Israel and Conservative Judaism. Thus, with renewed strength, we will carry onward the life of an eternal people, serving the Eternal God through His Torah. "Let us be strong and of good courage for the sake of our people and the cities of our God" (I Chronicles 19:13).

13

A CONSERVATIVE ZIONIST PARTY

I

I should like to preface the discussion of this important theme with some reminiscences that may be entitled "The Autobiography of a Homeless Zionist." Actually, I never really became a Zionist. I do not remember a time when the ideal of the restoration of the Jewish people to the Land of Israel was not part of my being. Perhaps it began with the blue and white *pushke* in my mother's kitchen into which we put our pennies and nickels throughout the week, and not merely before the lighting of the Sabbath candles. Then came selling imitation flowers on subways during Jewish National Fund days. In my eighth year came the Balfour Declaration, and I vividly remember the excitement and joy throughout the neighborhood. By that time, I had already studied *Ḥumash* and knew by heart God's call and promise to Abraham. As I grew older and studied the poetry of Bialik and the essays of Aḥad Haʻam, my emotional and intellectual ties to the Zionist ideal grew all the stronger.

My college career coincided with the rise of left-wing, pro-Communist sympathies among Jewish college youth. City College in the twenties and thirties was the Harvard of the seventies. It was filled with bright Jewish young men differing from their affluent successors in Cambridge today only by a passionate commitment to some overriding ideal and the possession of much more limited economic means. The alcoves at City College on Convent Avenue reechoed to the debates we carried on against our Communist adversaries.

Ultimately I joined the ZOA, the Organization of General Zionists, and my lifelong trek as a homeless wanderer in the movement began. My conception of the future of the Jewish people had been fashioned by the words of the Torah and the Hebrew prophets, who taught that social justice and mutual responsibility were the prerequisites for peace and freedom among men. I was therefore drawn to the social idealism of the *kibbutz,* which presented the world with an example of a cooperative society built on productive work in an atmosphere of liberty—poles apart from the repression and tyranny of Soviet Communism. In overwhelming degree the *kibbutzim* in Israel were the offspring of Labor Zionism, whose philosopher, Aaron David Gordon, had created *Dat Ha-'avodah,* "the religion of labor." I therefore joined the League for Labor Zionism, the American affiliate of the official Labor Zionist movement. My happiness, however, was less than complete, for I was aware of the general indifference, if not the hostility, to Jewish religious faith and practice in Labor Zionist circles.

Ever since my boyhood I had known Rabbi Meyer Berlin, the dynamic leader of the World Mizrachi movement. During my early years in the pulpit of Temple Beth El of Rockaway Park, he was accustomed to spend one Sabbath each year in the community with some mutual friends, members of my congregation, who were, incidentally, direct descendants of the Gaon of Vilna. During these visits, Rabbi Berlin would say to me, "Your place and that of other members of the Conservative rabbinate like yourself is in the Po'el HaMizrachi. Here is a movement dedicated to traditional Judaism with a progressive social orientation. Its philosophy of *Dat Va-'avodah,* 'religion and labor,' expresses the basic ideals you cherish." I found the reasoning highly persuasive, and a group of us, including, as I remember, Simon Greenberg and Ben Zion Bokser among others, became members of Po'el HaMizrachi. Then a ton of bricks descended upon us. While there were many members of Po 'el HaMizrachi who welcomed our affiliation, a campaign of vilification was launched against us. We were accused of a secret plot to subvert the organization and take over its leadership. Petitions and counter-petitions began circulating among the members. The only course open to us was to withdraw.

I had no alternative but to rejoin the Zionist Organization of America, to which the vast majority of Conservative Jews belonged. I became active in its work. Appointed Chairman of the National Education Committee of ZOA, which had not met for two years, I revived its activity and carried out several important projects, one of which, a serious Zionist journal, was not brought to fruition until several years later.

As years went by and the ZOA took on an increasingly right-wing political and economic orientation, I found its policies less and less congenial. At least equally disturbing was its indifference to the all-but-complete disenfranchisement of Conservative Judaism in the State of Israel. This in spite of the fact that the bulk of the membership and support enjoyed by the ZOA came from Conservative Jewish ranks, as did a great deal of its leadership, from Israel Goldstein to Joseph Sternstein.

II

Then came the great miracle of the century, which Theodor Herzl had prophetically foreseen. When the State of Israel came into existence in 1948, the only religious group that was prepared for the new order was Orthodoxy, which proceeded to organize as a political party both in Israel and in the Zionist movement.

The extraordinary success of Orthodoxy in establishing a monopoly in the area of religion derived from two factors. The first was internal. While Mizrachi constituted only a small minority in the State of Israel, the system of proportional representation governing elections to the Knesset gave it a great deal of leverage, since no single party commanded a solid majority. Labor, which ruled from the inception of the state in 1948 until May 1977, therefore entered into an uneasy alliance with Mizrachi, which had arrogated to itself the name of National Religious Party, Mafdal or NRP. Last May the Likud government of Menahem Begin established a similar alliance with the two Orthodox groups, Mizrachi and Agudat Yisrael, the latter having also discovered the advantages of political power. Qualitatively, the Likud government had much more enthusiasm for the compact than had the preceding Labor government. But neither Labor nor Likud nor the General Zionists ever raised their voice against the rightlessness of non-Orthodox Jews in Israel or against the concomitant campaign to relegate Conservative and Reform Jews to second-class status in the Diaspora.

The second factor that facilitated this process was external to the State of Israel; it lay with Conservative Judaism itself. We had been Zionists before the Zionist movement was born. In the first half of the nineteenth century, religious controversy was rife in German Jewry and a series of rabbinical conferences took place. One of the rabbis in attendance at the second rabbinical conference held in 1845 at Frankfort was Zacharias Frankel, the distinguished rabbinic scholar who was later to become the president and guiding spirit of the Jewish Theological Seminary in Breslau. He had come to the meeting with many misgivings and sat with little enthusiasm through the sessions of the first two days when various reforms were being discussed. On the third day, the assembly voted that the Hebrew language should be retained at religious worship "out of deference to the older generation." This obviously meant that Hebrew was expendable, if not immediately then within a few decades. When this decision was reached, Frankel walked out of the conference, because he recognized that the destruction of the Jewish national spirit meant the death knell of Jewish religious vitality. Frankel became the leader of the movement which he called "positive-historical" Judaism.

This philosophy had four fundamental postulates: (1) that Judaism, beginning with the Patriarchs and the revelation to Moses and Israel at Sinai, has a history, that is to say, that it has grown and developed through time; (2) that we are called upon to take a basically positive attitude toward the product of this history; (3) that the Jewish people and its national aspirations occupy a central position in the value-system of the Jewish religion; (4) that the ideal of a restoration of the Jewish people to its homeland in Eretz Yisrael is indispensable for the survival of Jews and Judaism.

This movement, carried across the Atlantic, has reached its greatest development in the United States and Canada, where Conservative Judaism, as all surveys have demonstrated, commands the allegiance of a far greater constituency than either Orthodoxy or Reform. The most recent figures are available in the National Jewish Population Survey of 1970. It revealed that 9.7 percent of American Jews regard themselves as Orthodox, 29.3 percent as Reform and 40.5 percent as Conservative (Fred Massarik, "Affiliation and Nonaffiliation in the United States Jewish Community: A Reconceptualization," in *American Jewish Yearbook*, 1978, page 265).

The organic link between Zionism and Conservative Judaism has characterized the movement throughout its history. The great Solomon Schechter, President of the Seminary during the first decade and a half of the twentieth century, in a historic address publicly declared himself a Zionist and called upon the Jewish community to follow suit. This was at a time when, as my distinguished teacher Professor Max L. Margolis used to say, no gentleman was a Zionist and no Zionist was a gentleman. Israel Friedlander, who served as Professor of Bible at the Seminary and who was to meet a martyr's death while on a mission of succor for his oppressed brethren in the Ukraine after World War I, became the great interpreter and advocate to the English-speaking world of the teachings of Aḥad Ha'am. Aḥad Ha'am's concept of "cultural or spiritual Zionism" saw the Land of Israel as the source of vitality and inspiration for world Jewry, as the creative center of Jewish culture influencing and reinvigorating Jewish life through the world.

Because Conservative Judaism and Zionism were related organically—it would be fair to say genetically—throughout their history, Conservative Jews had always been Zionists and always would be. They could, therefore, be taken for granted by office-holders and office-seekers both in the Zionist movement and in the government bureaucracy in the State of Israel, and their concerns could safely be disregarded.

The silent if unhappy acquiescence of Conservative Jews in the status quo could be counted upon for another reason as well. The State of Israel was in crisis, confronted by major problems at home and mammoth perils from without. Conservative Jews were surely too loyal to the interests of the new state to upset the apple cart because of slights and injuries which, relatively speaking at least, were minor. After all, does it matter overmuch whether Rabbi A or Rabbi B officiates at a wedding ceremony in Israel?

III

To be sure, the relationship of the State of Israel to Conservative Judaism and the impact of Establishment Orthodoxy upon the life of the people was punctuated by a series of incidents, many of which were successfully swept under the rug. Some, however, attracted widespread attention and evoked considerable agitation. Generally, these recurrent episodes were followed by explanations, clarifications, and extenuations in the best political tradition. Then the excitement would die down, and the calm would last until the next "incident." One or two may be recalled. The list can easily be augmented.

During the troubled days of the "war of attrition," a young Israeli soldier was killed in action. His family had been members of a Conservative congregation for many years and the young man had become Bar Mitzvah in that synagogue. He had always been close to the rabbi. The official Orthodox rabbinate, with the authority of the state behind it, denied permission to the rabbi to officiate at the lad's funeral. There was a tremendous outcry, and finally they relented and permitted him to speak as a "friend of the family."

Several years later a group in Rehovot took steps to organize a Conservative congregation to be launched at the High Holy Days. However, the place where the services were to be held was not announced in the press or made public until the eve of Rosh Hashanah, because of the well-grounded fear that there would be violent attacks upon them and efforts would be made to disrupt the services.

These dramatic incidents—and others could be cited—were perhaps less important than a steady and unrelenting campaign to relegate non-Orthodox Jews to the status of second-class citizens in Israel. For reasons that I have been unable to fathom, the *kapote* and the *shtreiml*, originally worn by Polish peasants and gentry in the Middle Ages and adopted as the garb of Hasidic Jewry, were "authentic" Judaism. But a felt hat or a Western-cut suit worn by an American Jew was assimilationist, alien, to be exorcised or at least decried as inferior and a threat to Torah-true Judaism. A dozen different liturgies were legitimate in Israel, but a Conservative or Reform ritual was to be fought at all costs as heresy. For more sophisticated advocates there was the blessed word "deviationist," as though there had never been any differences in biblical Judaism among priests, prophets, psalmists, historians, and sages, or any arguments in the pages of the Mishnah and the Talmud, or any divergences of opinion among medieval and modern authorities.

What is sad is that all too often we ourselves have succumbed to this propaganda. Recently a speaker addressed a governing body of our movement and warned his hearers against introducing American life-styles into Israel. I do not recall that Rabbi Kahanman hesitated to introduce the life-style of the Lithuanian *yeshiva* of Ponevez into Bnai Brak. Nor do I remember that Orthodox leaders warned their followers against bringing the life-style of Polish or Hungarian Jewry to Israel. On the contrary, they insisted on doing precisely that—reestablishing on Israeli soil—and often in total isolation from the world about them—replicas of Eastern European patterns in their schools and synagogues.

I do not decry this practice—quite the contrary. I believe that diversity enriches the color and the content of Israeli life and ultimately redounds to the benefit of Judaism. But it is only we who are bidden to refrain from introducing any aspect of American Jewish life into Israel, however worthwhile. Let me give one important instance. Israel in general and Israeli youth in particular could gain greatly from the example and the program of the American synagogue-center at its best.

Some members of the Orthodox Establishment in private conversation have been frank enough to confess that they would prefer to have Israeli Jews totally nonreligious than become adherents of Conservative or Reform Judaism. This attitude is entirely comprehensible, since the existence of a nonreligious majority in Israel, presumably indifferent to religion and the ethical questions involved, would leave undisturbed the privileges, positions, and perquisites of the Orthodox religious Establishment.

In the past, the wider implications for world Jewry of the religious situation in the State of Israel were not generally recognized in the United States and Canada, since a working arrangement has prevailed here among spokesmen and adherents of Orthodox, Conservative, and Reform Judaism. To be sure, hostility and estrangement are increasingly in evidence in the public life of American Jewry. But the tradition of urbanity and mutual respect is still very much alive.

The situation became clearer when the present government came to power in Israel. It established a close relationship with the right-wing Orthodox political party of Agudat Yisrael as well as with the centrist Mizrachi, which had always suffered from a bad conscience on the ground that its Orthodoxy was suspect because it cooperated with the heretical Zionists. This alliance was more than a marriage of convenience based on political necessity, such as had existed during the Labor government regime; now there was a genuine affinity of spirit.

The Orthodox religious Establishment was now ready for the decisive move—to disenfranchise officially and otherwise the millions of Jews in the Diaspora who are not Orthodox. The Orthodox political parties demanded, and Mr. Menahem Begin has supported, amending the Law of Return, which now permits any Jew to immigrate to the Land of Israel as a matter of right. The amendment calls for adding a phrase to the definition of a Jew as being anyone "born of a Jewish mother or converted to Judaism *'al pi hahalakhah,* 'according to the Halakhah.' " The strategy underlying the proposal was masterful. The proof is that some of our people have fallen into the trap and have failed to recognize the implications of the additional phrase "according to the Halakhah."

I must confess that I am not impressed by the cautions that have been addressed to us regularly for the past three decades in the name of a higher good. Some time ago, a group of leaders from our movement were admonished not to adopt a more militant course of action in these words, "Conservative Jews are concerned about Conservatism in Israel. Israelis are concerned about survival." I suppose one is forbidden to look a gift epigram in the mouth, but some gnawing doubts remain. Has the magnitude of the problem—literally war or peace—deterred the Mizrachi and the Agudat Yisrael from demanding the amendment to the Law of Return and thus introducing a major element of divisiveness in Jewish life in a critical hour? Is Menahem Begin, who is guiding the destinies of his country with such energy and devotion, indifferent to the fate of Israel? Yet he has not hesitated to declare repeatedly that he favors the amendment to the Law of Return.

The grave internal and external problems facing the State of Israel did not dampen the ardor of those advocating the disenfranchisement of non-Orthodox Jews. It is only we who are bidden, for the sake of Israel's interests, to suppress our concern and activity and submit to this new *démarche.* The truth is, of course, that however difficult the situation in Israel may be, normal life with its thousand and one concerns goes on both within the State of Israel and without.

We who live in the twentieth century should have learned long ago to recognize the use of "code words" in propaganda. When Stalinist Russia decided to embark upon an anti-Jewish campaign, arresting and convicting Jewish doctors of poisoning their patients, the hue and cry was raised not against Jews, but against "cosmopolitanism." Far be it from the socialist Fatherland to engage in anti-Semitism!

More recently, as the Arab states, abetted by the Communist bloc, took control of the United Nations, we witnessed the spectacle of resolutions declaring that "Zionism is racism." Nothing against Judaism and the Jewish people—only political Zionism was being attacked! But both the perpetrators of the move and their opponents understood the code language and recognized that the campaign was directed against the Jewish people not only in the State of Israel but throughout the world.

On a smaller scale, to be sure, but employing a similar tactic, the proposed amendment to the Law of Return, "according to the Halakhah," is code language. It means "subject to the pleasure and with the authorization of the Israeli Orthodox religious Establishment." Thus the entire power of the state would be mobilized to buttress their monopolistic control, not only in Israel, but far beyond its borders.

Two young people in Peoria, Illinois, planning to get married, might someday wish to go and settle in Israel. The validity of their marriage, performed by a non-Orthodox rabbi, might then be called into question. To be sure, it might not, but then who knows? Why take upon oneself a second-class, ambiguous status by being married by a Conservative rabbi or affiliating with a Conservative synagogue? Ultimately, no overt action might be taken, but bureaucratic paperwork, delaying tactics, and harassment would be enough.

A convert to Judaism in Atlanta, Georgia, after years of sincere and wholehearted adherence to Judaism, wishes to make 'aliyah to Israel. The convert then finds that he or she is outside the pale of the Jewish people—by the fiat of the Orthodox rabbinate in Jerusalem or Tel Aviv. If the convert is a woman, any children born to her subsequent to her conversion are also non-Jews. They have the choice of leaving the Jewish fold altogether or undertaking a new process of conversion under the direction of the Israeli rabbinate. This is no easy formality. The more liberal members of the group have set a minimum requirement of two years for the process; the others demand more. The sheer insult to human dignity involved, quite aside from the practical difficulties, hardly needs to be spelled out.

Once the restrictions and disabilities of Jews affiliated with Conservatism, Reform, or Reconstructionism are carried out in practice in Israel, the effects would resonate to the generality of American Jews. Who could then blame many of those contemplating marriage, conversion, or synagogue membership for avoiding affiliation with the Conservative movement?

The consequences of this second-class status would be equally damaging in Israel. As is well known, public education in Israel is conducted largely along party lines. The General School System (beit sepher mamlakhti) is secular in orientation. Often its practitioners are hostile to religious ideas and practices. It is generally conceded that it transmits little of the traditional religious culture we call Torah. Various attempts to remedy the situation, such as the introduction of courses in "Jewish consciousness" (Toda'ah yehudit), have met with little success. Parallel with that system is the Mizrachi-sponsored Government Religious Schools (beit sepher mamlakhti dati). It is flanked on the right by the Agudat Yisrael–sponsored Independent Religious System (hinnukh 'atzma'i). All of them receive government support, the last-named to a lesser degree, since it refuses to accept the authority and supervision of the Department of Education of the Israeli government. When Jewish parents in Israel wish to give their children a religiously oriented Jewish education based upon a modern interpretation of Jewish tradition, though they pay taxes like all other Israelis, their schools are unable to secure financial aid from the government. Only in June, 1978 was one Conservative religious school in Jerusalem officially recognized.

The same disabilities exist with regard to religious institutions and their leadership. While Orthodox rabbis are recognized by the state and their salaries are paid by the government, Conservative congregations in Israel, like their Reform counterparts, are outside the pale. They have no official standing and, what is more, receive no practical support.

The treatment accorded Conservative Judaism in the press is often little less than disgraceful. The most respectable organs of opinion do not hesitate to publish material reeking with ignorance and malice.

As Conservative Jews in Israel move into the areas of urban housing and the building of settlements, whether they be *kibbutzim* or *moshavim,* the same problem of discrimination and harassment prevails.

Wherever the possibility exists for downgrading Conservative Judaism and relegating Conservative Jews to an inferior status—and the range is almost limitless—the effort is being undertaken. It is likely to meet with substantial success—if we persist in our policy of inaction and silence, or even if we continue to employ the strategy of lodging a complaint after the damage is done and then waiting for the next incident to explode in our faces.

Power cannot be successfully confronted by persuasion. This bitter lesson we have learned to our cost after three decades of forbearance, patience, and understanding, none of which have elicited similar reactions from the other side. American Jewry, the majority of whom are affiliated with Conservative Judaism, continue to pour many millions into Israel through the United Jewish Appeal, Israel Bonds, and countless other campaigns for various institutions and projects in the Land of Israel. This loyalty and generosity, unparalleled in the history of mankind, is, we are assured, appreciated by Israel. It has, however, produced no improvement in the status of non-Orthodox Jews. On the contrary, our position gives every promise of deteriorating further, unless we are prepared, after much too long a delay, to participate actively in Zionist activity under our own colors, as Orthodoxy has done for three-quarters of a century, a course of action recently adopted by our Reform brethren as well.

IV

Are there problems and difficulties connected with our embarking upon the creation of a Conservative religious party in the Zionist movement? Unquestionably there are.

Conservative Jews, born and bred in the American tradition, are by and large convinced of the validity of the American doctrine of the separation of church and state. Speaking for myself, and in no chauvinistic spirit, I regard this doctrine, which is enshrined in the First Amendment to the American Constitution, as the single greatest American contribution to the democratic ideal. It has not only made possible the growth and progress of the American people and the survival of the American federal union. It has kept inviolate the total freedom of all the varied ethnic and religious groups to be found in our country. That is not all. Originally the doctrine was adopted in order to keep peace among the various religious sects and churches represented in the thirteen colonies. Separation of church and state has proved, however, to be not only a safeguard for the state, but a blessing for religion. It is no accident that in no European country, where varying degrees of official relationship between church and state exist, is religion as genuinely influential, as generously supported, and as highly regarded by the majority of the population as in the United States. Religious liberty is the key to religious vitality.

I profoundly believe that ultimately the separation of church and state will, perhaps with some modifications, become universal in the democratic world, and that includes Israel.

But we have not yet reached the days of the Messiah anywhere. In Israel we are confronted by a condition, not a theory. The condition is that of an entrenched theocracy which, conscious of its power, is unwilling even to mitigate the severity of its authority. Nothing plays more effectively into its hands than for us to continue to insist that we are opposed to "religion in politics."

There is another possible objection to the creation of a Conservative Zionist party. Politics is often a dirty business, and its participants are in danger of being soiled in the process. This is undeniably true, but there is no other way to achieve any worthwhile objective. It has been said, "The way for evil to triumph is for good men to do nothing." I am not suggesting that those whose actions I have been criticizing are evil—only that they are serving their cause by means which they consider legitimate and according to their lights. We can do no less. We, for whom ethics are central in Judaism, can set a higher standard, by utilizing honorable means to achieve honorable goals.

We need not plead with the Orthodox religious Establishment to recognize the legitimacy of Conservative Judaism. Not being afflicted with an inferiority complex, we neither need it nor want it. What we call for is that the State of Israel recognize the equal rights of all interpretations of the Jewish religion and accord freedom to all Jews to share equally in the rights and privileges of Israeli citizenship. In the religious field this means freedom from harassment, discrimination, and insult for their religious institutions. It means support for the professional leadership of Conservative congregations, our schools, and our adult education programs. It means fair and free access to the press, radio, television, and other opinion-forming agencies.

We want to cease being spiritually homeless in Zion and demand that the process relegating us to second-class citizenship in the Jewish people be halted and reversed.

V

In calling for the creation of the Movement for the Reaffirmation of Conservative Zionism, the acronym for which is MERCAZ, "the center," American Conservative Jews recognize both their need and their opportunity. MERCAZ will afford us a base of influence for the fulfillment of our goals for Israel and for world Jewry—the achievement of security, peace, and progress for the State of Israel. We are dedicated to the furtherance of social idealism, integrity in government and public life, tolerance and mutual understanding among all groups. We believe that a warm religious commitment is possible in an atmosphere of freedom. These goals we hope to advance by cooperation with all other Zionist groups and parties.

These objectives go far beyond the special interests of the Conservative movement. Approximately seventy to eighty percent of Israeli Jews are indifferent to religion as currently presented and practiced in the State of Israel. Their attitudes vary from indifference to outright hostility. The government has recognized that large sections of Israeli youth are totally estranged from the fundamentals of Jewish faith, the principles of Jewish ethics, and the practice of Jewish ritual. These tragic lacunae in education have produced growing cynicism, an erosion of the sense of the common good, and a search for instant gratification through drugs, alcoholism, and sexual immorality. For many in Israel it has also led to a sense of alienation from world Jewry and a loss of identification with the Jewish past and the Jewish present in the Diaspora.

Conservative Judaism, being composed of men and women of flesh and blood, does not claim a monopoly on truth and virtue, but it affirms that infallible truth and perfect righteousness are to be found only with God.

We ask no special privileges and refuse to accept special disabilities. The task of winning Jewish youth in Israel and throughout the world for Judaism is one that should enlist all groups dedicated to the survival of our tradition. Can Orthodoxy win the youth for its cause?

More power to it. Can Reform do so? They should be free to undertake the attempt.

We feel that large numbers of Israelis in all walks of life, young and old, male and female, if given the opportunity to discover the true meaning of Conservative Judaism, would wish to affiliate with the movement and thus find their place within Jewish tradition without resigning from the twentieth century.

A Conservative Zionist party, drawing its membership and support at present primarily from America, will not be a political party in Israel, but a constituent member of the American Zionist Federation. Obviously, it will not be able to achieve all its objectives. When Nebuchadnezzar laid siege to Jerusalem, the prophet Jeremiah could not prevent the burning of the Temple and the destruction of the Jewish state. But neither could Nebuchadnezzar prevent Jeremiah from lamenting his people's fate. At the time, one might well have asked, "What good do these tears and weeping achieve?" From the vantage point of history, we know that the prophet's fruitless words, treasured by later generations, helped preserve the Jewish people from destruction.

Though we are not prophets, we are children of the prophets, as the Sages remind us. By keeping the standard of justice and freedom aloft before the Zionist movement and the Jewish people, the Conservative party will be helping to assure Israel's future. If such an alignment helps to keep alive the goal of freedom and equality for Conservative Judaism in Israel, *Dayenu,* "that would be enough." If it can help to create a climate of religious freedom for all Jews in the Land of Israel, *Dayenu,* "that would be enough." If it helps to build the survival of Judaism in Israel and throughout the world, *Dayenu,* "that would be enough." An active Conservative Zionist party can play its part, so that the people, the state, and the heritage of Israel will not only survive but be worthy of survival. We shall then have fulfilled the blessing promised to our Father Abraham, "In you all the families of the earth will be blessed."

Before his untimely death, Theodor Herzl once addressed a group of indifferent Jewish college students in France, urging their adherence to the Zionist ideal. He said to them, "Je ne vous dis pas encore 'Marchons!' Je vous dis seulement 'Debout!' " "I am not yet saying to you, 'Let us go forward!' I am saying only 'Stand up!' "

This is the call of the hour.

14

A JEWISH PRAYER BOOK FOR THE MODERN AGE

I

When Solomon Schechter declared, "At a time when all Jews prayed, one prayer book sufficed their needs. Now when far less Jews pray, more and more prayer books are required," he was delivering himself not of an epigram but of an acute historical observation. The prayer book became a problem for Jews when Judaism as a whole became a problem. Hence the issues involved can be understood only in terms of this larger framework of Jewish life.

Prior to the Emancipation, the *nusha'ot*, or variants, in traditional prayer books were principally matters of local custom. Even the Hasidic controversy introduced variations without significant differences. The spiritual climate of the prayer book in all its forms was basically the same, exactly as the social, economic, and cultural character of the scattered Jewish communities varied only in the slightest degree.

When the Jews of Western Europe were granted civic and political equality, however hesitatingly, and new economic opportunities opened before them, a far-reaching spiritual revolution was set in motion. As they entered Western culture, they began to desert traditional Jewish life. One of the first consequences was that the prayer book, the classic expression of traditional Judaism, became increasingly unpalatable even to those Jews who retained a sense of attachment to the Jewish religion. There were, of course, thousands of Jews who regarded themselves as enlightened and advanced, for whom Jewish values and practices could not be made relevant under any circumstances, for whom the game was not worth the candle. Through conversion and intermarriage they and their descendants cut the links that bound them to Judaism. Only subsequent developments made it all too tragically clear that they had not succeeded in divorcing their destiny from their Jewish origins.

Many other Western Jews, however, found it impossible to dissociate themselves completely from their Jewish heritage, for a variety of reasons. In some instances, this reluctance had no theoretic basis, but stemmed from a deeply human desire not to hurt pious parents and grandparents. In others it was a sense of *noblesse oblige,* a conviction that self-respect forbade deserting the sinking ship of Judaism merely out of a desire to further one's own interests. For many more it was a genuine love for Jewish life, however unconscious and even shamefaced, in a world that doted upon novel intellectual fashions every day. Finally, for many Jews it was the lash of anti-Semitism which reminded them of their Jewish background. For all these groups, Judaism remained part of their heritage, but none of them were prepared to surrender their hard-won place in Western society or the enlarged vistas of modern culture. For them the problem of adjusting their Judaism to modern life arose.

"Adjustment" is a sonorous term that effectively disguises a process not altogether happy. All too often it resembles the procrustean bed of Greek mythology or the *mittat sedom* of Jewish legend. For the hospitable Sodomites, it will be remembered, fitted every wayfarer to the bed they had prepared by lopping off his limbs if they protruded or stretching him on the rack if his frame was too short. Generally the modern adjustment to Judaism followed this procedure—an amputation of the rich and variegated character of Jewish life or the stretching of one phase of Judaism out of all proportion to its place in the organic whole. By and large, adjustment meant reduction both in intensity as well as in extent, so that Judaism was reduced to the modest dimensions of a decorous near-Protestant cult.

Similar criticisms of the Reform movement have been made

before. However, it has usually been overlooked that these strictures notwithstanding, Reform was an expression of the Jewish will to survive. Basically its protagonists, however mistaken, were actuated by a genuine desire to preserve their heritage. Those who lacked that impulse found quicker and easier ways to escape their Jewish background. When this is recognized, it follows naturally that Reform has positive achievements of no mean order to its credit. Within its ranks, which originally included moderate as well as extreme views, were men like Abraham Geiger, whose brilliant reinterpretations of Jewish values and emphasis on development in Judaism are still significant; Leopold Zunz, the father of the science of Judaism, who favored necessary modifications,[1] and Leopold Löw, whose contributions to the problem of change in Jewish law are still valuable today. Even the patent errors and inadequacies of Reform Judaism have high pedagogic value. If we today strive to avoid them, it is in large measure because of the previous experience of "classical" Reform Judaism, which serves both as an example and a warning. Obviously, for us to repeat them would be the height of folly, but only because others have paid the price of experience.

Moreover, the contribution of Reform, used in the broadest sense, is by no means purely negative. Much of its achievement is today common property for all the modern schools in Judaism, Orthodoxy and Conservatism as well as Reform. It seems to us undeniable that Reform fulfilled a function which needed to be done. The emphasis upon decorum in worship, the elimination of many superstitious accretions in observance, the introduction of the sermon in the vernacular, the elimination of such abuses as the selling of honors in the synagogue, the reduction of the *piyyut*, the sanctity of which derived in large measure from its incomprehensibility, were each of them bitterly opposed as representing an affront to tradition. This in spite of the fact that for centuries leading rabbinic authorities had attacked some of these abuses to no avail. Even the production of properly printed prayer books, free from scribal errors and grammatical monstrosities, was an achievement of the modern trend in Judaism. These and similar changes do not seem radical today, appearing rather as part of the natural adjustment of Judaism to the modern age.

Other changes were not so easily or universally accepted. The introduction of choral singing by females or mixed voices aroused widespread objections among traditionally minded elements. The organ in particular became the symbol of both moderate and extreme Reform in Europe. On the other hand, family pews and bareheaded worship made practically no headway on the Continent. As a result, these characteristic practices of American Conservatism and Reform respectively remained virtually unknown in Germany, France, Italy, and England.

II

It is against this background that the efforts to modernize the traditional prayer book must be viewed. The motives that impelled a revision of the liturgy were both conscious and unconscious—that is to say, some were reasons and others were rationalizations. Among the conscious factors was a desire to reduce the length of the service by curtailing less important elements like the *Pesuke deZimrah* and the *piyyutim*. Closely related was the wish to make the service more intelligible by supplementing the Hebrew prayers or replacing them by prayers in the vernacular. Time revealed that this trend, like many other tendencies in Reform, had a dangerous spiral tendency. Once set into motion, the trend continued to gain momentum, so that beginning with comparatively minor inroads of the vernacular, it finally drove Hebrew almost completely out of the service. It was a prophetic recognition of this peril that led Frankel to withdraw from the Frankfort Rabbinical Conference of 1845, when the assembly voted to retain Hebrew only out of deference to the sentiments of the older generation.

While prayers in the vernacular were urged on the ground that they added greater meaningfulness to the service, in practice they created a new and unexpected complication. Hebrew prayers chanted in the traditional manner could be repeated on almost every occasion without producing a sense of monotony in the worshipper. In the first instance, the traditional congregant was an active participant in the ritual instead of being a member of a silent audience. The mass chanting and swaying might not be very decorous by Western standards. It had the virtue, however, of being alive. The old psychological principle of "no impression without expression" embodied in Jewish prayer made the experience emotionally vibrant and satisfying. Second, the characteristic musical modes and scriptural cantillations, which differ with the varying occasions of the year, served to create a distinct mood appropriate to the day and added variety and interest, even when the text remained the same.

All these unconsciously acquired resources were swept into the discard by Reform. The penalty was swift. As the different traditional modes and scriptural cantillations were abandoned or circumscribed and were replaced by responsive and unison readings in the vernacular, the monotony of the service became marked.[2] This new problem was now met by the device of varying the text of the prayers. Thus Samuel Holdheim's German Reform prayer book of 1856 contained nine cycles, the "classic" American *Union Prayer Book* contained five services for the Sabbaths of the month (obviously not the Jewish month!), as well as five additional services for special Sabbaths. The new Reform prayer book *Shaarei Tefillah* represents a radically different approach to the prayer book—it contains ten Friday Evening Services and six rituals for Sabbath morning—from the nearly traditional to the highly innovative. The English Reform prayer book prepared by Rabbi Israel Mattuck of London has no less than thirty distinct services. Nevertheless, the frequently voiced complaint that the Reform service is cold and uninspiring and the congregation inert and unresponsive gives grounds for doubting that the problem has been adequately met.

The objections noted above dealt with the language, the form, and the length of the service, problems in which the laity were interested, at least during the period of transition. On the other hand, modifications were also urged in the contents of the prayer book on dogmatic grounds. As Elbogen has acutely noted, these changes were of moment to theologically trained rabbis, but did not concern the laity much. Such features of the traditional liturgy as the resurrection, the personal Messiah, the reestablishment of the Davidic dynasty, the reintroduction of animal sacrifices, the restoration of the Jewish people to Palestine, the concept of the Chosen People, and the distinction between Israel and the nations, were opposed on the ground that they were not in harmony with the advanced religious ideas of the modern age. Elbogen, himself a leader of moderate German Reform, made a devastating comment on the motives behind much of this agitation when he noted that it was motivated by political considerations. He points out that

Western Jews did not hesitate to trim their religious ideals and were quite willing to sever the link binding their destiny to their brothers elsewhere in the world, in order to render unassailable, as they thought, their political rights and economic opportunities as citizens.[3] That identical tendencies appeared in modern American-Jewish life is evidence of the truth of Koheleth's words, "There is nothing new under the sun," or, to cite a more recent philosopher, George Santayana, "He who does not know the past is doomed to repeat it."

In the name of universalism, Reform leaders raised a hue and cry against Jewish "particularism," quite unaware of the fact that the dichotomy between these two polar forces has no objective reality in Hebrew thought. Actually, it is an invention of German theologians and their disciples, who sought a method for preserving the Bible while condemning the people that had created it. Now this passionate advocacy of universalism and excoriation of nationalism by Reform spokesmen was strictly limited to the Jewish scene. Nowhere did the accredited leaders of "modern" Judaism cry out against the aggressive and militaristic nationalism of Germany, France, England, and Italy, which plunged nineteenth-century Europe into war after war and brought civilization to the brink of extinction three times in the twentieth. On the contrary, it is hard to find anywhere more fervent preachers of patriotism and boundless loyalty to the state than among those Jewish apostles of "universalism."

There is another proof that practical considerations rather than philosophical ideals were at the roots of the objections to the traditional liturgy. It lies in the procedure adopted by Reform with regard to the passages dealing with the reintroduction of sacrifices and the restoration to Zion. Elsewhere prayer book editors had had no difficulty in excising or modifying the traditional text, preserving what they thought worthwhile and eliminating the rest. But it did not occur to them to make a distinction between these two ideas, which are often linked in the traditional prayer book, to be sure, but are by no means inseparable. Reiterating that no modern person could pray for the restoration of sacrifices, they proceeded to eliminate with these prayers all petitions for the restoration of the Jewish homeland. The conclusion is inescapable that the objection to sacrifices served as a cloak for eliminating the hope of a reestablishment of Israel in its ancestral home.

It is noteworthy that only in two instances was it recognized that these two ideas were not necessarily interdependent, both times within Conservative ranks.[4] Zacharias Frankel stated that he favored the elimination of the petition for the restoration of sacrifices but not the deletion of the Messianic hope. Unfortunately, here, as in so many other respects, Frankel contented himself with negative criticism rather than positive action. In England, the West-London Synagogue, whose minister was Morris Joseph, the author of *Judaism as Creed and Life,* actually proceeded to delete the passages dealing with sacrifices but retained the prayers for the restoration to Zion.

To revert to the main theme, all these objections to the language, length, form, and content of the traditional liturgy were so far-reaching that they necessitated a radical transformation of the *Siddur* and the *Maḥzor.* In Germany, Reform was unable or unwilling to break so violently with tradition, and so it produced a prayer book which made some adjustments along these lines, but later reintroduced many traditional features.[5] In America, where there was little Jewish learning among the laity and no deeply rooted tradition of practice, Reform was able to follow its logic to its consequences or go to extremes—the phrase used depends on the point of view! The natural consequence was the creation of the *Union Prayer Book,* which bears only a slight resemblance to the traditional liturgy throughout its many revisions until the last.

As a result, the prayer book became one of the most important dividing lines between the traditional and the anti-traditional elements. Since Reform had made a modification of the prayer book one of its cardinal planks, the adherents of traditional Judaism made the retention of the original a matter of principle. Frequently recourse was had to the rabbinic utterance (Tosefta *Berakhot* 4: 5, ed. Zuckermandl, p. 9) כל המשנה ממטבע שטבעו חכמים בברכות לא יצא "Rabbi Jose said, 'Whoever deviates from the form established by the sages for the blessings has not fulfilled his religious duty.' " It was generally overlooked that this statement refers only to the ברכות הנהנין, the blessings recited over food and drink and similar experiences, as is clear from the text itself, as well as from the context in which it is cited (Babylonian Talmud, *Berakhot* 40b; Jerusalem Talmud, *Berakhot* 62).[6] The very genuine problems of a Jewish prayer book in the modern age were ignored merely because the solution of Reform was found inadequate.

As in so many other aspects of Judaism, there is a need of a synthesis of the old and the new, the traditional and the contemporary. That the difficulties are tremendous, even without the problem of adjustment, is graphically indicated by two very sound judgments on the art of translation expressed in the Talmud. One declares: אין מקרא יוצא מידי פשוטו "The literal meaning of a text cannot be disregarded" (*Shabbat* 63a and often), and the other: המתרגם פסוק כצורתו הרי זה בדאי "Whoever translates a text literally falsifies it"(*Kiddushin* 49a). Yet, complex as is the task of making traditional Judaism vital and creative in the modern world, we cannot desist from it—for nothing less is the historical mission of our movement.

III

The slow gestation of Conservative Judaism and the lack of clarity in its outlook during its early stages is reflected in its approach to the prayer book. Historically, it was the "left-wing" of modern traditional Judaism which first emerged on the American scene. The close relationship of this group to Reform is to be seen in its procedure with the prayer book. Two of its great leaders, Marcus Jastrow and Benjamin Szold, produced the "Jastrow Prayer Book," which is still used in some congregations. These great scholars and lovers of traditional Judaism, one of whom, at least, was a pioneer of the Zionist ideal in America, produced a prayer book that can only be described as mildly Reform. The reason is surely to be sought in the conditions of the time. These pioneers saw the rising tide of extreme Reform, which seemed to sweep everything before it. They doubtless believed that only some kind of modified Reform had the faintest chance of success in America.

This consideration would seem to explain why their work is more radical in many respects than *Minhag Amerika,* the prayer book of Isaac M. Wise, the builder of Reform Judaism in America.[7] Wise's strength lay far more in his zeal for unity and his organizational skill than in philosophic depth and consistency. In fact, his desire for unity in American Israel had led him to subscribe to the statement of principles adopted at Cleveland in 1855, in which the talmudic legislation was accepted as binding!

At all events, the Jastrow Prayer Book eliminates all references to a restoration to Zion and reduces the *Pesuke DeZimrah* very drastically. It does not hesitate to paraphrase the Hebrew original in a manner which bears only the slightest relationship to the traditional text, a procedure Geiger had adopted in 1854 in his prayer book. Its traditional character resides largely in its retention of the Hebrew language and the basic structure of the service, as against the Reform prayer books, which were rapidly reducing the use of the sacred tongue to the vanishing point.[8]

In appearance and spirit these "left-wing" Conservative prayer books show a marked affinity with Reform, from which they stem. Similarly, "right-wing" Conservative congregations, which derived from Orthodoxy, retained the traditional prayer book unchanged, except for the omission of some technical passages like *bammeh madlikin* and *pittum haketoret*. The early contributions of Conservative Judaism to the Jewish liturgy lay principally in better-printed editions, more attractive English versions, and the preparation of songs and supplementary readings.

These works, though often drawing from the collective experience of our colleagues, were issued on individual responsibility. The first collective enterprise in the field was the *United Synagogue Maḥzor for the Pilgrimage Festivals,* which, at the time, was the most attractive traditional prayer book yet issued. The volume is distinguished by a sharp reduction in the extent of the *piyyut,* the addition of several supplementary prayers, many felicities in translation, and a beautiful setting of the Hebrew prayers, particularly the Psalms, in a manner calculated to reveal the poetic beauty of the original.

In the fall of 1944, the Rabbinical Assembly and the United Synagogue agreed to adopt a manuscript prepared by Rabbi Morris Silverman as the basis for a prayer book to be issued jointly by them. A commission was created by the two bodies with complete authority to revise, supplement, and edit the material. This Joint Prayer Book Commission consisted of the following rabbis: Robert Gordis, Chairman; Morris Silverman, Editor; Max Arzt, Secretary; Simon Greenberg, Jacob Kohn, Israel H. Levinthal, Louis M. Levitsky, Abraham A. Neuman, Elias L. Solomon. The *Sabbath and Festival Prayer Book* was issued in 1946 on the collective responsibility of the Joint Prayer Book Commission.

In the course of the concentrated, day-by-day labors of the Prayer Book Commission, certain fundamental principles evolved. Obviously, opinions will differ with regard to the degree of success the commission achieved in implementing these principles. But they remain, I believe, significant for our approach to the problem of the Jewish liturgy, as well as for the philosophy of Conservative Judaism as a whole. They must, it seems to us, constitute the basis of a Jewish prayer book in the modern age. It is, therefore, of more than academic interest to set forth these guiding principles:

1. *Continuity with Tradition.* Important as tradition is for every faith and culture, it is infinitely more significant for Judaism and the Jewish people. This is true, not only because, as Ranke declared, Jews are the most historical of peoples, but also because of the limitless centrifugal forces that threaten Jewish survival, and against which loyalty to tradition is the strongest bulwark.

This continuity has "horizontal" as well as "vertical" aspects; that is to say, there must be a strong sense of association, not only with the generations gone before, but with our brothers the world over, whom Schechter called "Catholic Israel." Nor is it merely a matter of the retention of the words that is involved. Generally, the spirit of the Jewish service inheres far more in the Hebrew language, in the traditional melodies, and in the well-known and well-loved customs—one is almost tempted to say, in the easy familiarity that our ancestors displayed in the house of God. This, unfortunately, degenerates too easily into mere lack of decorum among their descendants!

This emphasis upon continuity is no mere ancestor-worship on our part. As Israel Zangwill declared, ours is not a religious generation. Whatever other virtues we may possess, we lack that genius for religious expression which is so beautifully exemplified in the traditional prayer book. This consideration cannot free us from the obligation to strive perpetually after fresh and creative devotional forms. But it should prevent us from rashly laying hands on the product of the piety of earlier generations.

A striking illustration of the superiority of traditional religious thought over our modern conceptions lies in the awareness of evil. Modern prayer books of all types tend to minimize and soft-pedal the existence of evil in the world. Sin, wickedness, and evildoers have all but disappeared from their pages. In this respect they reflect the melioristic, comfortable philosophy of the nineteenth century, which looked forward to a painless and automatic progress guaranteed to end in the millennium. The absence of the recognition of evil gives to most modern prayer books an air of unreality and saccharine sweetness. This attitude reaches its apogee in the first important new cult of our century, Christian Science, which denies evil completely, and in the various cults, Oriental and Occidental, both within the Establishment and without, that guarantee salvation or peace of mind or freedom from worry, while dismissing any concern with the world and its problems.

In the case of Jewish prayer books, political considerations, as noted above, played an important part in the process. It was completely overlooked that the political emancipation of Western Jewry was not synonymous with the Messianic Age, but merely the first step toward liberation. It was not even suspected that civic equality is a mockery unless it includes the right of spiritual self-determination, the maintenance of group loyalty protected by law and exemplified in life.

By the elimination of "disturbing" passages, modern redactors sacrificed the manliness of the old prayer book, which expressed the conviction that evil must be recognized, fought, and conquered. A specific example is afforded by the *shefokh hamatekha,* which both the *Union Haggadah* as well as the Reconstructionist version have eliminated. Only a few years ago it seemed blind obscurantism, if not worse, to pray for the destruction of "nations who do not know God and kingdoms that do not call upon His name, who destroy Jacob and devastate his habitation." It has unfortunately turned out to be one of the basic realities of the life of our generation. Few sections of the liturgy are more truly geared to the Nazi and post-Nazi era and are more tragically relevant in our day, when our civilization is threatened by the new barbarism. Even if such passages were merely historical reminiscences, a sense of continuity would dictate their retention. Alas that they qualify as contemporary history!

It is undoubtedly true that we must not underestimate the changes in thought which separate the modern from earlier periods. It is equally important not to overestimate these differences. Frequently, when we penetrate the spirit of traditional literature and reckon with the genius of the Hebrew language, we discover that the gulf is by no means as wide as seemed originally to be the case.

For all these reasons, the sense of continuity with a living tradition in time and space must be a fundamental principle in a Jewish prayer book for the modern age.

2. *Relevance to the Needs and Ideals of Our Generation* is the second criterion. A prayer book is not a museum piece. It must express our own aspirations rather than merely those of our ancestors, however much we may revere them. As the traditional phrase אלהינו ואלהי אבותינו indicates, He must be "our God" rather than only "the God of our fathers."

This problem of relevance has two aspects. There are modern ideals that are expressed inadequately or too briefly in the traditional liturgy. This lack can be met by supplementing the accepted service and thus incidentally stimulating creativity in the liturgy. The more difficult aspect of the problem of relevance lies in the undeniable fact that there are passages in the traditional prayer book that do not seem to express our present-day convictions and hopes. Such passages must be carefully studied and dealt with through a variety of procedures, as will be noted presently.

3. *Intellectual Integrity,* the third criterion for a modern Jewish prayer book, demands that we do not yield to the temptation, to which some editors have fallen victim, of printing a traditional Hebrew text and a parallel English version that has practically nothing in common with the original. This has been done most recently in the revised edition of the *Union Prayer Book,* which reintroduces the *Kol Nidre* while ignoring the text in the English version.

IV

These basic principles—continuity with tradition, relevance to the modern age, and intellectual integrity—are obviously not easy to harmonize. The extent to which one or another principle ought to prevail in a given instance will naturally be the subject of differences of opinion. The touchstone of their validity lies in their application to the most crucial issue—those traditional passages that do not seem to square with modern attitudes. The problems posed by these passages must be met in varying ways:

1. In many cases, apparent divergences of outlook disappear when the true intent of the prayer book is grasped and its mode of expression is understood. The doctrine of the Chosen People, which

is so prominent in Jewish tradition, is a case in point. Undeniably this idea has been vulgarized in many circles, so that it is often confused with the myth of racial superiority and the doctrine of national chauvinism. But the remedy does not lie in eliminating it from the prayer book. For that means surrendering to the vulgar distortions of the concept and, incidentally, perpetrating an injustice upon the prophets and sages of Israel, who understood it aright.

Moreover, we today affirm the election of Israel because it is historically true. The great religions of Christianity and Islam, modern humanitarian ideals, and the principles of democracy are all rooted in the Hebrew Bible. They testify to the central role that Israel has played in the religious and ethical development of Western man.

Not only is the doctrine in accord with objective truth; its reaffirmation today is required on psychological grounds. It may be true that a normal people living under normal conditions needs no rationale for survival beyond the instinct for self-preservation, which stems from the fact that it is alive. But that is not likely to suffice in the case of Israel, and for obvious reasons. Jewish survival is hazardous, demanding untold sacrifice, even during the thirty years since the establishment of the State of Israel. Moreover, modern Jews have the belief—even if it be an illusion—that escape from the Jewish group is possible, at least for themselves individually.

If our generation is to accept Jewish fellowship and loyalty to Judaism willingly and joyously, accepting the disabilities of Jewish life and rejecting the temptation to desert, it requires a sense of consecration—a conviction that the Jewish people has played and yet will play a noble and significant role in the world. Many of our finest young people have inherited a profound idealism, a "Messianic complex," if you will. They must be taught to feel that Jewish loyalty is nothing petty and insular, but that, on the contrary, it ministers to the progress of humanity. The doctrine of the Chosen People is therefore a psychological necessity as well as a historical truth, an indispensable factor for Jewish survival today.

Moreover, when the ideal is studied in classic Jewish thought, it becomes clear that the prayer book has interpreted it properly by linking it invariably with the great instruments of Jewish living, the Torah and the *mitzvot*. This has often been overlooked by modern editors, who failed to note, or draw the proper conclusions from, the fact that the prayer book is written in a classical Hebrew, midway between biblical and mishnaic style. It therefore follows the syntax of classic Hebrew, which uses coordinate structure where Indo-European tongues would use subordinate clauses. This fact, well known to all competent Semitists, is clearly expressed by Professor Theophile J. Meek:[9]

> "The Hebrew language is a more primitive, less complex, language than our own, and where we use grammatical subordination in our sentence and structure, Hebrew is more likely to use grammatical coordination. . . . At other times they introduce a grammatically coordinate clause, which, however, is logically subordinate (that is, subordinate in meaning) and has to be so translated into English, because a true translation must reproduce the idiom of one language, not in literal terms, but in the idiom of the other language."

To cite one instance out of many, biblical Hebrew will say, בצלו חמדתי וישבתי (Song of Songs 2:3), which must be translated into English, "In his shadow have I desired to dwell." Similarly, the *Berakhah Aḥronah* says, אשר רצית והנחלת לאבותינו, which means, "which You did desire to cause our ancestors to inherit." This same characteristic of Hebrew syntax occurs in the Blessing over the Torah, אשר בחר בנו מכל העמים ונתן לנו את תורתו, which means for us, as it has for all the thinking generations of Israel, "who has chosen us from among the peoples by giving us His Torah." Similarly, אשר נתן לנו תורת אמת וחיי עולם נטע בתוכנו means, "who has given us the Torah of Truth, thus planting (or, and thus has planted) in us the seed of eternal life." Other instances are to be found in the *Kiddush* and the *Amidah:* אשר בחרתנו מכל העמים ואהבת אותנו ורצית בנו ורוממתנו מכל הלשונות וקדשתנו במצותיך וגו'.

In every instance the prayer book associates the election of Israel not with any inherent personal or group superiority, but with the higher responsibilities which come to the Jew as the custodian of Torah and the devotee of the Jewish way of life. This is no modern reinterpretation, merely an instance of the correct understanding of the letter and the spirit of tradition.

2. There are other instances where our attitudes now vary from older concepts. In many cases, it is possible to reinterpret traditional phrases in order to express our own convictions. There is no need

for us to fall prey to the genetic fallacy. Words may mean for us more than they originally meant. Thus the word *'abodah,* "religious worship," which our ancestors equated with the sacrificial system in the Temple, may quite properly mean for us the entire system of public religious observance, even the reestablishment of a great religious center on Mount Zion without the reintroduction of sacrifices. We are therefore not called upon to eliminate such phrases as השב את העבודה לדביר ביתך because in the consciousness of Israel the idea of the spiritual restoration to Zion remains one of undeniable power. The mode of worship we envisage differs from that of those who look forward to animal sacrifices. But the phrase here cited says nothing of that, and it can therefore continue to speak for us with sincerity and force.

The same connotation of *'abodah* exists in the Festival Musaf prayer והשב כהנים לעבודתם ולויים לשירם ולזמרם וגו׳. There our rendering voices our aspiration for the restoration of Temple worship on Mount Zion with *kohanim* pronouncing the Priestly Benediction and Levites offering song and psalmody as elements in the historical continuity of Israel's religion.

The phrase מחיה המתים, rendered "who calls the dead to everlasting life," is linguistically sound. It serves admirably to express the faith of those who believe in the immortality of the soul as well as that of believers in physical resurrection. It may be added that the older rendering is itself a reinterpretation of a biblical idiom, which usually meant "to restore to health those near death," as in I Samuel 2:6: ה׳ ממית ומחיה מוריד שאול ויעל. Words are symbols, and it is of the nature of symbols to represent more than one idea or conception.

3. With all our striving for intellectual integrity, it must always be remembered that the prayer book is couched in poetry and not in prose. It must therefore be approached with warm emotion and not with cold intellectual detachment. Thus, the emphasis in the prayer book upon the Messiah need not mean for us the belief in a personal redeemer. The Messiah remains for us the vivid and infinitely moving symbol of the Messianic hope. To have deleted the references to the Messiah would have meant to surrender one of the most picturesque elements of Jewish belief, culture, music, and art. Similarly, the petitions of the prayer book for the restoration of the House of David are felt and are regarded by most modern Jews as poetry. There are no Davidic pretenders alive today! Most Israelis

today are not stubbornly wedded to ancient religious tradition. Yet the modern *halutz* sings with fervor and sincerity not only the old אליהו הנביא, with its reference to משיח בן דוד, but countless modern melodies like *Yerushalayim,* with its plea יבא המשיח יבוא, and מתי יבוא המשיח. To have eliminated all such passages from the prayer book would have meant the impoverishment of the Jewish spirit. The prayer book, like all poetry and truth, has things in it too exalted for literalness.

4. There will naturally be instances, however, where legitimate reinterpretation is impossible because the traditional formulation cannot be made to serve our needs. Such preeminently are the passages dealing concretely with animal sacrifices, which are central to the Musaf Service. Passages like '*ezehu mekomam* and *pittum ha-ketoret* can be dropped without injuring the rubric of the service, but the elimination of the Musaf Service as a whole means destroying the entire structure of the traditional liturgy. Moreover, it would mean sacrificing several fundamental ideas contained in the Musaf which ought to be preserved, and if possible made even more vivid and explicit. We surely cannot afford to throw out the baby with the bath-water.

What procedure should be adopted? Even before the appearance of our prayer book, a step in the right direction was made in one edition of the *United Synagogue Maḥzor,* which changed the phrase נעשה ונקריב from the future to the past: עשו והקריבו. It thus made תכנת שבת express what untold numbers of modern Jews have found in it—a recollection of the ancient glory of Jerusalem and the Temple, not a plea for the reintroduction of animal sacrifices on the Holy Mountain. Prayer must be more than historical reminiscence.

Moreover, imbedded in the Musaf Service are several other ideas and implications of value. Primarily, there is, of course, the passionate hope for the restoration and preservation of the Land of Israel as the homeland of the Jewish people. The extraordinary achievements of our people in the State of Israel constitute a miracle of God in our day. But our brothers are still in need of our prayer and our concern.

That is not all. The Musaf reminds us that more than prayer is needed; it is a law of life that sacrifice is essential for the fullfillment of our ideals.

Then, too, we cherish the hope that Eretz Yisrael will again become significant not only for the Jewish people, but for the spiritual life of mankind as a whole. The sacred soil that nurtured the prophets and the sages will, we pray, prove the center for a world-order based on faith in God and obedience to His law of justice, brotherhood, and peace, as the seers of Israel have foretold.

Finally, the recollection of the sacrificial system is characteristic of the spirit of Judaism. As Israel Abrahams wrote, "This is the virtue of a historical religion, that the traces of history are never obliterated. . . . The lower did not perish in the birth of the higher, but persisted."[10] Animal sacrifices were a legitimate stage in the evolution of Judaism and of religion generally. For all these reasons the deletion of the Musaf, no less than its retention unchanged, would violate the basic principles of a Jewish prayer book for the modern age.

The Prayer Book Commission accordingly decided upon the following procedure with תכנת שבת and ומפני חטאינו. The phrase נעשה ונקריב, "where we will offer sacrifices," was changed to read עשו והקריבו, and 'avotenu was added to supply a needed subject, "where our ancestors offered sacrifices"; the mere change of tense is inadequate. Two suffixes were modified and 'alenu was dropped from the phrase כמו שכתבת עלינו בתורתך, since we do not look forward to the restoration of animal sacrifice in the future. Thus the essential traditional structure of the Musaf is retained as a reminiscence of Israel's glorious past. The ideas we wished to stress are then expressed by a *Bakashah* preceding the תכנת שבת and the ומפני חטאינו, which it was the privilege of the writer to compose with the counsel of his colleagues. Both for the sake of variety and in order to interpret the distinctive spirit of the Sabbath and the different festivals, two distinct *Bakashot* have been included.

The text for the Sabbath is as follows:

אלהינו ואלהי אבותינו יעלה לפניך זכרון אבותינו בעמדם לפניך בחצרות קדשך. מה רבה אהבתם לך בהביאם לפניך את קרבנות חובותיהם. אנא ה' אלהינו האצל עלינו מרוחם רוח דעת ויראת ה'. כן נזכה למלא חובותינו לבנין ארצך ולחידוש בית חיינו ויתברכו בנו כל משפחות האדמה.

Our God and God of our fathers, may there ever rise before Thee the remembrance of our ancestors as they appeared in Thy sacred Temple. How deep was their love for Thee as they brought Thee their offerings each Sabbath day. Grant us the spirit of knowledge and the fear of the Lord that lived in their hearts. May we, in their spirit of sacrificial devotion, fulfill our duty toward the rebuilding of Thy Holy Land, the fountain of our eternal life. Thus may we ever be a blessing to all the peoples of the earth.

The text for the Festivals reads:

אלהינו ואלהי אבותינו זכר נא את צדקת אבותינו בעלותם מימים ימימה להראות לפניך בירושלים
עיר קדשך. מה רבה שמחת לבבם בהביאם לפניך את קרבנות חובותיהם. אנא ה׳ אלהינו האצל
עלינו מאמונתם בך וששונם בעולמך, מאהבתם לתורתך ושאיפתם לחרות ולצדק. כן נזכה למלא
חובותינו לבנין ארצך ולחידוש בית חיינו ולעבדך ביראה כימי עולם.

Our God and God of our fathers, remember the merit of our ancestors,
who from year to year appeared before Thee in Jerusalem, Thy Holy
City. How deep was their rejoicing as they brought their offerings to Thy
sacred altar. Imbue our hearts, O Lord our God, with their faith in Thee
and their joy in Thy world, their love for Thy Torah and their yearning for
freedom and justice. May we, in their spirit of sacrificial devotion, fulfill
our duty toward the rebuilding of Thy Holy Land, the fountain of our
eternal life. Thus may we serve Thee in reverence as in days of yore.

It will be noted that the effort has been made to follow the
traditional style of the prayer book without making it a mere echo of
older and more familiar passages. It has been our hope that this
Bakashah, in Hebrew or English, will be utilized for private
devotion like the congregational *Modim,* or be read publicly by the
rabbi and perhaps ultimately become part of the *Amidah* like *Tal* or
Geshem. We hope it is not an unworthy attempt to create that
modern *piyyut* to which we have been looking forward.

In *Retzeh,* which is itself a modification of the ancient prayer
utilized by the priests officiating at sacrifices in the Temple, the
words *Ve'ishei Yisrael,* "the fire-offerings of Israel," cannot be
reinterpreted. When these two words are deleted, the prayer
becomes a fervent plea for restoration of the center of our faith to
Jerusalem.

Another section of the prayer book where reinterpretation did not
suffice is to be found in the Preliminary Blessings שלא עשני גוי, עבד,
אשה, in which thanks are expressed to God, "who did not make me a
Gentile, a slave, or a woman" (Jerusalem Talmud, *Berakhot* 9:1,
63b, ed. Vilna; Tosefta, *Berakhot* 7:15, ed. Zuckermandl, p. 16). As
the position of these benedictions near the prayers and blessings
dealing with the Torah indicates, they express the sense of privilege
that the male Jew felt in being able to fulfill the Torah and the
mitzvot, which were not obligatory in equal measure for non-Jews,
slaves, and women. But these blessings have been the source of
widespread misunderstanding because they phrase negatively what
is stated elsewhere far more effectively in the positive, in such
prayers as אשרינו מה טוב and והערב נא ה׳ אלהינו את דברי תורתך בפינו
חלקנו ומה נעים גורלנו ומה יפה ירושתנו "O Lord our God, make the

words of Your Torah sweet in our mouths and "Happy are we, how good our lot, how pleasant our destiny and how beautiful our heritage."

The negative formulation of these Preliminary Blessings caused Jewish leadership much concern through the ages. The censor had already compelled a change in the talmudic passage (B. Menaḥot 43b) to read שעשני ישראל instead of שלא עשני גוי. While older talmudic editions and commentators, like Asheri and Tur, still read the blessing in the negative form, which is undoubtedly the original, it is noteworthy that the Gaon of Vilna accepted this changed reading.[11] Similarly, the blessing שלא עשני עבד has a uniquely Jewish variant שלא עשני בור, "who did not make me an ignoramus." Particularly interesting is the attempt of Rabbi Judah Mintz to explain homiletically why the blessings are put in the negative rather than the positive form. Finally, Prof. Louis Ginzberg called attention to an interesting liturgical fragment found in the Genizah:

ברוך אתה ה' אלהינו מלך העולם אשר בראת אותי אדם ולא בהמה איש ולא אשה ישראל ולא גוי מל ולא ערל חפשי ולא עבד...

ברוך אתה ה' אלהינו מלך העולם אשר בראת אדם הראשון בדמותו ובצלמו.

Supported by this trend of tradition, the Prayer Book Commission decided to rephrase the first three Preliminary Blessings in the positive: she'asani betzalmo, "who has made me in His image," she'asani ben ḥorin, "who has made me free," and she'asani Yisrael, "who has made me a Jew."

The first of these blessings, "who has made me in His image," is a brilliant suggestion presented to the Prayer Book Commission by Rabbi Max Gelb. This new text is more than a mere rewriting of the traditional form. It voices our thanksgiving to Almighty God for having made us human. We are grateful for being sentient and conscious creatures, rather than animals, in spite of the tragedies and frustrations that inevitably inhere in our human estate. It underscores the basic insight of Judaism on the nature and potentiality of men and women. For Judaism, both are fashioned in the divine image, a truth expressed in the opening chapter of Genesis.

It is noteworthy that these Preliminary Blessings parallel the categories of the noble statement in Yalkut Shimeoni, Judges, sec. 42; "I call heaven and earth to witness that whether one be Gentile or Jew, man or woman, slave or free, the divine spirit rests on each in accordance with his deeds."

5. In a few instances, the problem of the traditional elements of

the liturgy disappears, not by changing or reinterpreting the text, but by supplementing it. Thus, *Yekum Purkan,* with its prayer for the welfare of scholars, is in the best tradition of Judaism. The reference to Palestine and Babylonia gives it an archaic flavor, which does not render it irrelevant. All that was required was the addition of the phrase *ubhekhol 'arat galvantana,* "and in all the lands of our dispersion."

Similarly, in *Sim Shalom* it was felt that a more universal note would be desirable, but not through the device of a paraphrase that would not be in keeping with the original. The *Siddur* of Rabbi Saadia Gaon here proved to be of great service. For Saadia's expanded text of this prayer includes שים שלום בעולם (ed. Davidson-Asaph-Joel [Jerusalem, 1941], p. 19). The Prayer Book Commission therefore modified our passage to read: שים שלום טובה וברכה בעולם חן וחסד ורחמים עלינו ועל כל ישראל עמך. In the *Mi Sheberakh* we read: וכל מי שעוסקים בצרכי צבור ובבנין ארץ ישראל באמונה since the rebuilding Eretz Yisrael is for us a cardinal *mitzvah* in Judaism.

6. The creative approach to tradition means not only the surrender of outworn material and the reinterpretation of what can still be made viable, but also the supplementing and enrichment of the prayer book by new material. Consequently, a large number of supplementary prayers, both for unison and congregational reading and suitable for special occasions throughout the year, were included. This material, both in prose and verse, draws upon all the fundamental elements of Israel's life and thought, and, in accordance with our principle, was selected from Jewish authors of all periods. This material is being utilized successfully to enrich public worship and make it more meaningful, besides creating variety and heightened interest in the service.

Thus, the endeavor to maintain the principles of the continuity of tradition, relevance to the modern age, and intellectual integrity have led us to a deeper understanding of the prayer book. The results include more adequate renderings, legitimate paraphrases in terms of the modern outlook, a small number of changes and deletions in the traditional text, and a good deal of supplementary material drawn from our rich literature.

V

While the content and ideas of the prayer book are naturally the first concern, the forms of expression, both in the Hebrew original and in the English version, are scarcely less important. Here, too, certain principles and techniques emerged in the course of the work.

1. Obviously a modern prayer book should contain as accurate a text as possible, and here S. Baer's *Abodat Yisrael* was generally followed. The excellent innovation of the *United Synagogue Maḥzor* of printing poetry in verse form was gratefully adopted and extended. The sections of the service, as well as necessary directions, have been indicated for the guidance of congregations and individuals.

2. The spirit and structure of English and Hebrew are generally dissimilar, and each must be adhered to. Reference has already been made to the characteristic use in Hebrew of coordinate rather than subordinate clauses. This is not all. Hebrew is an Oriental language abounding in imagery. The use of many synonyms, which was stimulated by biblical parallelism, is a characteristic feature in such prayers as יעלה ויבא and אמת ויציב. To eliminate some of these synonyms in the Hebrew, as is done in some modern versions, means to commit the literary sin of judging Hebrew style by Western standards. To translate them all, as in most English versions, violates the spirit of English. Obviously a briefer formulation is required in the English, in accordance with the genius of the language. Equally obviously, the Hebrew text requires no change.

In general the reader deserves an idiomatic English version, exactly as the worshipper requires an idiomatic Hebrew text. Hence long phrases may be shortened, the word order may be varied, and parataxis may be recast in hypotactic form. The changes of person that are characteristic of biblical literature and hence are frequent in the prayer book should be brought into harmony with one another in the English. For the requirements of an attractive English version are that it be clear, succinct, and true to the vigor of the original.

3. A comment is in order on the treatment of the biblical passages in the prayer book. The Masoretic text, which has been hallowed through centuries, should not be emended in a work intended for popular use, but the English version offers an excellent opportunity for new and better interpretations, especially where the accepted view is manifestly unsatisfactory and the tacit change is slight, if any.

Thus Psalm 29 is a magnificent description of a storm in which the thunder, "the voice of the Lord," is heard over the sea, the mountains, the desert, and the forests, In verse 9 יחולל אילות ('ayalot) is usually rendered "The voice of the Lord makes the hinds travail," an interpretation which, even if sound biologically, is surely not calculated to add to the intelligibility of this magnificent Psalm. It is clear that all that is required is a slight modification of the Hebrew vocalization to read יחולל אילות ויחשף יערות ('eilot) and translate the passage, "The voice of the Lord makes the oak trees dance and strips the forests bare."

In Psalm 147:17 the phrase lifnei karato mi ya'amod is generally rendered "before his cold who can stand?" However the parallelism with משליך קרחו כפתים and the plural suffix in the next clause, ישלח דברו וימסם, indicates that mi is either an apocopated form or a variant for mayyim. At all events, the passage is to be translated: "He casts forth ice like morsels; before his frost, the waters congeal. He sends forth His word and melts them; He blows His wind and the waters flow again."

Psalm 116 is a great hymn of thanksgiving for deliverance from death. Verse 15, יקר בעיני ה' המותה לחסידיו, as generally rendered by modern exegetes, is exceedingly inappropriate to the context, however stimulating to homiletic ingenuity. "Precious in the eyes of the Lord is the death of his saints" is practically the reverse of what we should expect. The key lies in yakar, which is an Aramaism meaning "heavy, burdensome, grievous." Thus Genesis 48:10, ועיני ישראל כבדו מזקן, is translated by Onkelos and the Jerusalem Targum יקרן מסיבו and הכבד לב by the same root (Exodus 7:14, 8:11, 28, etc.). Our verse is to be rendered: "Grievous in the eyes of the Lord is the death of his saints!" This natural and appropriate rendering is the view of Rashi, Ibn Ezra, and Kimhi ad locum. Both the idiom in the passage and its idea are parallelled in such rabbinic utterances as כך אמר הקב"ה קשה בעיני לומר לצדיקים שימותו (Yalkut Shimeoni, ad loc.) and קשה לפני הקב"ה בשעה שבניהם של צדיקים מסתלקין בחיי אביהם (Yalkut Shimeoni on Leviticus 10:2).

In Numbers 10:36, ובנחה יאמר שובה ה' רבבות אלפי ישראל, the usual rendering "Return, O Lord" is inappropriate, since the Ark is already at rest. The verb shubh in biblical Hebrew possesses the meaning "halt, rest, dwell, be at peace," as in such passages as Isaiah 30:15, בשובה ונחת תושעון בהשקט ובבטחה תהיה גבורתכם. This meaning suits our passage admirably: "When the Ark rested, Moses said; 'Mayest Thou dwell, O Lord, among the myriads of the families of Israel!' "[12]

In two biblical passages, Psalms 116:19 and 135:9, both of which occur in the prayer book, the form בתוככי occurs—generally rendered "in the midst of thee," on the assumption that we have an archaic second-person feminine suffix. The parallelism, however, of בתוככי ירושלים with בחצרות בית אדני and of בתוככי מצרים with בפרעה ובכל עבדיו, as well as the entire context, makes it clear that no direct address to Jerusalem and Egypt is here intended. It is evident that the form is a construct and is to be translated simply as "in the midst of Jerusalem (or Egypt)."

In a responsive reading based on Psalm 15, we have rendered verse 3 as "He speaks no slander against his enemy, nor does evil to his fellowman, nor bears shame for mistreating his kinsman."

4. Finally, practical utility has been taken into account at many points. The Minḥah and Maariv Services for weekdays have been added to make it convenient to use this prayer book both at the inauguration and the conclusion of the Sabbath and festivals. Hymns both in Hebrew and in English have been added for the further enrichment of the service. Being a repository of a rich religious culture, the Jewish prayer book cannot be understood or appreciated by analphabets. Some knowledge of background is essential. This is supplied by brief introductory notes at important points of the service as well as by titles for some prayers. Where a subject requires somewhat more extensive treatment, supplementary notes have been added. These themes include the *Shema*, the Preliminary Blessings, Sacrifices in Judaism, the Chosen People, and the Messiah idea in Israel.

Countless other innovations that will aid, we hope, in the effective use of the prayer book have been introduced in content, form, and arrangement. These cannot be detailed here. Through the indices of themes, sources, and occasions given in the volume, it will be easy to make fruitful use of the supplementary material.

Acutely conscious of our limitations, we yet venture to hope that this prayer book will advance the great cause of spiritual revival in Israel. Our keynote was sounded by Rabbi Kook of blessed memory in his great words: הישן יתחדש והחדש יתקדש —"the old must be renewed and the new become sacred." For the privilege of sharing in this enterprise, we are humbly thankful to Almighty God.

15

THE PHILOSOPHY OF THE CONSERVATIVE DAY SCHOOL

The progress of the day school movement within Conservative Judaism may be measured in terms of the growth of the Solomon Schechter Schools, both elementary and intermediate, throughout the country. It was not always so. When, in 1950, I organized the Beth El Day School (now called the Robert Gordis Day School) in Belle Harbor, Long Island, its existence during the first five or six years of its history was virtually ignored in the publications of our movement and by its official spokesmen and agencies. Whatever interest Conservative Judaism had in the day school was then being devoted to the Foundation School for kindergarten and pre-kindergarten children. That we now give the day school so high a priority is, I think, a recognition of the truth that the Jewish day school is a central element in any viable scheme of Jewish education.

The future historian of American Judaism may well regard the day school as the greatest contribution of Orthodox Jewry in America. We owe a debt of gratitude to those elements in Orthodoxy who pioneered the Jewish day school, often in the face of substantial opposition both from within and without.

There are several reasons which have led to the widespread acceptance of the day school idea, not only in Orthodoxy but in Conservative Judaism and latterly in some circles of Reform as well.

These factors, demographic, ideological, and social, are of more than historical interest.

A few decades ago, there were great Talmud Torahs, or afternoon Hebrew schools, in New York, Brooklyn, Boston, Chicago, and several other cities, notably in Minneapolis and Winnipeg. Most of them have declined or disappeared as the concentrated Jewish neighborhoods of the past disintegrated. These were indeed "great Talmud Torahs," in which the idealism of the teachers, the large number of hours and years of instruction, and the intensive character of the teaching program were such as to produce a Jewishly learned generation. From them came much of the professional leadership in Jewish life, including many members of the Rabbinical Assembly. These communal Talmud Torahs have all but disappeared, and our congregational Hebrew schools, with very few exceptions, are no adequate substitute for them.

The breakup of the older Jewish neighborhoods was only one factor in the decline of the Talmud Torah. The frequent assertions to the contrary notwithstanding, these schools were not "secular" or anti-religious; they were, to be sure, not synagogue-oriented but focused on Zionism and on the Bible and Hebrew language and literature. As Jews became increasingly acculturated to the American scene, the Jewish group, at least vis-à-vis the larger community, took on the lineaments of a religious denomination in the well-known tripartite conception of America as the land of "the three major faiths"—Catholicism, Protestantism, and Judaism. The synagogue now became the center for all those Jews positively committed to the content and values of Judaism and its transmission to the coming generation. The congregational religious school now naturally served as the educational arm of the synagogue and its membership. The communal Talmud Torah lost its constituency as Jews moved to new areas of population.

Unfortunately, another factor gravely undercut the effectiveness of the religious school. Built into its structure was an inherent weakness, its supplemental character coming after a long public school day. This problem had confronted the communal Talmud Torah a generation or two earlier. That institution had been able to surmount the difficulty. Now, however, parents were no longer willing to subject their children to ten or fifteen hours a week of Hebrew school instruction after the public school hours. To be sure, all Jewish children—or most of them—are geniuses, but a minimal number of hours of instruction for a few years cannot possibly transmit even the elements of the rich Jewish heritage to which all Jews continue to pay lip service.

The disappearance of the communal Talmud Torah and the low level of achievement of the congregational religious school have made the day school appear as the ideal solution. Here, within the framework of a normal school day, a substantial number of hours can be allocated for Jewish studies, including an intensive study of the Hebrew language. The effort can be undertaken to integrate the Jewish and general aspects of the curriculum, instead of perpetuating a dichotomy between the "Jew" and the "human being," of which the Maskilim had been acutely conscious a century ago in Eastern Europe. Progressive methods and other innovations can be attempted in a school free from the bureaucratic control of governmental agencies.

A less positive factor has also played its part in the growth of day schools. The flight from the public schools by the white middle class has been both a cause and an effect of the declining level of achievement in public elementary and intermediate education.

All these factors, positive, negative, and neutral, have won for the day school widespread acceptance as the linch-pin in the structure of American-Jewish education.

However, dedicated as I am to the day school, I do not believe it to be the one and only solution to all the problems in this area. Jewish education is best conceived of as a pyramid. Its broad base at the bottom must remain the Jewish home, incomparably the most effective educational instrument yet devised. New and more vigorous efforts must be directed toward strengthening its historic role, which is, as all surveys indicate, irreplaceable by any other agency. The second layer in the pyramid is the afternoon Hebrew school, which will continue to enroll the largest number of Jewish children in a formal educational program. Above it is another layer, somewhat narrower, representing informal Jewish educational instrumentalities, the chief of which is the summer camp, which can combine the virtues of the Jewish home and the Jewish school at their best in a natural, virtually ideal environment. The apex of the pyramid, narrowest of all, is the day school, for the training of a Jewish intellectual elite from whom effective and knowledgeable Jewish leadership in the next generation will hopefully emerge.

Before turning to the day school, it should be underscored that the potentialities of the afternoon or supplementary Hebrew school that exists in most congregations and in many community centers must not be underestimated. The largest number of Jewish children from Orthodox and Conservative backgrounds are still enrolled in the Talmud Torah or afternoon school after public school hours. A great deal more can be achieved in these institutions than is generally recognized.

In this regard, an interesting fact may be cited, though it goes back a few decades. When the Jerusalem Examinations were given by the Hebrew University, thirty-four students in all of North America passed them. Thirteen of these students came from the Canadian city of Winnipeg, which has a Jewish population of only twenty thousand. New York City did not produce more than four students who passed the examination, and all four were Hebrew teachers of mature years. The explanation for this lies in the fact that Winnipeg long maintained an outstanding Hebrew school, with a group of dedicated teachers.

The afternoon Hebrew school has one other social advantage which is generally overlooked today—it is the ally and not the competitor of the public school system. Basically the public school has played a very important role in building the spirit of American unity. There is no institution that can compare with the achievement of the public school in earlier decades in creating direct personal contact among the various racial, religious, and ethnic groups, and in creating an atmosphere in which a child, be he Jewish, Protestant, or Catholic, Italian, Pole, Irish, or Russian, feels himself at home and at ease with fellow Americans of other groups.

Unfortunately, the public school has fallen tragically from its once high estate. It has become a pawn of self-serving politicians speaking in the name of mutually antagonistic racial and ethnic groups in our major cities, thus exacerbating hostilities rather than cementing unity and fellowship. This major problem has been aggravated by the serious economic crisis of the great urban centers, which have felt themselves compelled to reduce their educational budgets, dismissing many of their most experienced administrators and teachers. The rising climate of violence has converted school buildings into virtual battlefields in which teachers and pupils alike fear for their safety. A large number of Jewish parents, like other members of the middle class, have fled to the suburbs or enrolled their children in private schools of various types.

Many Jewish parents were now led to send their children to modern Jewish day schools, whether or not they had previously given Jewish education a high priority in their system of values. As a result, the Jewish day school movement, both on the elementary and high school levels, has grown at a phenomenal rate during the past two decades. There is today a crying need for substantially increased support for the day school movement from federations, synagogues, individuals, foundations, and other communal institutions. It is universally recognized that the day school offers the best hope for the rearing of a truly literate, knowledgeable, and committed laity in the years ahead, and that from their ranks the future Jewish leadership will largely be recruited.

To be sure, the formal school, basic or supplemental, is not the only instrumentality available to us for dealing with Jewish education. Our movement, like other groups in Jewish life, has created a very significant agency in the form of summer camps with an intensive educational program. It is almost impossible to exaggerate the contribution which the network of Ramah camps throughout the United States, Canada, and Israel created by Conservative Judaism has already contributed to Jewish life.

Hebrew high schools and colleges of Jewish studies in cities like New York, Boston, Baltimore, Chicago, Detroit, and Los Angeles have helped to educate a cultural elite among our youth.

In addition, the extraordinary growth of Judaic studies in colleges and universities throughout the continent constitutes one of the most remarkable phenomena on the contemporary Jewish scene. Today thousands upon thousands of Jewish youth have spent a summer, a term, or a year in Hebraic and Jewish study at institutions in the State of Israel.

Finally, youth and adult study and discussion groups in synagogues and centers are on the increase—though not increasing fast enough! They embody the basic Jewish life-style that one studies as long as one lives. We must, therefore, recognize that Jewish education does not find its only solution in the day school.

What are the essential advantages of the day school? I think that they are largely self-evident and may therefore be set forth briefly.

Most important of all, it creates a natural environment for the child's Jewish education. It no longer becomes an added burden after the public school day, either in point of time, interest span, or approach.

Second, it offers the opportunity for an integrated education. I am going to qualify this a little later, being by temperament very skeptical about popular slogans. By and large, the fact that a child can get his entire education as a single organized, unified unit is itself a great good.

Third, and most important, the day school make adequate content possible.

Fourth, a subordinate but not unimportant factor, it offers the opportunity to create and maintain a cadre of truly professional teachers who can earn a living wage because they can be fully employed. In many, if not in most, cases, day school teachers are able to supplement their basic income by teaching in an afternoon Hebrew school.

Day school teachers also enjoy another great benefit. They have the psychological satisfaction of working creatively in the field of Jewish education. These boons the teachers in the afternoon Talmud Torah can rarely experience. Let us remember that over and above the fine salaries we pay (or think we pay), the dignity of a Hebrew teacher and the sense of creative achievement are too often lacking in the afternoon school. This has much to do, I think, with the shortage of competent and dedicated Hebrew teachers in the field today.

The next question is fundamental: Should there be anything distinctive about our schools as compared with the best of the modern Orthodox schools? Let me say at the outset that the answer is not necessarily "yes." If what we want done is being done and being done very well, then the honest thing for us to do is to follow the same pattern. And there are certain fundamental elements that we do have in common with the finer Orthodox schools.

First of all, every day school should place a maximum emphasis upon the transmission of content. This may sound extremely reactionary in these progressive days, but I cannot help expressing my views on the subject. If our day school is nothing but a private school with some Jewish atmosphere, then it has no claim, moral or financial, upon either the energies or the substance of the Jewish community and its leaders. Such day schools do exist today on the American scene. They are private schools for children of Jewish parentage with a kind of Jewish flavor. For that alone, the very substantial sacrifices which a day school requires are not justified. I think we ought not to yield to our Orthodox brethren in our zeal for traditional Jewish knowledge. Our schools should emphasize Torah and Rashi, Prophets, Mishnah, and Gemara. This, indeed, is what we attempt to do in all our better day schools. It is gratifying to note that this emphasis is growing in Conservative day schools. I know of no way to create positive attitudes except through Jewish knowledge. Hence, only if we transmit a sufficient amount of Jewish knowledge can we justify the heartache and the strain of the sacrifice which the day school requires.

Secondly, the day school should have a strong Hebrew orientation. The goal must be not only a reading knowledge but a speaking knowledge of the language, because the language is not natural for the student who cannot speak it.

In the third place, there must be an emphasis upon standards of personal observance. This involves probably the most difficult problem in education: the carry-over from school and camp into the home. It is true that no existing school can hope to succeed perfectly, but the emphasis upon inculcating Jewish practice and Jewish observance is one from which we cannot turn aside simply because it is difficult.

In all these respects, therefore, our goals will not differ significantly from those of the finer Orthodox schools. What should be distinctive about our Conservative day schools? First, I would say, is the principle of motivation. Our motivation is not isolationism, but preparation for Jewish living in the context of general life, in America or anywhere else in the world. The first day schools or *yeshivot* began with a clearly avowed desire to separate the youngsters from any contact with the outside environment. I remember that in my own days at the *yeshiva*, we had a very saintly teacher who urged the students not to take any secular studies where they possibly could avoid it. Even within the Jewish curriculum we were told that it was a *mitzvah* not to attend the three hours of classes on Friday morning that were set aside for all Jewish studies outside the Talmud. These subjects, which included the Bible, Hebrew grammar, Hebrew literature, and Jewish history, were of no importance at best and downright heretical at worst. Skipping these classes was a *mitzvah* many of us were only too eager to observe.

This goal of isolationism remains as a very important motivation, Incidentally, it is an important factor in Catholic parochial schools. A good friend of mine, a dedicated monsignor of the church, said to me: "We do not wish to have our children's faith weakened by mixing with children of other backgrounds."

There is an element of validity in this standpoint. In the earliest years of his life, a child should not be exposed to a conflict of cultures, such as the Christmas syndrome in December. On the contrary, during this formative period the child should develop deep emotional ties to his own tradition and practices, which should become basic to his personality. The patterns of behavior should precede the rational analysis or critical challenges which are inevitable as he attains to adolescence and maturity. This period of immersion in a total Jewish environment in the early years of schooling is particularly important since Jews constitute a minority in many of their areas of residence.

Nonetheless, this motivation, acceptable for early childhood, cannot serve as a permanent principle of thought and action. It, therefore, cannot constitute the central rationale for the day school, which must educate and inspire its students to lifelong devotion to Judaism both in thought and in practice within the context of modern life and thought.

Our conception of Judaism is one which has not only the capacity of surviving in the marketplace of ideas but the ability to be enriched and deepened by such contact. We do not regard a Judaism which is at home in the world as a "compromise" or as a "diluted" form of Judaism. We do not denigrate this type of Judaism as "unauthentic." It is well known that Jewish thinkers, scholars, and writers in ancient Alexandria, medieval Spain, and modern Germany had an intimate contact with the world. It is equally true, though often ignored, that both the Bible and Talmud are not products of closed communities. On the contrary, they demonstrate the increased vitality arising from the interaction of Judaism and its environment.

The great creative aspects of Judaism were never lived in isolation. This is not simply yielding to the environment, making compromises with necessity. Not only the civic and political position of Jews, but our understanding of the true nature of Judaism, demands that we regard isolation from the general community and world culture as a goal devoutly to be shunned.

In the second place, our day schools should be dedicated to the inculcation of the philosophy of Conservative Judaism. This is a very difficult area, because sometimes one has the feeling that we possess a tremendous apparatus of institutions with far too little of the momentum of a movement. We certainly cannot inculcate an attitude on Judaism until Conservative Judaism makes its point of view clear. I am thoroughly aware of the differences which exist within our group. At the same time, there is a sufficient core of fundamental principles for Conservative Judaism upon which virtually all of us agree. These ideas ought to be presented without apology, as a fundamental aspect of the program of the day school.

We must resist the temptation to engage in the currently popular pastime of "nostalgic Judaism," a kind of glorification of the *shtetl*, beyond recognition and beyond reality, indulged in particularly by those who never knew the *shtetl*, either at first or at second hand. We have to set our house in order and see that Conservatism is not regarded as a halfway house between certain forms of Orthodoxy and certain forms of Reform.

We need to reaffirm that Conservative Judaism represents a distinctive point of view which must be expressed and embodied in life. Its essence may be found in the rather ponderous phrase of the founder of the movement a century and a half ago in Germany. Zacharias Frankel defined his philosophy as "positive-historical Judaism." In this formulation Frankel was trying to say: (1) that Judaism has a history, it is a historical religion, the product of growth and development, and (2) that we must take a positive, affirmative attitude toward this product. Therefore, the concept of one Jewish people the world over, the binding character of Jewish law, the recognition of tradition as living and growing, and the combination of continuity and change, these are all aspects of Judaism fundamental to our outlook.

In the day school I organized, I introduced a course on *Yesodot Hayahadut*, "The Foundations of Judaism," which set forth clearly and forthrightly the viewpoint of Conservative Judaism, while dealing fairly and sympathetically with Orthodox and Reform

Judaism. The course also included the points of similarity and difference between Judaism and Christianity. This course was made part of the requirements for the eighth year in our day school.

There is another point I think our schools need to emphasize. In far too many day schools, there is a blatant attitude of hostility to those Jews who differ with their official viewpoint. I know a day school at first hand where Bialik was dropped from the curriculum on the ground that he was an '*okher yisrael,* and where a teacher was dismissed because he taught a poem by Tchernichovsky.

This kind of bigotry and hostility to all those who do not share one's viewpoint is fraught with tragic consequences for Judaism as a whole. Perhaps there was a time when tolerance could be taken for granted, but unfortunately not today. Our schools must be dedicated positively to our convictions, but they must couple this loyalty with a willingness to have other people's points of view treated with respect and understanding.

Our schools should emphasize not only the ritual aspects, but the spiritual content of Judaism, its ethical and religious principles. I am sorry to say that all too often in day schools and other schools, religion is taken to be equivalent to ritualism. Reform Judaism, to be sure, stresses ethics, but it has paid a high price in minimizing ritual.

Sometimes it seems that we need to be reminded that truth and honor, peace and love are also a part of Judaism. Some years ago two articles appeared in an Orthodox Jewish periodical. The first article, from the pen of an Orthodox rabbi, made the point that no Orthodox teacher should teach in a Conservative day school or Hebrew school. He reasoned that, aside from the heresy which is involved, if all Orthodox teachers were to withdraw from Conservative schools, then Conservative Judaism would collapse under its own weight for lack of personnel.

The next issue of the magazine published a "liberal" point of view. It contended that it is perfectly proper for Orthodox teachers to teach in Conservative day schools because the rabbis never know what is going on in the classroom anyhow, and the teacher can therefore teach Orthodoxy *sub rosa.* Obviously the learned rabbi who wrote the second article did not believe that a breach of faith or a lack of elementary honesty (accepting payment for a job one has no intention of doing) is a violation of Jewish tradition.

It is perfectly clear to me that Conservative Judaism represents the totality of Judaism in time and space. It is what our Israeli friends like to call *yahadut kollelet,* "all-inclusive Judaism." Our educational philosophy is all-inclusive because it draws upon the achievements of Alexandrian and Babylonian Jewry in the ancient world, upon the medieval communities of Spain, Provence, and Italy, and upon the cultural achievements of the modern German-Jewish culture sphere. These free—or at least open—communities were far closer in structure and spirit to us who live in the democratic world than the closed ghetto societies of Eastern Europe, which were the home of our immediate forebears. This, of course, is not to suggest that our educational philosophy will fail to incorporate the rich spiritual and cultural treasures created by Central and East European Jewry during the medieval and modern periods.

Let us not fall prey to the baseless contention that only isolationist Judaism is "authentic" Judaism. It is true that ancient Alexandrian Jewry and modern German Jewry were destroyed, but so were Russian and Hungarian Jewry in our time. Wherever the genius of Israel was at work, Judaism was enriched. It is we and not the enemies of the Jewish people who determine what enters the treasure-house of the Jewish heritage.

Our educational philosophy is all-inclusive because it incorporates all aspects of Judaism, for Torah is law, lore, and literature. It encompasses the world-view of Judaism, its ethical insights and commandments, as well as the observance of the ritual *mitzvot* "between man and God."

Finally, and perhaps most important, our educational philosophy is all-inclusive because it will be dedicated to *'ahavat Yisrael,* "the love of our fellow Jews," and *'ahavat haberiyot,* "the love of our fellow human beings." Our children will be taught these two ideals in every aspect of their studies and called upon to practice them in every aspect of their lives.

Having said all this, I would like to revert to my original statement, which seems to be unassailable. We cannot put all our eggs in one basket, even a basket as promising as that of a day school. We have very many problems that cannot be met through a unitary solution. What is required is a very determined and dedicated effort to strengthen the quality of our educational endeavors in all forms and on all levels.

How is a day school to be organized? Some of us are unfortunate enough to be in an isolated area. That was my particular problem. I was surrounded by water on three sides, and so our school had to be a congregational school. What we lacked in external conditions we tried to compensate for in zeal and effort.

Fortunately, most day schools are situated in large Jewish areas, enabling them to draw on the support of several congregations. But certainly in a city or community of any size it ought to be possible to organize a Conservative day school which would command the loyalty of all the congregations in the area that are involved.

A few closing observations. I heartily endorse the feeling that integration of the Hebraic and general curriculum is an advantage. But it is not simply a matter of black and white. There happens to be great practical advantage in having the Hebrew studies in the morning. If you wish to create an all-Hebrew atmosphere, it makes a great difference if the child knows that for three hours a day he is living in an all-Hebrew-speaking environment. On the other hand, in the integrated program the transition to Hebrew becomes more difficult because the child finds it easier to speak English and the Hebrew atmosphere is dissipated to a great degree. The dilemma posed by this problem must be confronted and solved by the staff and parent body of each school in accordance with their own convictions and insights.

Second, I do not see any difference between a child-centered and a book-centered school. I remember an old-fashioned teacher I had in a Talmud Torah who made the closing chapters of Exodus and the laws of sacrifice in Leviticus fascinating for us. He took a cardboard which came from a laundry. He made cut-outs and tied a string around them. Then he wrote down the names of the twelve tribes and had that worn by the children as the *Ḥoshen* with the *Urim vetumim*. We also drew up charts about each of the sacrifices and how different parts of the animal went for various purposes. A good teacher makes book learning a living experience for the child.

With regard to phonic and mechanical reading, I do not believe that reading requires comprehension, particularly in Hebrew. The present tendency is to doubt the theory of "understood reading" even in connection with English, but it certainly does not hold true for Hebrew. If we are going to wait until our children are able to understand every line of the prayer book before we teach them to read, they will never learn to read—and never pray!

Here again, everything depends on how you teach it. A skillful teacher can make the experience of mechanical reading a fascinating experience for children. I do not believe that the child's "reading readiness" ought to be glorified and made an end-principle. We want the child to participate in ritual, even if he does not understand every word of the text. They should learn to sing a large number of songs, the vocabulary of which may not be perfectly clear to them.

I should also like to express my hesitation with regard to the idea of getting teachers who will teach both the Hebraic and the general studies program. I believe it is not only difficult but well-nigh impossible to get teachers properly trained in both divisions. We may as well face the fact that if we can get good teachers for the general studies program and other good teachers for the Hebrew studies curriculum, we should get up and thank God, *erev vavoker vezohorayim,* "morning, noon, and night." Good teachers are as rare as geniuses. They *are* geniuses.

The problem of teacher orientation is, of course, a very real one. In our school we used to conduct a series of meetings for our entire faculty, both general studies and Hebrew studies. We discussed problems of religious outlook and personal philosophy. These were extremely interesting sessions. The teachers welcomed them because the school became an instrument for their education as well. Though there was a long way to go, the teachers of the general studies program became increasingly sympathetic to what we were attempting to do in the Hebrew program. And some of our Hebrew teachers, whose background is Orthodox—and whose convictions we respect—began to develop an understanding and a respect for the goals and approaches of Conservative Judaism.

The time has come for us to go forward with love and zeal, with courage and faith.

We have a viewpoint which is positive, intensive, all-inclusive, and creative. In the true sense of the term, it is authentic because it is rooted in the totality of the living Jewish tradition. The Jewish day school can help supply the leadership, both lay and professional, for the American Jewish community of today and tomorrow and produce a laity that will be both knowledgeable and loyal.

16

THE RABBINATE: ITS HISTORY, FUNCTIONS, AND FUTURE

In this volume we have been concerned with the content of Judaism and the forms in which the tradition has been embodied in time. One of the unique contributions of the Jewish people to religion has been the creation of a type of leadership that we take for granted today, because it is universal in the great monotheistic religions of the West: Judaism, Christianity, and Islam. At its inception, however, it marked a revolutionary departure from the accepted pattern. In the ancient world, religious authority reposed in the priesthood, a closely-knit professional caste often hereditary in character. The priests were the custodians of culture, the officiants at the sacrificial cult and other rituals, the medical and legal experts, and the dispensers of justice. Biblical Judaism had its counterpart in the *kohanim,* who were the descendants of Aaron. They performed these functions in the Jewish community during the period of the First and Second Temples (ca. 960–586 B.C.E. and 516 B.C.E.–70 C.E.).

According to our historical sources, Ezra (5th cent. B.C.E.) took the revolutionary step of creating a new class of religious leadership. Indeed, he was the first exemplar of this new type, the *Sopherim.* The word, which is usually translated "scribes," is better rendered "masters of the Book." This new leadership was not hereditary, being open to all levels of society. It was not concerned with officiating at the sacrificial cult in the Temple. Its basic activity lay in studying and interpreting the Torah and applying it to life.

A few centuries after Ezra, shortly after the destruction of the Second Temple (70 c.e.), a new title, "rabbi," literally "master," was applied to these leaders, which accurately reflected their teaching role. For the past twenty centuries, the rabbinate has been recognized as the classical Jewish leadership. In the modern secularized world more than in the past, the rabbi—for good or for ill, and often for both—is the living symbol of Judaism. His level of learning and piety, his dedication and sensitivity to the world about him, constitute one of the principal spiritual resources of twentieth-century Judaism. The battle for meaningful Jewish survival will be won or lost largely through the activity—or lack of it—of the rabbinate. It is, therefore, both important and interesting to explore its past, analyze its present, and contemplate its future.

I

The full history of the rabbinate as an institution is yet to be written, yet a striking paradox is already clear. On the one hand, the title "rabbi" is the oldest honorific designation in continuous use, far older, indeed, than any honorary degree or academic distinction in vogue today. On the other hand, the functions designated by this ancient title have undergone so far-reaching a transformation in modern times that it may be said to represent virtually a new calling. The term "rabbi," it may be suggested without irreverence, is an old label on a bottle of new wine.

The rabbinate has undergone at least five principal phases, reflecting the kaleidoscopic character of Jewish history. Disregarding fine distinctions of time and space, we may describe these stages in the rabbinate as follows: (1) talmudic (Palestine and Babylonia); (2) medieval (Western Europe); (3) pre-modern (Eastern Europe); (4) post-Emancipation (Western Europe); and (5) contemporary (predominantly United States and Canada).

The exalted station that is accorded the rabbi in the Jewish tradition is highlighted by the fact that its greatest son, Moses, liberator, lawgiver, creator of the Jewish nation, and architect of the Jewish religion, is not called by any of these titles, but is most affectionately referred to as *Moshe rabbenu,* "Moses, our master, our teacher." It need hardly be added that this title was not applied to him until millennia after the period of the historical Moses. All the extant evidence indicates that the term "rabbi" did not come into use until after the destruction of the Second Temple in the year 70 C.E.[1]

In the period of the *Tannaim,* the teachers of the Mishnah (70–217 C.E.), two related titles were in use in Palestine. One, *rabban,* "our master," was restricted to the Patriarchs who served as heads of the academy and as official representatives of the Jewish community vis-à-vis the Roman government. The other, *rabbi,* "my master," was applied to every accredited teacher of Torah who was ordained by an older scholar.

In this, the first stage of the rabbinate, the term was used exclusively in a nonprofessional sense. All the talmudic sages earned their livelihood by some other occupation. The great Hillel was a woodchopper, Shammai a builder, Joshua ben Hananiah was a blacksmith, who complained with good reason that the highly placed patriarch Rabban Gamaliel knew nothing of the tribulations of scholars.[2] Akiba was a shepherd, Johanan was a cobbler, while others were tailors, tanners, laundrymen, and even water-carriers. Higher in the economic ladder were the farmers and the merchants among the rabbis. At one period, the rabbis devoted one-third of the day to their livelihood and the remainder to study, but later the situation deteriorated. Rabbi Judah ben Ilai complained that earlier generations spent most of their time in study and less in gainful labor and succeeded in both, while his own contemporaries reversed the emphasis and failed in both.[3] Nonetheless, no salaries or other forms of public support were made available to the rabbis.[4]

With the compilation of the Mishnah by Rabbi Judah the Patriarch (170–217), at the beginning of the third century C.E., the tannaitic period came to a close, and with it ended the hegemony of Palestine as the center of spiritual authority. The Patriarch had striven to prevent the transfer of influence to the more prosperous community of Babylonia by denying full ordination (*semikhah*) even to its most distinguished scholars, Rab and Samuel, who had studied in the Palestinian academies. As a result, the Babylonian *Amoraim,* "expounders of the Mishnah," unlike their Palestinian confreres, did not have the title *rabbi,* "my master," but *rabh,* "master," but that interfered little with their activity as teachers of the Torah (200–500 C.E.). The massive record of their creative labors is the Babylonian Talmud.

It should not be overlooked that their teaching included not only Halakhah, which encompassed civil, criminal, and religious law, but also Aggadah, nonlegal material, religious and ethical in character. The Aggadah occupies a substantial, if subordinate, part of the Talmud, but it predominates in the vast expanse of the Midrashim. As Zunz showed in his pioneering masterpiece, *Die gottesdienstlichen Vorträge der Juden,* the Midrash is often a written record of the homilies delivered in the synagogue and thus bears witness to the antiquity of preaching in Judaism. The interpretation of Scripture had its inception in the days of Ezra and Nehemiah, early in the period of the Second Temple.[5] The process produced both the Targum, the Aramaic translation of the Bible, which generally went beyond the literal text, and the Midrash.

In Hellenistic circles the influence of the Greek rhetoricians was marked in the structure of the sermons preached in the Alexandrian synagogues and elsewhere.[6] It is likely that the many brief treatises of the philosopher Philo represent transcriptions of sermons he delivered in Alexandria.[7] The great preachers of the early church, Gregory, John Chrysostom, and Ambrose, followed some of these Hellenistic-Jewish models.

In Palestine and Babylonia, preaching was an important activity. Throughout the talmudic and gaonic periods, sermons were delivered every Sabbath and festival, as the extant Midrashim demonstrate.[8]

Throughout the mishnaic and the amoraic periods (200–500), as well as the succeeding saboraic (500–540) and gaonic ages (589–1038 C.E.), the rabbinate remained an avocation in the great centers of Babylonia and Palestine. Only the officially appointed judges were paid for their work, which was primarily a governmental function rather than a spiritual activity. Certain special privileges were accorded scholars by law, such as the remission of taxes, preference in the marketplace, and other marks of social deference.[9] But the rabbinate did not become a profession until the later Middle Ages. As compact Jewish communities, isolated from the general population, increasingly came into being, there was a growing need for a permanent functionary to supervise the life of the congregation, be available for religious guidance, and exercise a judicial role in civil suits among members of the community.

The payment of a salary to a rabbi, however, posed a grave problem from the standpoint of the Halakhah. The tradition was clear—the teaching of Torah was a *mitzvah* from which no material gain might be derived. "As I have taught thee freely, so teach thou freely," God said to Moses, according to an old Aggadah,[10] and the warning against "making the Torah a hatchet to chop with or a crown to glorify oneself with"[11] was taken very seriously. Medieval rabbis in Spain supported themselves by trade, investments, or moneylending, while a very considerable proportion earned their livelihood as physicians.[12]

In a characteristically vigorous statement, Maimonides declared that, though he knew that not all the scholars would agree with him, it is best for practitioners of Torah not to be supported by public funds.[13] He himself was a silent partner in the trading enterprise of his brother David and was free to dedicate himself to study and writing. When his brother was drowned in the Indian Ocean, Maimonides continued to practice what he preached. He now undertook the arduous profession of physician to the court of Saladin in Egypt. The rigors of his calling Maimonides described in a vivid letter addressed to his beloved disciple Joseph ibn Aknin, whom he dissuaded from visiting him, because he would have no leisure to spend with him, even the Sabbath being occupied with communal affairs.

II

Few rabbis, of course, possessed the professional eminence of a Maimonides. The deterioration of the economic position of the Jews that followed in the wake of the Black Death of 1349, and the increasing number of massacres and persecutions from the fourteenth century onward, made it ever harder for rabbis to support themselves by some other livelihood, and so salaries came into vogue. The imperious demands of life met the challenge of the Law by defining the salary of the rabbi as *sekhar battalah*, "compensation for being prevented from engaging in a gainful occupation," just as the theory was that teachers were being paid *sekhar shimmur*, "payment for taking care of the children consigned to their care"—a glorified anticipation of the modern occupation of baby-sitting! Yet as late as the fifteenth century, Rabbi Simon Duran, who was, incidentally, not "the first Spanish rabbi to take pay," felt constrained to offer a public apology for accepting a salary for his services.[14]

From the fifteenth century onwards, salaries for rabbis were all but universal. The emoluments of the rabbi were, however, minimal, and resourceful spirits sought to make ends meet by auxiliary occupations. The colorful Leo da Modena, who served as rabbi of Venice, kept the wolf from the door by being a printer, a letterwriter, an author, a marriage broker, and, it seems, also a cardplayer, but whether this last occupation proved a financial asset or a liability is not clear.

Most rabbis, who did not possess talents as varied as these, were supported by a small salary, supplemented by communal taxes on wine, meat, or salt, and by fees received for sitting as judges. Their functions included, in addition, the supervision of the *shohetim*, or ritual slaughterers, the maintenance of the ritual tradition in the synagogues of the community, and the responsibility for the system of elementary education in the most general terms. The principal function of the rabbi was to be an exemplar of Torah, to spend his days in studying the Talmud, the Codes, and the vast expanse of other rabbinic literature, and be available to answer questions of law posed by the congregation. If he possessed the requisite learning, he would be consulted in writing on religious questions by other rabbis and by laymen, and his responsa (*teshubot*) to these questions (*she'elot*) would untimately be gathered together as a corpus. If his gifts were of a still higher order, he might himself enrich rabbinic literature by writing commentaries on the Talmud and on the Codes, independent halakhic treatises, or all-encompassing Codes of Jewish law.

The old tradition of regular preaching, however, underwent a decline in the Middle Ages. The addition to the Sabbath and festival services of the *piyyutim,* complicated religious hymns, often quite lengthy, left less and less time for a sermon. Besides, the ever-greater preoccupation of the rabbis with halakhic details left them little opportunity for, or interest in, developing homiletic skill.[15] Nonetheless, the sermon did not disappear completely from the medieval synagogue. It continued to be cultivated most regularly in

Spain, less commonly in France and Italy, and least frequently of all in Germany. The published sermon collections of such gifted preachers as Nahmanides, Shemtob ben Joseph, Isaac Arama, and Moses of Coucy[16] are evidence that preaching remained a significant activity in the synagogue, whether by the permanent rabbinical incumbent or by specially gifted itinerant preachers.

The intellectual attainments of the rabbis in Spain, Italy, and the Provence were not limited to the Talmud and its commentaries. Many of them were interested in biblical research and Hebrew philology. Some commanded Arabic, valuable as an adjunct to philosophic studies. Some knew Latin, which they needed for consulting the Vulgate and for participating in the frequently held compulsory public religious disputations. Latin proved useful also in the examination of legal documents in suits coming before them.[17]

III

There is a tragic paradox running through Jewish history. The earlier part of the medieval period, often described as the Dark Ages, was the happier period of the European Jewish experience. On the other hand, the later Middle Ages, which saw the breaking of the walls for Western Europe through the forces set into motion by the voyages of exploration, brought about a narrowing of the horizons in Jewish life.

In the later Middle Ages, the ghetto came into being, forcing the Jew, through legal enactments, into limited segregated areas of the cities and towns. The ghetto, established in Germany after the Black Death in 1348–49, was first introduced into Italy in Venice in 1516. It served effectively to isolate the Jew from the general population. It barred him from the general economic and social life, in which he had previously shared, and deprived him of the challenge and enrichment of the broadening intellectual horizons that came with the dawn of modernism.

As though the isolation imposed by the ghetto were not enough, the worsening of Gentile-Jewish relations led to the physical elimination of Jews from Western Europe. In 1290 they were expelled from England, not to return until the seventeenth century and then only furtively as nominal Christians. In France they had been expelled and readmitted time and again as cat's-paws in the shifting financial policies of the kings, but in 1394 they were finally and permanently forbidden the rights of domicile. As for the Iberian peninsula, their expulsion from Spain in 1492, and from Portugal four years later, was the climax of a long series of persecutions that had converted the "land of delight," as Spanish Jews had loved to call their homeland, into a "vale of tears."

The elimination of the Jews from England, France, and Spain meant their concentration in Eastern Europe, where there was neither challenge nor inspiration to be derived from the low cultural level of the general environment. As a result, Jewish life retreated into the four ells of the law, the Talmud and its "armor-bearers," commentaries, supercommentaries, Codes, and responsa. Such disciplines as philosophy, poetry, history, biblical philology and exegesis, which had shared the interest of Western Jewry along with rabbinic studies, now all but disappeared from the orbit of Jewish traditional life. Soon desuetude passed into distaste, so that these studies became suspect as passports to irreligion. The basic intellectual enterprise now became the "battle of the Torah," the legal disputations and casuistic refinements of the German-Polish talmudists.

The function of the rabbi underwent a corresponding change. There emerged the traditional figure of the Rav, whose presence was the very symbol of the Torah, impressive in appearance, revered for his learning and piety. His communal duties were few: to answer ritual questions, to act as judge in lawsuits between Jews, and to deliver two discourses a year. On Shabbat Shubah he exhorted the congregation to repent of its sins before the Day of Atonement, and on Shabbat Hagadol, the "Great Sabbath" before Passover, he discussed the laws of *ḥametz* and *matzah,* which are basic to the traditional Passover. His major occupation was to busy himself with the study of the Torah. As was the case in the earlier period, a more distinguished rabbi would be consulted on legal questions by laymen and rabbis in other communities, and he would write responsa. A gifted scholar would organize and preside over a *yeshiva,* or academy, that would attract students in proportion to the greatness of its teachers. Essentially, however, his existence was more important than his activity. The average Jew might apostrophize his rabbi in Emerson's words, "I cannot hear what you say, for what you are speaks a thousand times louder."

In the traditional Jewish communities of Eastern Europe—

Germany, Austria, Hungary, Rumania, Poland, and Russia—Jewish life might be narrow in compass, but its roots were deep. The rabbi was not needed to stimulate Jews to Jewish living—no other pattern was conceivable. His basic function was that of the highest religious and legal authority, and the sole patent of his authority was his learning. His scholarship was more significant than his possession of the traditional *semikhah,* or ordination, which he received from his teachers and which was considerably more limited in scope and power than the *semikhah* of the Palestinian rabbis of the talmudic period. In fact, at times the *semikhah* took a decidedly unconventional turn, as when it read, "So-and-so is empowered to serve as rabbi in any place where there is no scholar greater than he."

The rabbi's lot was not necessarily an easy one. Frequently, the rabbi had to deal with aggressive lay leaders, and nearly always his meager income posed substantial economic problems for his wife, who generally managed household affairs. But as long as the community itself survived, he was assured of a position of dignity and a modicum of security. For the vast majority of East European Jews, the traditional way of life, with the Rav as its crowning symbol, remained all but unchanged until the beginning of the twentieth century, and in many cases until the First World War and beyond.

IV

For the Jews of Western Europe, however, the Middle Ages came to an end with the force of an earthquake in the closing decades of the eighteenth century. The Age of Reason had challenged accepted ideas everywhere, particularly in the fields of religion and morality. As the new ideas of the Enlightenment percolated into the Jewish communities of Germany and France, first in the upper economic strata and then to the lower levels, the authority of the Jewish tradition was gradually undermined. In the wake of the French Revolution came the Emancipation of the Jews, which, hesitating and half-hearted though it often was, brought political citizenship, enlarged economic opportunities, and new cultural influences into the life of the individual Jew. At the same time, it effectively destroyed the hegemony and cohesiveness of the organized Jewish community.

For the first time, defection from Judaism and the Jewish people became not merely a possibility for isolated individuals, but a reality for hundreds and thousands of the most ambitious, gifted, and aggressive members of the community. Thousands more, who did not formally replace Judaism by another faith, found their Jewish loyalties and attitudes and, even more, those of their children, being steadily reduced toward the vanishing-point. The ancient commination of Moses became a tragic reality, three millennia after his lifetime: "Your sons and daughters will be handed over to another people, and your eyes will behold them and pass out with longing for them all the day, and you will be helpless."[18]

But not altogether helpless. The process of defection and decline was powerful and overwhelming, but it was not complete. There were considerable sources of loyalty in the Jewish community which, after the initial shock of the onslaught wore off, reacted against the forces of dissolution. A variety of religious movements came into being, all designed to preserve the Jewish tradition in greater or lesser degree and make it viable in the modern world. And all these schools of thought, conventionally subsumed under varied designations, such as Reform or Liberal, positive-historical or Conservative, and Orthodox or Torah-true, transformed the traditional Rav into the modern rabbi, who was catapulted into a new and challenging environment. In Western Europe, as the Jewish community became a religious group, largely paralleling other denominations, the rabbi took on many of the functions, and often even the garb and appearance, of his Christian counterparts, particularly the Protestant pastor. But his duties were always more extensive than those of the Christian clergyman. They were almost never limited to purely religious functions, such as preaching, conducting services, and officiating at marriages and funerals.

This condition was true even in Western Europe. Here the Jewish community retained a quasi-official status, which often included the all-important rights to tax its members and to be maintained by the state. The change in the function of the rabbi was particularly marked in the United States. Here no religious group enjoyed any official position, so that the Jewish community was completely "voluntary," adherence to it, or alienation from it being a matter of free choice by the individual.[19]

There were three principal reasons for the vast extension of the field of operations of the modern rabbi. First, Judaism faced far greater challenges than Christianity; there were more powerful forces weaning its devotees away, not merely ideological in character, but social and psychological as well. It would, therefore, not suffice for the rabbi to *supply* the religious demands made upon him; generally he had to labor to *create the demand* before seeking to fill it. The modern rabbi might believe that he was needed; he rarely had the feeling that he was wanted. His major task now became the stimulation of Jewish life and loyalty on all sectors, in the face of vast, if often impersonal, obstacles.

Second, the expansion of the scope of rabbinical activity found a large measure of warrant in the tradition as well. Judaism had always embraced more than religion. The organic link in Judaism between faith and folk could be loudly denied, but it could never be destroyed, even among those who proclaimed most shrilly that they were merely Germans or Frenchmen or Britons of the Mosaic persuasion. The realities of Jewish life, therefore, compelled the rabbi to concern himself with areas like education, culture, community relations, local philanthropy, overseas aid, and the ubiquitous problem of anti-Semitism. As Zionism became an increasingly dynamic factor in Jewish consciousness, more and more rabbis of all schools were caught up by its vision and hope.

The third factor which revolutionized the rabbinical calling was the weakening of religious ties among modern Jews, the surrender of the traditional way of life, and the decline of Jewish learning among the laity, so that the rabbi's expertness in the law became less and less relevant and less respected. The vacuum thus created had to be filled with new content.

In sum, core and circumference reversed roles. Instead of the rabbi being the scholar and teacher *par excellence,* with a few peripheral functions, his scholarship became secondary, or less than that, and his peripheral functions became central, and these in turn proliferated into a vast complex of activities.

Perhaps the most obvious phase of the rabbi's work lay in his preaching, which now became a regular task, once or even twice each Sabbath and on the festivals. This represented an extreme extension of a function which had existed in earlier phases of the rabbinate. Many of the talmudic teachers were "masters of the Aggadah," and many medieval rabbis of the West were distinguished preachers. The East European rabbi had, as we have seen, contracted this activity almost to the vanishing point. The need for exhortation and inspiration was met, not by the rabbis located in the various communities, but by wandering preachers called *maggidim,* some of whom, like the famous Rabbi Jacob of Dubno, were men of extraordinary spiritual and forensic gifts. The modern rabbi, impelled both by the needs of his community and by the example of the Christian minister, was called upon to become a regular preacher.

The older tradition of preaching, traced by Zunz through the medieval period back to the Midrash, had so far disappeared during the latter centuries of the Jewish Middle Ages that its restoration seemed to many to be a "reform" based on Christian models. Thus, as late as 1829 the rabbinical seminary founded in Padua made no provision for the teaching of homiletics in the curriculum. Before the nineteenth century was over, every rabbinical school, whatever its orientation, gave considerable attention to the art of preaching. The ultimate proof of its importance is that the touchstone by which laymen evaluate and choose a rabbi is his sermonic ability, with a greater or lesser secondary interest in his other qualifications. Speaking perhaps *pro domo,* Maybaum, who was professor of homiletics in the Hochschule in Berlin, did not hesitate to say, "In small communities as in large, the rabbi is equally obligated to *dedicate the greatest part of his strength and time to the sermon"* (italics his).[20] He goes so far as to caution the rabbi in Germany to be sure not to devote too much time to philological, historica. and philosophic studies, but to keep his eye on the sermon as his major goal.[21] The first part of the injunction, at least, is now unnecessary!

Theoretically, the function of the pulpit discourse is the exposition of Judaism, based upon its classical sources in general, and the scriptural reading of the day in particular. This type of "text-sermon" has survived largely at the Sabbath morning service, when the *sedrah* of the Torah is read and where the worshippers are largely traditionally inclined. At the late Friday evening service and—during its brief heyday in Reform—at the Sunday morning service, the themes were drawn from the current scene and the treatment was generally that of the lecture or secular address, with relatively little reference to Bible, Talmud, or Midrash. Social, political, and economic issues that were treated, were illumined only rarely by the light of Jewish teaching. Often, books and plays of current interest were utilized as sermon topics. Sermon titles were advertised in the metropolitan press, as well as in the congregational bulletins, in an effort to attract the floating population of "sermon shoppers," who sought the stimulation of sensationalism rather than the spiritual re-creation of religion.

V

The past decade has seen a distinct diminution in these latter types of rabbinic preachment though they are far from extinct. The new media of mass communication, notably the radio and television, have brought the most eloquent and the most skillful platform orators into every home, so that the appetite for sensationalism has been jaded by surfeit and the individual rabbi can no longer attract a "following" by such devices.

On the more positive side, the new intellectual climate of the age has had a marked effect upon the pulpit. Men and women who previously could not be attracted to a synagogue or a church on any but the most secular terms, are today manifesting a new interest in religious ideas and values, even if they are unprepared for intellectual acceptance or personal commitment. Increasingly, therefore, the pulpit is concerning itself with religious themes, broadly conceived to include the entire gamut of Jewish problems, to be sure, but no longer eschewing theological issues.

The second great area of rabbinic activity lies in the field of education. With the rise of the economic level of most congregations, fewer of the rabbis are called upon to teach children in the classroom, professional teachers being the norm, but the rabbi frequently serves as principal of the religious school. He is generally regarded as its titular head, responsible for the broad policies of the institution, such as the content of the curriculum, the number of days and hours of instruction per week, and the general spirit of the school. Special groups of older children, like Confirmation classes and high school groups, will generally be taught, in whole or in part, by the rabbi, on the assumption that his personal influence ought to be brought to bear upon the youth during these formative years.

While important aspects of the educational program thus continue to occupy the rabbi's attention, the tendency is to reduce his work in this area. This trend has been accelerated with the growth of the congregational school at the expense of the communal Hebrew school. A few decades ago, when the more intensive afternoon Hebrew school was conducted under independent auspices, the average congregation contented itself with a Sunday school, often intended for the girls, concerning whom the old prejudice persisted that a minimum program of Jewish education was sufficient. Since the Sunday school met only on Sunday mornings, the rabbi could be expected to devote himself to its supervision. But as the congregational school systems gain in size and complexity, with weekday afternoon Hebrew schools becoming the norm and day schools on the increase, it becomes clear that most rabbis lack both the experience and the technical knowledge, as well as the time and energy, required for school administration. Were the shortage of competent educational personnel less acute, the process of transferring school supervision from the rabbi to the professional educator would have proceeded even more rapidly than it has, but the trend is unmistakable.

It is in the field of adult education that the rabbi has found a congenial and challenging area of service. Professionals in the field are few, and the conduct of study courses and discussion groups remains a fertile field in which the rabbi may exercise his historical function of teacher.

The uphill struggle to create viable programs of adult education has produced various devices for attracting students, aside from the standard technique of the platform lecture and the classroom. These include Sunday morning lectures, often accompanied by breakfast, and Friday evening study groups, which replace or supplement the sermon at the formal worship period. The social emphasis, which is not always free from "snob appeal," is utilized in the home study project, where a limited number of families meet at one another's homes for study and discussion. Recent years have witnessed an extensive growth of the *Kallah,* or the Laymen's Weekend Institute, sponsored by congregations or by a group, as well as the Institutes on Judaism created by national organizations like B'nai B'rith, which recognize that adult education is the basic need of the American Jewish community. In the Laymen's Institute, a group, ranging from thirty to one hundred men and women, spends a weekend or a week away from home, generally at a resort-hotel or a summer camp, under the guidance of the rabbi, who generally serves as a member of the faculty. The institute, under whatever sponsorship, devotes itself to Jewish study, accompanied by a detailed observance of the traditional Jewish way of life, including prayers, grace after meals, Sabbath rest, and *zemirot,* elements that are otherwise remote from the lives of most American Jews. The impact of these institutes on the lives of the participants is undeniable—it still remains to be determined to what extent they affect the pattern of their year-round living and influence the community at large. To meet this concern, congregations frequently sponsor a *Kallah* or weekend study program, with a visiting scholar as teacher, in the synagogue, so that larger numbers may participate.

The fourth area of the rabbi's functioning today probably affects the largest segment of the Jewish population, if only at rare intervals—his role as a minister. In traditional communities as well as in Reform circles, it is a far cry today from the time when a *brith milah* was performed by a *mohel* with no other "clergyman" needed; when a *pidyon haben* required only a first-born male child, the father, and a *kohen* in the presence of a *minyan;* when a Bar Mitzvah was called to the Torah immediately after his thirteenth birthday, even on a Monday or Thursday morning, with no attendant pomp or circumstance; when a wedding could be solemnized by any Jew who knew the ritual; and when a funeral was conducted by the family and friends of the departed, who read the order of service themselves.

Today all these *rites de passage,* especially the Bar Mitzvah, the wedding, and the funeral, as well as the unveiling of the monument approximately a year later, have become rabbinic functions. Undoubtedly, the example of the Protestant minister and the Catholic priest has not been without influence. Even more potent in encouraging the process has been the widespread ignorance among the Jewish laity. On the positive side, it may be conceded that there has been a gain in the dignity and impressiveness with which these significant occasions in life are invested by the participation of the rabbi.

It would be captious in the extreme to oppose a state of affairs merely because it has its analogue in the non-Jewish community. The fact is that, over and above all else, the rabbi has become an ecclesiastic and is regarded by many of his flock as possessing sacramental powers—and this trend represents a transformation of the rabbi's role that is a violent distortion of Jewish tradition.

Closely associated with this clerical function is his role as pastor. In ratio to the reputation that the rabbi enjoys for practical wisdom and human sympathy, men and women turn to him for consultation on their personal and family problems, especially when religious aspects enter into the issue, though by no means only then. This aspect of rabbinic service is growing rapidly, as more and more Jews become permanent members of congregations and develop long-standing associations with their rabbis. As against this trend, the increased activity of the personal counsellor and of the psychiatrist has raised important questions with regard to the precise delimitation of function between religion and psychology and the possibility of cooperative endeavor between them.

The modern rabbi's functions have not yet been exhausted. As religious institutions have grown in size, with larger membership rosters and constantly expanding programs, annual budgets have skyrocketed, often reaching six figures. The rabbi has therefore been catapulted into the arduous role of fund-raiser, whether directly in the form of pulpit appeals or personal solicitations from affluent individuals or indirectly by enlarging the membership, "building goodwill," and attracting income from other sources. The mechanics of a large institution, with various affiliated groups, has created a new professional, the synagogue executive director, but the rabbi's role in this area is still very pronounced.

Finally, the modern rabbi in America a generation ago won his spurs as the Jewish representative to the larger community. This function as "ambassador to the Gentiles" was particularly important when most American Jews were of foreign birth and limited general education. Within less than half a century, the bulk of American Jews are native-born, with college-trained men and women now reaching over eighty percent. Today, Jewish lay leaders in every area of the national life meet their counterparts in the general community. Nonetheless, this function of the rabbi is far from spent. The generally accepted religious stratification of the American nation along the tripartite division of Catholics, Protestants, and Jews makes the presence of a Jewish religious representative imperative at public functions and in interfaith activities. The efficacy of the "goodwill movement" has been questioned in various quarters, but it continues to be favored by most American Jews. There can be little doubt that even when stripped of the exaggerated claims incidental to publicity and fund-raising efforts, interfaith activity has a vital function to perform in keeping the bridge of communication open among the various elements of the American people.

The capstone in the arch of the rabbi's manifold activities is his role as Jewish spokesman and community leader on the national and international scenes. The preservation of the Jewish people, the physical succor of the oppressed, the economic rehabilitation of the destitute, the resettlement of the homeless, have created large and complicated agencies that need financial support, administrative direction, and statesmanlike leadership. The State of Israel, in spite of its yeoman achievements during its brief history, is not yet a self-sufficient entity. It continues to be confronted by the herculean task of peaceful reconstruction, which must go on simultaneously with the heroic struggle it has had to wage against its hostile neighbors. Great significance, therefore, continues to attach to the various instrumentalities, financial, educational, and political, created by the Zionist movement. These institutions, too, require leadership. The Jewish cultural equipment of the rabbi, his forensic gifts, his total absorption in Jewish affairs, his communal experience, and his prestige in the general community, make him an ideal public servant of the Jewish community, a statesman at his best, or, alas, merely a politician.

To be sure, the highest level of leadership is, by its very nature, open to only a few chosen individuals. It is noteworthy that many of the national and international leaders in American Jewry have been drawn from the rabbinate. Figures like Stephen Wise, Abba Hillel Silver, and Israel Goldstein—*lehavdil bein hahayyim ubhein ha-hayyim*—come to mind in this category. Other rabbis of more modest talents or lesser energy have served on a more limited scale, but virtually every member of the rabbinate is expected to be a Jewish spokesman and arbiter of policy at least in his own local community.

It will be noted that in this bewildering catalogue of activities, no mention has yet been made of the one function that once characterized the traditional rabbi above all others, Jewish scholarship. The truth is that for many modern practitioners of the rabbinic calling, scholarship has been a prime casualty, crowded out of the program by the imperious demands of an activistic age. With pardonable exaggeration, it might be said that while the old Rav did nothing but study, the modern rabbi does everything but study! The loss of scholarly stature has not passed altogether unwept and unhonored. It is significant that at least a minority of rabbis—and their number is growing—do sacrifice their hours of leisure and relaxation to maintain the tradition of learning in the rabbinate. Some few do original scholarly research of high quality in Bible, rabbinics, history, and theology. Many more interpret and present the results of technical scholarship to the general public in popular books and through articles in the press. Others seek to give the permanence of print to their more effective pulpit discourses. Still others, like their confreres in Germany before World War II, compile the history of their own congregations and communities and thus supply the sources for the future historian of American Jewry.

Now it is undeniable that a decline in the scholarly attainments and personal piety of the modern rabbi, as against his traditional predecessor, cannot be compensated for by concrete practical achievements; they belong to different levels of being. Yet the change in the character of the rabbi has not been a total loss. There has been a broadening of cultural outlook, and not merely a lowering of the level of Jewish learning, in the transformation of the rabbinical calling. Creative scholarship and serious philosophic and theological thought, which had largely been absent from the life of the traditional East European rabbi, have emerged once more in the pattern of activity and thought of a growing number of American rabbis.

VI

In surveying the changing role of the rabbi in the modern world, nostalgia for the past is not merely useless; it may prove positively harmful if it prevents a realistic appraisal of the situation. The metamorphosis of the rabbi's role, from passive contemplation to active leadership in the community, was absolutely called for by the conditions of modern life. Whoever doubts the need for this transformation has only to observe the situation in the State of Israel, where the old rabbinic pattern has been retained in the face of a new and dynamic situation. As a consequence, the rabbi in the State of Israel has sunk to a position of relative insignificance, being little more than a state functionary for registering vital statistics, possessing no vital connection with a congregation of men, women, and children. In Israel, the synagogue frequently serves only as a prayer house, playing no dynamic role in the fashioning of Jewish personality or in the solution of the manifold spiritual and ethical problems of a nation in travail.

There are strong grounds for believing that if religion in Israel is to become a vital force and prove an influence for good in the life of the people as a whole, it will come to pass only through the medium of a revitalized synagogue and an active rabbinate. Both can learn more than a little from American synagogues and rabbis at their best. The value of the American synagogue-center at its best is not limited to America.

In the closing quarter of the twentieth century, Jewish life is in violent flux. The rabbi, who is the living symbol of the deeply rooted desire of Jews to survive meaningfully through their tradition, is accordingly undergoing a new transformation, the end of which is not yet in sight. Prophecy is often as much an effort of the will as it is an enterprise of the mind; the wish is usually father to the thought. But certain trends seem clear with regard to the future of the rabbinate.

All signs point to the growing significance of the rabbi as the symbol of Judaism and hence as the central figure in the Jewish community. As Jewish acculturation in America continues to move forward with seven-league boots, American Jewry will increasingly take on the form of a religious group. Whether this will mean a narrowing or a deepening of Jewish life, only the future will reveal. In no small measure the vitality or the decay of the Jewish community will depend on the character of its leadership, both lay and rabbinic.

To be sure, the restructuring of West European Jewry in the post-Emancipation period as a *Religionsgemeinde* or a *Consistoire* was accompanied by a progressive decline of vitality. Growing religious indifference, mounting cultural illiteracy, and widespread alienation from the community were everywhere in evidence as elements of an extended process, the end of which was marked by mass intermarriage and conversion. The fault lay, however, not in conceiving of Judaism as a religious tradition, but in severing the organic relationship of faith, culture, and peoplehood which has always characterized Judaism.

It is fair to say that the modern rabbi, whatever his "denominational" leaning, is increasingly dedicated to such an all-embracing conception of Judaism. His zeal in furthering Jewish life in all its phases will strike a responsive chord among most American Jews. For intuitively they grasp this organic view of Judaism and the Jewish people, an insight which both the theologians of West European Jewry and the secularist theoreticians of East European Jewry often failed to achieve.

At the same time, it is likely that while cherishing this all-embracing view of Jewish life, the rabbi will increasingly be freed from many of the tasks that now harass his days and often give him the frustrated feeling of being a glorified jack-of-all-trades, master of none. The emergence of the educator, the executive director, the social worker, and latterly the psychiatrist will relieve him of certain facets of his local work. The professionalization of fund-raising by Federation, United Jewish Appeal, Israel Bond Drive, and countless other agencies is making his participation in these areas less central and time-consuming than before.

Finally and most important, the much discussed "return to religion" has a vital bearing on the future role of the modern rabbi. While this much-touted revival is often exaggerated, it is real; its basic drawback is that, genuine as it is for many, it has often remained superficial, lacking deep roots in Jewish knowledge. Modern Jews, young or old, seeking to "return" are often at the mercy of the many voices—siren or strident—that compete in the marketplace for Jewish souls, and many are victimized in the process. Nevertheless, the new interest in religion will make it possible for the rabbi to become, in ever greater degree, the teacher and interpreter of Judaism as a world-view and as a way of life for those men, women, and young people who are intelligent in their quest for *hama'or shebayahadut,* "the light that is in Judaism."

This religious revival is not of one piece. It takes the form of a pyramid consisting of three layers. The broad base at the bottom constitutes the new, widespread interest in the message of religion; the middle, narrower segment above it represents an intellectual acceptance, in whole or in part, of the content of religion; the apex, narrowest of all, but the crowning glory of the pyramid, consists of those who have made a personal commitment to practice and observe the imperatives of religion. Each section of the pyramid poses a challenge and an opportunity for the rabbi, summoning up all his learning and piety, his sympathy and wisdom, his energy and patience.

Evidence is mounting of a radical transformation in the future structure of the synagogue as well, affecting the role of the rabbi as its spiritual leader. Organized religion does not lack for critics today, many of whose strictures have a substantial measure of justice. It is often pointed out, sometimes in sorrow and often in anger, that organized religion today has become a massive insitution, mechanical, impersonal, and expensive, particularly for young people early in their careers. It is unfortunately true that the church and the synagogue repel many of the most sensitive and potentially most valuable elements in the community. All too often, the million-dollar temple fails to establish those intimate links between the individual Jewish child, youth, or adult and his faith which are the essence of the religious experience. Unfortunately, the remedy is harder to come by than the diagnosis.

One obvious suggestion would be for the large congregations, consisting of many hundreds of families, to be broken up into smaller independent units. However, such a procedure, even if it could be carried out, would have major drawbacks. If one large congregation were replaced by six small, independent entities, the maintenance of an effective school for the young would become virtually impossible. If the children were graded properly, classes would be too small to be economically viable; if age-groups were combined, the classes would be too heterogeneous to be educationally effective. As a general rule, even a large school may be of inferior quality; a small school can rarely achieve excellence.

Many other activities would suffer by the dissolution of large congregations. An effective school for adult education requires both large enrollment and funds which small congregations could hardly muster. Well-functioning programs for the youth or for the rapidly growing group of Jewish singles, or for social services for working mothers or senior citizens, all require substantial budgets which only a large congregational membership can support.

Is there any escape from the Scylla of large aggregates that are often religiously sterile and the Charybdis of small units that are not socially and economically viable? The alternative is to maintain the structure of congregations that have been built with so much sweat and tears and to have them encourage and maintain the formation of smaller worship and study groups within the total membership.

In many, if not in most, instances, the large formal services now conducted on Friday evenings, Sabbath mornings, and the festivals will continue to attract substantial portions of the community who find in them a satisfaction for their spiritual needs, especially since these services would enjoy the benefit of the rabbi's discourse. But in addition to the main services, the synagogue would sponsor several parallel and independent Friday and Sabbath morning services geared to various groups in the community. Some of these services might be more traditional, others more innovative. Some would cater to adolescents or to young adults, some to singles or younger couples, while others would meet the needs of older men and women. Still others might focus on special-interest groups of various kinds. Services conducted by smaller groups would have the major virtue of permitting active participation by larger numbers of persons. They would bring a sense of involvement and a medium of expression to the individual which is difficult, if not impossible, to achieve in mass congregations, with hundreds of worshippers at a single service. The service would permit the use of several cantors and Torah-readers and extend the distribution of *aliyot* and other honors to many more congregants than is possible today—a recurrent complaint through the years.

Such smaller groups would not be limited to prayer and worship. They would be particularly effective in youth activities, in adult education involving many, both in the teaching and the learning process, and in various types of social service on a volunteer basis—"religion in action."

Nearly two decades ago, a noticeable movement toward the creation of *havurot,* "fellowships," arose in several major cities, generally sponsored by college students living on college campuses. These early *havurot* had few if any links to the organized religious community. Nevertheless, they helped point the way a little later toward the creation of *havurot* that would be associated with an existing religious institution and would reap the benefits of its professional staff, its experience, and its facilities.

Larger, unified services might continue to be conducted on the festivals and on other stated occasions in order to reinforce the sense of unity in the congregation. Major educational efforts, like public forums, would also be geared to the congregation as a whole.

The rabbi would continue to be the preacher and teacher of the congregation as a whole. It is true that the preaching function is often attacked today as artificial and useless. One is tempted to reply that, like religion as a whole, the sermon has not failed; it has generally not been tried. Where the preacher approaches his task with a high sense of responsibility and devotes adequate preparation, the sermon can prove both inspiring and enlightening in the future as it has been in the past.

Prescriptions for the future are even more futile than projections. Undoubtedly varying patterns of congregational structure and function will be emerging in different communities. It does seem clear, however, that a greater emphasis than at present will be placed upon intimacy, fellowship, and personal participation.

While other phases of his present activities may pass away, the functions of the rabbi as teacher, preacher, pastor, and personal counselor show no signs of diminution in the future. Quite the contrary, they give every evidence of bulking ever larger. If the modern rabbi succeeds in adding to his life the dimension of "love of Torah," on however modest a level, he will have established the vital link of continuity with his predecessors in spiritual leadership. He will thus prove himself not altogether unworthy of being called "master, counselor, and friend."

PART FOUR

A Vital Judaism for
Our Day

17

ON THE SPIRIT OF JUDAISM

At the 1969 Convention of the Rabbinical Assembly, my colleagues honored me by tendering me a Testimonial Dinner marking, at a slight remove, my sixtieth birthday. I was asked to prepare an address for the occasion. It was suggested that I include not merely personal reminiscences from my years of service in the rabbinate, but some broader, more embracing theme that would be of interest to my colleagues.

My entire scholarly career has been concerned with language, which is the manifestation of the human spirit in all its limitless variety. Where would our age be without "commitment" and "confrontation," without "identity" and "alienation"? About as badly off as the preceding generation would have been without "concept," "values," and "ideology." Particularly characteristic of our day is the death of the notion of dirty words or obscene acts in modern life. Today there is no word left in the English language that can be described as pornographic and therefore out of bounds.

Perhaps, however, this assertion ought to be qualified. There is one word which is a dirty word today—the word "liberal." Yet I believe it is no mere perverseness or contrariness of spirit that impels me to describe myself as a liberal. I am using the term here not with regard to politics or economics or even religion, but in a philosophical sense as embodied in the definition, "A liberal is one who believes that all legitimate ends are compatible with one another." Liberalism so conceived, it seems to me, is the great liberating principle in human life and thought. It sees life as virtually limitless in its possibilities for good. It has boundless faith in the capacity of man's spirit to explore ever-wider vistas in a universe which is miracle as well as mystery.

To the extent that any of us can speak of having a philosophy of life, I think it fair to say that this outlook has actually been my guiding principle, the conviction that all legitimate ends are, or can be, compatible with one another. I know that in some quarters of the current literary and theological scene, this attitude would be regarded as a very "simplistic" and naively optimistic view. Hopelessness and despair of man and the world are the marks of profundity for many theologians.

But I fall back upon some rather august authority for this conception of liberalism. I find it in the opening chapter of the Bible, where it is attributed to no less than the Almighty Himself, "God saw everything that He had made, and behold, it was very good" (Genesis 1:31). Note that the word "everything" applied to the entire range of creation. Our sages fearlessly spell out the implications of this acceptance of the world, with all its limitations, when they comment: "Very good—that includes death itself."

Optimistic this view of existence may be, but not naive, when it challenges head-on the theological nay-sayers of our time. I am reminded of the utterance of one of my private heroes, Samuel Johnson: "When I was young, I wanted to devote myself to philosophy, but I found cheerfulness always breaking in." Johnson knew frustration and loneliness, bereavement and illness and death at first hand. To teach men to be sensitive to the limitless tragedies of life and yet to rejoice in its boundless glories is the high role of vital religion.

This basic approach, which seems to me to have shaped the various events and activities of my life, is of more than personal relevance. Thus I have always felt that scholarship and the practical rabbinate are, or must be, compatible with one another. I do not for a moment, after all these years, think that harmonizing these two goals is particularly easy within the present structure of Jewish and modern life. But as some of you may remember from my Seminary classes, I have always underscored my conviction that a rabbi who is not a scholar or at least a student is either a fool or a charlatan. If a rabbi is to retain the respect and esteem of the community and, what is more important, if he is to maintain his own self-respect and sense of worth, he must make the study of Torah, broadly conceived and zealously pursued, an integral element of his rabbinic career.

Moreover, Torah is, if possible, more essential to the rabbi today than in the past. Our people are no longer foreign-born immigrants glorying in their rabbi's "accentless" English. In twenty years, virtually all our congregants will be college graduates. They will know that the rabbi cannot match the competence in psychology, literature, politics, and economics possessed by the professor they had in college or, for that matter, by many laymen in the congregation. Our laymen will turn to the rabbi, if they turn to him at all, for expert, sympathetic, and significant exposition of Judaism, its literature, history, religious ideas, and ethical insights. The rabbi will stand or fall on his knowledge of Torah, his capacity to communicate the content and significance of the Jewish tradition. In a far more personal and immediate sense than Saadia Gaon intended, the rabbi may echo his sentiment: *'ein lanu shi'ur ella hatorah hazot,* "We have no claim to survival or significance except for this Torah."

On the other hand, if Jewish learning continues to be the private preserve of a handful of professional scholars living in ivory towers, far removed from the marketplace of ideas or the valley of human struggle, if scholars speak in their own particular jargon only to one another and do not go beyond their circle, scholarship stultifies itself and loses whatever value or pertinence it once may have possessed.

This relationship between scholarship and life is validated in the millennial experience of Israel. Consider, for example, the alleged contradiction posed by the logician between thought and action, between the timeless and the timely, the recondite and the relevant. As we study the history of our people, we find that our greatest teachers and most creative spirits were those who were able to combine a concern for the life of the spirit with an active involvement in the daily world. We need call to mind Moses, Isaiah and Jeremiah, Ezra and Hillel and Saadia, Rashi and the Tosafists, the Rambam and Nahmanides, the Hasidic masters and Rabbi Israel Salanter, Solomon Schechter and Israel Friedlander, Rabbi Kook and Abraham Joshua Heschel.

In our tradition, Torah appears under two aspects. The first is

Torah lishmah, "Torah for its own sake," disinterested study for the joy of understanding, for the delight of glimpsing the great mystery and miracle of the universe, which is the embodiment of God's will, and thus thinking God's thoughts after Him. But Torah is also *Torat hayyim,* Torah ministering to life, deeply immersed in all the problems and perils of Jewish and human existence. When it was at its best, our tradition never found any conflict between the two aspects of Torah.

The tragedy of our time, it seems to me, is largely due to the dichotomy that has developed here. In the realm of scholarship, we have developed the impression that objective, disinterested scholarship means uninterested scholarship, which quickly becomes uninteresting, pedantic, and essentially useless.

I believe that the principle that all legitimate ends are in harmony with one another was characteristic of Judaism long before the term and concept of liberalism came into being. In various books and papers, I have sought to deal with significant aspects of Judaism that are examples of this approach to life. You will surely forgive me if I do not supply a bibliography! Here I can briefly cite only one or two instances. There is, for example, the difficulty that has been felt by theologians and scholars, by many Jews and non-Jews alike, in understanding the truth that particularism and universalism are both integral to the world-view of Judaism and are compatible, not contradictory.

Consider the difficulty that confronted St. Paul, who could not grasp the fact that in Judaism the letter and the spirit are not antagonistic but compatible elements, complementing and reinforcing each other.

There is more than a merely theoretical interest in the fact that the Jewish tradition at its most authentic recognizes no dichotomy in the Paulinian sense between *sarx* and *psyche,* between body and soul, between the material and the spiritual. In this day and age, when so many of our Christian brothers both within the Establishment and without are seeking to find a role for religion in the "secular city," the Jewish tradition speaks with special authority to the human condition here and now. For in Judaism the secular and the religious have always been inseparable, or more precisely, the religious tradition has been at the same time secular, deeply involved in the *saeculum* in which men live, suffer, and struggle. In sum, it has been of the very genius of Judaism, as adumbrated in the first chapter of

Genesis, to regard all legitimate ends as compatible with one another.

I believe that it is no mere coincidence that this approach, in special degree, has been true of our school of thought, the Conservative movement in Judaism. If, as I profoundly believe, it is we who stand in the mainstream of the tradition—and I have a very high regard for the contributions of Orthodoxy and of Reform to the treasure-house of Jewish life and thought—it is because our movement has strikingly exemplified this same capacity for seeing all legitimate ends as compatible with one another.

That is why Conservative Judaism seeks to combine ritual and ethics, without downgrading either, whether in theory or in practice. That is why it strives to develop loyalty to Halakhah within the context of freedom, and why its concern for the preservation of our specific tradition goes hand in hand with an involvement in the agonies of the world at large.

I am not suggesting for a moment that ours is an easy position to formulate or, what is an even more formidable task, to translate into reality. It is much easier, for example, to turn one's back on the world, at least in theory, and to concentrate on one's own group exclusively. Or one may, on the contrary, yield completely to the outside world and surrender whatever is distinctive about one's own way of life. It is we, standing at the center, who are called upon to combine disparate goals which seem to others to be contradictory and mutually exclusive. We must constantly call attention to the fact that these varied elements are all legitimate and, therefore, inherently compatible. Hence we are committed both to Israel and humanity, and seek to cultivate both Torah and *Hokhmah*. Our philosophy of Judaism embraces both observance of the *mitzvot ma'asiyot* and dedication to the religious and ethical goals they embody, faith in God and in man, whom He has created in His image.

This our movement has attempted to achieve. As many of us have felt, we have not yet fulfilled our destiny, and all too often have not acted upon our convictions. But these lapses do not flow from a lack of sincerity or a failure of will or an absence of creative ability. If we continue to keep the goal before us, we shall, God willing, move toward our objectives and make of our movement a blessing for Judaism and make Judaism a blessing for the world.

A long time ago, in thinking about our movement, I came across a

Midrash which, in my youthful enthusiasm, I thought I was the first to discover. Later I learned that Zacharias Frankel had used exactly the same Midrash, and for the same purpose, over one hundred years ago—a tragic example, you will agree, of plagiarism by anticipation.

The Midrash tells the following parable: "An army was walking between two roads, one a road of fire and the other a road of snow. If the army gets too close to the road of fire, it will be burnt. If it gets too close to the road of snow, it will be frozen. What is the army to do? Let it walk in the center and take care not to be burnt by the fire or frozen by the cold" (*Aboth di Rabbi Nathan*, first version, chap. 28, ed. Schechter, p. 86).

This Midrash Frankel utilized in order to expound his conception of "positive-historical Judaism." Incidentally, ponderous as is the designation "positive-historical Judaism," it is another example of the harmony of all legitimate ends. "Historical" represents a recognition of development, of growth in a living tradition, which includes both continuity and change. "Positive" means that we adopt not a negative or even a neutral attitude, but a positive relationship to the tradition, which is the product of history.

This is what our movement has sought to achieve. We certainly have not accomplished all that we would have wished, but neither have we failed to make significant progress. On the contrary, the signs are multiplying of a religious awakening both within our group and in our sister movements that indicates the extent of our impact upon the future of Judaism in America. We may legitimately hope that our younger colleagues and the generations to come of our laymen will carry forward this process of creating a viable and meaningful Judaism in America. In the language of our sages, "We shall have left room for our successors to achieve greatness."

There are among us, as there should be and I hope always will be, varying interpretations of our tradition and divergences of view with regard to the procedures to be adopted by Conservative Judaism in dealing with the problems of life. We shall, God willing, always keep open the roads of communication among us and, what is even more important, the paths of mutual influence and mutual esteem.

If we preserve this characteristic of our movement, we shall become a *Yisra'el biz'er 'anpim*, a kind of Israel in miniature. The various tendencies and emphases within our movement will all contribute to making it not only a worthy heir of a great past, but an instrument for the enhancement of life in the present and future. In this unending task we have all attempted to play a part.

As I stand here before you, I realize that I may, perhaps, have given a picture of a consciously ordered and tidy existence, which is, of course, not given to any human being to achieve and certainly not to me. Much in my life, as in yours, has, from our limited perspective, been accidental—perhaps it was the hand of God. A good deal has been left undone, and much that I would wish to accomplish I shall probably never be able to do. But while I have any life and strength, I hope to do what I can *lehagdil Torah ulha'adirah,* "to magnify the Torah and enhance it." If I can do this even in part, knowing that I have the esteem and affection of my colleagues and friends in the Rabbinical Assembly, whom I love as my brothers, I shall feel that my life will not have been in vain. There is comfort as well as command in the supremely wise words of Rabbi Tarphon: "It is not incumbent upon you to complete the task, but neither are you free to desist from it" (*Abot* 2:16).

For all that you have meant to us and done for us, above all for the blessing of my family and Fannie, who has been my life's companion and my abiding inspiration through the years, I offer my heartfelt thanks to Almighty God.

18

JUDAISM: THE SECRET OF ITS VITALITY

The origin of great movements in history can rarely be pinpointed with specific dates, and this is true of Conservative Judaism as well. In 1902 Solomon Schechter arrived on these shores and was inaugurated as president of the Jewish Theological Seminary. Though the Seminary had been founded a decade and a half earlier, Schechter's assumption of the presidency may properly be described as the beginning of Conservative Judaism as a dynamic, self-conscious movement dedicated to the perpetuation of traditional Judaism within the context of the modern world.

The eight decades that have elapsed are probably the most eventful in the long epic of Jewish history, only the period of the destruction of the Temple rivaling it in its tragic and revolutionary import. The twentieth century has witnessed the brutal destruction of the greatest center of Jewish life in the last five hundred years, in Eastern and Central Europe, which served as the mighty heart of world Jewry for centuries. On the plus side of the ledger has been the miraculous emergence and extraordinary progress of the State of Israel, perhaps the only authentic miracle in our age, without which the Jewish present and future would be bleak indeed. The third great event, the dimensions of which Schechter clearly foresaw, was the growth and development of American Jewry.

Beginning in the 1880s, American Jewry had begun to grow astronomically through the mass immigration of East European Jews fleeing tsarist oppression and the grinding poverty which characterized their lives. By the turn of the century, American Jews were divided into two widely disparate and basically hostile groups. On the one hand was the community of German Jews who had come to these shores a few decades earlier. In relatively short order, they succeeded in establishing themselves economically in the land of liberty and in achieving a high measure of integration into American cultural and public life. Though there were many exceptions, the German Jews who came to America brought with them limited Jewish cultural resources and religious loyalties. Here they encountered both the opportunities and the temptations of a free and open society. The individualism and pluralism of American life were particularly evident in the field of religion, where hundreds of sects and denominations proliferated on the American scene. Lacking strong roots in their Jewish heritage, German Jews in America became the seed-bed of a type of Judaism which proudly called itself "American Judaism" and which had relatively few links with the tradition.

Ranged on the other side—and the phrase is not casually chosen—were the masses of East European Jews huddling in the great ghettos of our country; living in squalor and poverty, exploited in sweatshops or eking out a meager existence as petty tradesmen. Coming from lands of intense Jewish life, these East European Jews brought with them memories of the *shtetl,* which they tended to idealize with the passing of time. They were imbued with a powerful desire to reproduce on these shores what seemed to them the only authentic version of Judaism.

But as their children came into the world, it soon became painfully apparent that the poverty-stricken synagogues and the antiquated teaching methods of the *melamdim* would prove powerless to withstand the blandishments of assimilation and the temptations of the bright new world beckoning outside. In his classic *Autobiography,* the famous American reporter Lincoln Steffens, who possessed a deep interest in the Lower East Side of New York, describes Yom Kippur in the first decade of the twentieth century: "Outside the synagogues, the young men stood laughing and telling jokes, while inside, the old men sat, reading their prayers, gnashing their teeth and weeping bitter tears. Two, three thousand years of sacrifice, devotion and loyalty to a cause lost in a single generation." Virtually all observers of the American scene, Jewish and Christian, sympathetic or otherwise, saw no prospect for Judaism save extinction or emasculation.

However, the fundamental truth of Jewish history was expressed long ago by the psalmist: "The Guardian of Israel neither slumbers nor sleeps." The pessimistic appraisal, which seemed the only realistic outcome to be expected, has proved mistaken. A variety of factors led to the forging of the instruments of salvation. Among these, the emergence of Conservative Judaism under the dynamic inspiration of Solomon Schechter was surely not of the least importance.

The new movement showed American Jews that the genuine tensions between Americanism and Judaism, between the modern world and religious tradition, between devotion to Torah and responsiveness to life, between loyalty to Israel and concern for humanity, far from being destructive, could prove richly creative of Jewish and humane values. As a result, Conservative Judaism experienced an efflorescence without parallel.

Reform and Orthodoxy, the two other great movements in American Judaism, were greatly influenced by Conservatism. During the past seven decades, Reform Judaism has been all but transformed, and the progress that has been registered goes beyond the differences between the Pittsburgh Platform of 1885 and the Columbus Program of 1915. While isolated pockets of "classical" Reform still remain, contemporary forms of Reform Judaism exhibit a new recognition of the significance of tradition, the importance of religious practice, the basic role of the Hebrew language, and a warm attachment to the Land of Israel as indispensable to the Jewish future.

As for Orthodox Judaism, it has made great progress since its early, poverty-stricken days in developing self-confidence, organizational strength, and cohesion. It has mastered successfully the techniques of American mass-culture, is energetic in propagating its cause, and is militant in defending its interests. It boasts many institutions of higher learning and takes legitimate pride in its greatest contribution to Jewish survival, the establishment of the day school as a basic feature of Jewish education.

It is not unfair to say that during the twentieth century, Reform has become more traditional and Orthodoxy more modern, both because of the impact of world events and the example of Conservative Judaism.

These religious movements are not the only weapons in the arsenal of Jewish survival in America. There were other significant factors—the rise and progress of Zionism, the earlier development of the Yiddish press, drama, and literature, the all-too-brief flowering of American Hebrew literature, and the growth of Jewish scholarship, both in older traditional and in modern critical forms. Above all, the harsh lessons of history in the twentieth century, spelled "Hitler," conspired to deepen Jewish consciousness and impelled millions of Jews to seek a religious affiliation for themselves and their families. We may humbly offer thanks that the forecasts of virtually all honest observers at the turn of the century, that a meaningful and recognizable Judaism was impossible on this continent, have not been fulfilled.

It would, therefore, be easy for us to indulge in self-congratulation. We can call attention to the millions of Jews associated with synagogues and other basic Jewish organizations and institutions. We may point to the magnificent buildings in which our synagogues, Jewish centers, philanthropic and communal agencies are housed. We may point to the many millions of dollars in the budgets of federations and welfare funds and to the imposing structure of philanthropic agencies created by American Jewry, which has no parallel in the past annals of our people or in the life of our fellow Americans today. We may observe the elaborate facade of Jewish education on this continent, for preschool children as well as on the elementary and secondary levels. It is undeniable that Judaism has made far more progress than anyone dared dream when Schechter first came to America seventy-five years ago.

These are unquestionably genuine achievements. Those who are tempted to dismiss them are invited to try to create an alternative pattern. Yet there is far less comfort and reassurance than we like to believe in structures of bricks, chrome, and stainless steel, in conventions, conferences, and million-dollar budgets. At no time within living memory has there been a deeper sense of unease with regard to the future of Judaism than today. To put it clearly, though illiterately, "If you've got it so good, why is it so bad?"

To be sure, this sense of concern and foreboding is not limited to Judaism. On the contrary, it is all-pervasive today. Several years ago Professor Peter Berger, addressing representatives of eleven leading Protestant denominations of the United States, decried the loss of confidence and the erosion of faith in the future of the church characterizing contemporary Christianity. The decline in Sunday school enrollments, the lack of growth in church memberships, the reduced seminary enrollments, the virtual disappearance of inner-city churches, and above all the empty pews need no documentation.

As for the Roman Catholic Church, perhaps because it formerly presented to the outside world a picture of impregnability and immobility that no other group could emulate, the changes here are even more sensational. To cite a few cases in point, a survey some years ago by *Newsweek* magazine disclosed that more than a third of American Catholics do not attend Sunday Mass regularly. Two out of three Catholics acknowledge that they have not gone to confession in the past two months. Even more significant than these infractions of time-honored ritual practices is the shift on fundamentals in the field of faith and morals. A majority of American Catholics believe that a "good Catholic" can ignore the Pope's stand against contraception. According to one study, the church is currently losing five priests for every two seminarians it enrolls. These trends have been accelerating steadily.

It is, therefore, clear that the contemporary challenge to religion is not directed against one tradition alone, be it Judaism or Christianity, or against a single denomination within that tradition. What is more, the attack against all established religion is many-faceted, in fact even self-contradictory.

On the one hand, organized religion is charged with being indifferent to the burning problems of the real world, having immersed itself in ritualistic and theological concerns. On the other, the church and the synagogue are attacked on the ground that they have surrendered to activism and "secularism" and, therefore, offer the genuinely troubled spirit of man no refuge from the turmoil and materialism of the world.

Many critics decry the inability or unwillingness of religion to reckon with the insights and attitudes emerging from contemporary science, technology, and philosophy. Yet there are probably louder and more articulate voices today blaming religion for trying to reckon with doubt and denial. Authentic religion, they declare, means a firm, immovable faith in divine revelation, free from equivocation and doubt, insulated from the challenge of reason and the conclusions of critical scholarship.

The massive frustrations and terrors of life in the twentieth century have engendered a profound disenchantment with man's reason and character, a loss of confidence in his capacity to understand his own nature and his place in the universe, or to grapple with the problems of life that press on our generation.

Such phenomena as existentialism and occultism, the preoccupation with sex and drugs, the interest in Zen and Yoga, the worship of Satan, the interest in astrology, the search for new forms of religious expression—these contemporary phenomena are radically different from one another, but they are at one in having surrendered the heart of the biblical faith that man is created in the divine image, little lower than God.

Finally, there is a far-flung socio-political challenge from many quarters directed against the religious "establishment." They see in organized religion a self-serving defender of the status quo in a world in which war, oppression, corruption, cruelty, and group hatred are the dominant motifs of society.

It is no wonder that religion is reeling under this bewildering barrage of criticism. It is clear that no single body of doctrine can retrieve the position of religion in the modern world or win back all those who have left the fold. Since every genuine religious faith is a personal faith, and as our sages reminded us, all men are divinely endowed with different temperaments and backgrounds, no single answer, be it rationalist, existentialist, activist, or mystic, will succeed in restoring or creating loyalty to religion among all our youth and their elders.

Is there, then, no underlying approach capable of dealing with all these varied responses? I believe that there is. We may seek for it in the history of the greatest creative periods of Judaism, notably the biblical and the talmudic eras.

There is one basic fact which helps explain the survival and creative capacity of the Jewish religion while all other ancient religions were overtaken by decay and death. Modern archaeological research has revealed the existence of lofty religious ideas in ancient Egypt and Mesopotamia. The Mari excavations have disclosed the existence of prophets who, in their techniques, bear more than a little resemblance to the biblical prophets. The ancient law codes of the Middle East reveal the presence of humanitarian ideals even in pagan cultures. We now know that an institution as remarkable in its social idealism as the Sabbatical year in the Bible has its analogue in Akkadian society. Why have all these resplendent civilizations and colorful religions been relegated to the dustbin of history? Why, on the other hand, has an unimportant people clinging precariously to the eastern shore of the Mediterranean survived two thousand years of exile, persecution, and mass murder? How was it possible for this faith of a weak and harried people to engender two of the mightiest religions of all times, Christianity and Islam, while retaining its own individuality and potential for creativity and growth? If I may propound a naive riddle, what have Abraham Lincoln, Josef Stalin, and Moise Tshombe in common? Not to keep the reader in suspense—their first names, Abraham, Joseph, and Moses, are all biblical. Their biblical names testify to the world-wide influence of the spirit of Israel and its Holy Writ, cutting across continents, races, cultures, and social systems. *After all the explanations of scholars, legitimate as they are, have been heard, the eternal life of the Jewish people remains a mystery for the nonbeliever and a miracle for the man of faith.*

Yet even divine miracles have their basis in human realities. What set biblical religion apart from all others was the fact that its classical spokesmen were not priests, the custodians of religion everywhere else in the ancient world, but prophets and sages. Judaism is not the legacy bequeathed to us by the *kohanim,* but our heritage from the *neviim* and *hakhamim,* both biblical and rabbinic. The Torah, the foundation-stone of Judaism, comes to us from Moses, who was not a priest but a prophet.

Now the dichotomy of prophet and priest has, of course, long been remarked upon, but it has not been properly understood. It is not that the priest was preoccupied with ritual and the prophet was concerned with morality. The Torah, which was the province of the priests, contains many of the most exalted ethical imperatives in the world. Thus, the Holiness Code in Leviticus enshrines not only the justly famous Golden Rule, "Thou shalt love thy neighbor as thyself" (Leviticus 19:31), but the tragically relevant injunction,

"Thou shalt not stand idly by the blood of thy neighbor" (Leviticus 19:16). Equally significant is the provision (19:34), "Thou shalt love him, i.e., the stranger, as thyself, for ye were strangers in the land of Egypt." The priests, who served as the judges of the people, were not impervious to ethical considerations.

Conversely, it is now generally recognized—indeed often in exaggerated form—that the prophets were by no means hostile to ritual. Actually, the biblical prophets reflect a full spectrum of possible attitudes. On the left stands Amos, who, in his relatively few speeches, does not betray any favorable attitude toward ritual. At the center is Isaiah, whose inaugural vision of God came to him in the Temple of Jerusalem. The "right" is represented by Ezekiel, whose book contains a law code that includes ritual enactments for the New Jerusalem that he envisioned for the future. Fundamentally, all the prophets evaluated ritual in terms of its relationship to the moral law—if it became a substitute for righteousness, it was evil; if a stimulus, it was good.

The essential distinction between the biblical prophet and the Hebrew priest was not in the confrontation between ethics and ritual. The priests in Israel were official spokesmen for religion, respected, recognized, and compensated, a position analogous to the one they occupied in all ancient religions. The shrines and temples in ancient Israel also had prophets, soothsayers and foretellers associated with the sanctuaries. These two groups represented the professional religious leadership, who derived their material support from the king and the people.

Opposed to these professionals was a group of passionate dissidents, who made no claim to the chain of Aaronide legitimacy but spoke out of the immediate consciousness of God's presence, "Thus saith the Lord." Far from being well compensated—or even respected—these proclaimers of God's will were scorned as madmen, reviled as trouble-makers, and persecuted as subversives and traitors. They were imprisoned, exiled, or assassinated by the defenders of the status quo. But out of their total commitment to God and their wholehearted love for their people, they could not remain silent in the face of the inequities they saw all about them and the inevitable disaster they saw before them. They had no choice but to attack all aspects of the national life, its politics and international affairs, its social and economic structure, its religious observance and its cultural pretensions. They weighed everything in the one scale of God's law of righteousness, and found it wanting.

What makes the Bible unique is that it is the repository not of "mainline Establishment religion" but of these rebels and nay-sayers. When these "enemies of the people," to use Ibsen's phrase, attacked the optimism of those crying, "peace, peace" when there was no peace, they were penetrating beneath the superficial prosperity and well-being of the kingdoms of Judah and Israel to the rot of moral decay and national destruction beneath.

What characterized the biblical prophets and set them apart from their professional counterparts? Jeremiah described the word of God as "a burning fire pent up in my bones, that I cannot contain" (Jeremiah 20:9). In the Song of Songs, love is compared to "sparks of fire, a mighty flame of God" (8:6). Love in its deepest sense is concern, and passionate love was the driving force behind the prophets' heroic and tragic activity. They were, in the basic sense of the term, *amateurs,* lovers of their God and His people.

We use the word "amateur" today to describe nonprofessional activity. Twenty-seven hundred years ago Amos indignantly proclaimed, "I am neither a professional prophet nor a member of the prophetic guild" (7:14). Many centuries later, a medieval work, *Sepher Hasidim,* declared that the most perfect prayer was that of an illiterate shepherd: "O God, if You had sheep, I would guard them for You for nothing." What the Hebrew prophets introduced into the fiber of Judaism was the spirit of the amateur in its etymological sense, "one who serves a cause or an ideal out of love rather than for gain." Undoubtedly, great-souled and sensitive spirits existed among other peoples and religions, but their influence was minimal. They were at best isolated voices, crying in the wilderness. In no other ancient society did an ongoing group of men arise sufficiently influential in confrontation with the status quo to become the architects of the accepted, normative tradition.

The stamp of the amateur, the nonprofessional, remained a distinguishing mark of Judaism in its second great creative era, the period of the Talmud, as it had been with the prophets in the biblical epoch. During the days of the Second Temple, only the priesthood, the descendants of Aaron, could legitimately officiate at the Temple ritual in Jerusalem. They, therefore, remained the official representatives of Judaism, as is clear from Hellenistic and Roman sources.

Yet the vital spiritual leadership was exercised not by the priests, but by the scribes and their successors, the rabbis, whose activity was centered in the *bet hamidrash,* the House of Study, which served as the *bet hakeneset* and the *bet hatefillah,* the House of Assembly and Prayer. The vast majority of the sages occupied no official position and received no emolument for their labors. The destruction of the Temple and the cessation of the sacrificial system all but eliminated the role of the priesthood as officiants. Yet the rabbis of the Mishnah did not become professionals on that account. They remained amateurs, supporting themselves by various callings and occupations. They carried on the study and the teaching of the Torah in the spirit of the rabbinic Aggadah, according to which God said to Moses, "As I have taught you freely, so teach you freely" (*Nedarim* 37a; *Bekhorot* 29a).

In fact, not until the later Middle Ages did the rabbinate become a profession, when there was a growing need for a functionary to supervise the life of the community, be available for religious guidance, and exercise a judicial role when required. Even then rabbinical authorities had great difficulty in justifying the payment of salaries to rabbis. Maimonides, who was personally situated rather fortunately, as long as his brother's business operations supported him, expressed himself very vigorously in opposition to compensating rabbis from public funds (*Commentary on the Mishnah, Abot* 4:5).

The march of events and the pressure of circumstances made it inevitable that a group of men should dedicate themselves completely to communal needs, religious and cultural, thus being precluded from earning a livelihood elsewhere. Yet the nonprofessional spirit in the rabbinate continued to survive virtually until our own day in traditional Jewish communities. In fact, the emoluments received by most East European rabbis were so minuscule in character that they could well qualify as amateurs—in both senses!

The great *yeshivot* in Eastern Europe, Volozhin, Slobodka, Vilna, Mir, were not institutions for the training of rabbis, but rather for the education of scholars. Most of their students remained laymen, bringing their learning to bear upon the life of their communities. These unique academies eminently deserved Bialik's epithet, "the potter's house where the soul of the people was fashioned." From these *yeshivot* came the communal rabbis, to be sure, but also most of the great Jewish scholars, both traditional and modern, the creators of modern Hebrew and Yiddish literature and the leaders of such varied movements as Zionism, Diaspora nationalism, and socialism.

It is fair to say that all that has proved most creative in modern Jewish life bears the stamp of the amateur, who, whether or not he earns his livelihood from his activity, is basically motivated by a love and dedication to the cause. The line of descent from the biblical prophets and the rabbinic sages is clear and unbroken.

It is, of course, entirely possible, and indeed frequently the case, that the professional is, in this higher sense, an amateur. This held true of the prophets Jeremiah and Ezekiel, who were priests by descent. Similarly, the descendants of Hillel became the patriarchs in the Roman period, serving as the official heads of the academy and as the recognized representatives of the Jewish community vis-à-vis the government. Occupying officially recognized positions, the patriarchs undoubtedly received the emoluments of office, yet the wholehearted dedication of men like Rabban Gamaliel the Elder, Rabban Gamaliel of Yavneh, and Rabbi Judah Hanasi is beyond question.

It is, however, in the very nature of things that when men are charged with the care and administration of an institution, they are likely to develop a preoccupation with its short-term, immediate interests. They tend to identify the material well-being of the institution with the advancement of the ideal which the institution was originally designed to maintain and develop. In this connection, we may recall the homely fact that the English verb "preserve" has two meanings—it means "to safeguard" and also "to pickle." The history of religion demonstrates how often institutions have preserved the ideal in both senses of the term!

As we have noted earlier in our discussion, there is a widespread and varied attack upon religion today. These divergent and even contradictory manifestations of hostility are united in one basic respect—it is religion as an institution that is under fire, not religion as a body of ideals. People today are disenchanted with religion because they see it as a visible and central element of the Establishment. The term is used loosely and inexactly today to refer to the dominant forces in society, government, industry, commerce, education, and culture. It is generally overlooked that the term was originally applied to the church which was established and maintained in certain European countries, like Great Britain and Scandinavia. Many of us remember that in the days of our youth, the longest word in the English language was "Antidisestablishmentarianism," a term applied to those who opposed "disestablishing" the church, that is to say, removing its position of influence, power, and support from the government.

The United Synagogue has demonstrated its awareness of the crisis confronting Judaism by setting as the theme of this convention the great utterance of the sainted Rabbi Abraham Isaac Kook, *Hayashan yithadesh, hehadash yitkadesh,* "The old must become new, and the new must become holy." These words, incidentally, are cited in the conclusion to the Introduction to the *Sabbath and Festival Prayer Book* of the Rabbinical Assembly and the United Synagogue, which appeared in 1946, the first official Conservative prayer book in our movement.

There is more than an accidental relationship between the two elements of Rabbi Kook's injunction. The old can be renewed only if there is an openness of spirit, a willingness and a capacity to welcome the new and make it holy. Conversely, the new can be brought into the orbit of the holy only if we retain our link with the old, but in no mechanical and external way—rather by imbuing it with new vitality and spirit.

How is this dual process of revival to be achieved? The entire history of the Jewish tradition points to the answer—it lies in accentuating the positive role of the amateur spirit which is to be found in those laymen, rabbis, and scholars who love their people and their faith and are prepared to labor and sacrifice on their behalf. I said "laymen" and "rabbis," but let us remember that in Judaism the rabbi is a layman. He cannot function successfully without the support and understanding of knowledgeable and dedicated laymen who will be *bnei Torah,* "men of Torah," and *hovevei Torah,* "lovers of Torah."

One of the basic tragedies of modern Jewish life has been the increasing growth of ecclesiasticism, the patterning of Jewish life after Christian hierarchical models. All too often the rabbi becomes a clergyman, an administrator of sacraments, an intermediary between the individual and his God, or what is surely no better, a fund-raiser, a coordinator of activities, a public relations expert.

Jews are like other people, only more so. We can, therefore, understand why official Jewish leaders, weighted down by the cares and burdens of the institutions they were administering, all too often were averse or at best indifferent to creative and vital innovations in Jewish life. The last great folk movement in the Jewish religion, Hasidism, was bitterly opposed by the official leadership of East European Jewry. It was the achievement of inspired lay leaders, far removed from the seats of power and influence, who were able to quicken the spirit of religious vitality among the downtrodden and depressed masses of the poor.

When Herzl was about to convene the first Zionist Congress, a group of German rabbis, who have gone down in Jewish history as the *Protestrabbiner,* issued a statement opposing the holding of the congress in Munich on the ground that it would impugn the wholehearted loyalty of German Jews to the Fatherland. They prevented the Zionists from meeting in Munich; they were not equally successful with the Nazis four decades later.

The long record of opposition to Zionism by large sections of the Orthodox rabbinate and most of the official agencies of Reform Judaism is happily a thing of the past. But the impetus for Zionism, the most dynamic Jewish movement in modern times, did not come from the religious Establishment. Today, the central role of Zionism and Israel in the revitalization of contemporary Jewish religion and culture for all Jews needs no demonstration.

The greatest contribution of American Orthodox Judaism to Jewish survival is without question the creation of the *yeshivah ketannah,* or day school. But the first *yeshiva,* the Rabbi Jacob Joseph School, and its early successors were created by Orthodox laymen who enjoyed—if that be the word—only lukewarm support from most of the rabbinate.

To the slight extent that order and dignity have been introduced into the supervision of Kashrut in the United States, it is to be attributed to the lay Union of Orthodox Jewish Congregations rather than to the professional leaders in the movement, individually or collectively.

For decades American Jewry has been neglecting our college youth and their religious, cultural, and social concerns, spending pennies on their Jewish and human needs, and allocating dollars to public relations and civic defense activities. Then one day the discovery was made that the college campus was a "disaster area" for Judaism. The problems are still massive and in part intractable, but some rays of light are penetrating the darkness. The creation of *havurot,* or student communes, Jewish student coffee houses, the establishment of hundreds of chairs in Judaic studies on college campuses, the setting up of free Jewish universities where students voluntarily come to study Judaism with no college credit, the burgeoning Jewish student press—these developments all over America are the work of amateurs who love Judaism or are trying to love it and striving to live by it.

The record makes it clear that the same principle holds true in Conservative Judaism as well. Many of the most significant and creative achievements in our movement go back to farsighted laymen and a few courageous and creative rabbis. The Camp Ramah movement, which has helped create a youth for Conservatism, began at the initiative of lay leaders.

The first official prayer book in our movement, the *Sabbath and Festival Prayer Book,* became a reality only when the United Synagogue and the Rabbinical Assembly joined forces. The work was produced by a Joint Commission consisting of ten rabbis, five chosen by each agency. Whatever its imperfections, this pioneering prayer book strove to give honest expression to the genuine attitudes of Conservative Judaism toward the role of women, both in life and the synagogue, toward the sacrificial system, and toward the vital role of the Land of Israel for modern Judaism.

The Seminary Center in Jerusalem was, at first, only a dream in the hearts of a tiny handful of rabbis and lay leaders. The oldest existing day school in the Conservative movement is now nearly thirty years old. At its inception, it received no encouragement or recognition from the official leadership of our movement. The entire network that has developed since owes much of its progress to dedicated laymen, working hand in hand with rabbis in our congregations.

These instances, drawn from many diverse areas in modern Jewish history, are not intended to impugn the *bona fides* of Jewish leadership or their sincere devotion to Jewish interests. Our purpose is only to indicate what has been insufficiently recognized, how often it was the unofficial amateur, the layman, who represented the cutting edge of progress, the stimulus to creativity, and by that token, the hope for the future.

On the other hand, the professional and official leadership has all too often construed its task by telescoping Rabbi Kook's utterance, combining the first and last words, and reading *hayashan yitkadesh,* "the old shall be regarded as sacrosanct." Undoubtedly the preservation of the traditions, rites, and sancta of the past and the maintenance and support of our institutions are important tasks, for which the official custodians of religion deserve our gratitude and support. But these activities may be a necessary condition; they are not sufficient for the survival of Judaism.

If more is to be preserved than the empty shell, we need to recapture the excitement, the novelty, the sense of urgency, which characterized religion in its greatest hours. In the words of the sages, the Torah must become for us *diatagma ḥadasha,* "a royal edict newly proclaimed." The wisdom of vital, relevant scholarship, the guidance of our rabbis, the idealism of our youth, the dedication of our laity—all are needed if the institutions of Jewish life, the home, the synagogue, and the school, are to become instruments of survival, not for their sake alone, but for the cause of God and man.

It is not enough to honor the extraordinary achievements of the synagogue in the past. We must create for it a potential role in the future by having it take on new forms. The synagogue must reverse the trend toward automatism, depersonalization, and all the ills to which Louis D. Brandeis referred as "the curse of bigness." Its activities and its worship must be forged out of the crucible of our experiences, our trials, our triumphs, our fears, hopes, and ideals.

A few steps in this direction may be indicated. Large congregations are unavoidable if large budgets are required for massive plants, elaborate educational programs, and large-scale services. Whether these are necessary is a moot question. But there is no reason for one mass service in a congregation. Five services on Friday evening of one hundred worshippers each, perhaps different in spirit and tone, traditional and modern, conventional and creative, can involve scores or hundreds actively in planning and conducting the service. A rabbi is only one human being; lay preaching and expounding of the *sidrah* can make it possible to "staff" a half-dozen worship groups. We need to utilize our more knowledgeable and committed young people for work with their peers. This is particularly essential in the face of the growing need and the lessened supply of leaders and teachers.

Undoubtedly small schools cannot function well, since they do not permit adequate classification of students, sufficient variety in the curriculum, and specialty instruction. The solution lies in sharing the resources of several congregations to create large, better staffed, more efficient schools, and in the process, breaking down petty, meaningless loyalties. This is already being done increasingly in adult Jewish education.

I often feel that there is too much "unselfishness" among us, especially in the higher echelons of Jewish life. We honor, as we should, the donor, the leader, the active worker, who give of their means, their energies, and their talents to keep Judaism working— for the other fellow. All too often our active workers are much like stagehands—so busy taking care of the curtains and the props, they have no time or energy to enjoy the production.

I would like to see the United Synagogue initiate a program to give public recognition, both at regional and national conventions and locally in our congregations, to laymen who are Jewish scholars or are active in advancing Jewish education, including those young people who enrich the spiritual life of their peers by their dedication to Torah in both senses as Jewish study and as the practice of the Jewish ideals of justice, freedom, and peace. We honor men of wealth and power who use their gifts for the common good. I would suggest, in addition, conferring such titles as *ben Torah, rabh po'olim,* and other designations on scholarly, dedicated laymen. Our most precious resource lies in the laymen—men, women, and young people—who are not only our greatest hope for the future, but our only reason for being.

We cannot eliminate professionalism in twentieth-century Jewish life, but we must be perpetually on guard against its seductions and corruptions. Eternal vigilance is the price of vitality.

In order that the old may be renewed and the new become holy, the amateur, the lover of God and Torah, of Israel and mankind, must reassert his active role in Jewish life, whether he be a rabbi or a layman, a scholar or a lover of learning, a businessman or a professional, a man or a woman, a youth or an adult. It is not easy to fulfill Rabbi Kook's great injunction, but if we pool our human resources of heart and mind, we shall not fail. For as the Talmud reminds us, if we are not prophets, we are at least the descendants of prophets.

19

SEVEN PRINCIPLES OF CONSERVATIVE JUDAISM

American Jewry is becoming increasingly conscious of its historic role, not only as the partner of the State of Israel and the defender of Jewish rights in the Soviet Union and throughout the world, but as the last major center of Jewish life in the Diaspora. In this sacred task, the movement popularly known as the Conservative movement has a significant role to play.

As a matter of fact, the founders of the Conservative movement, the youngest group in moden Judaism, had no wish to create a new alignment in Judaism. They sought, rather, to unite all Jews who had a positive attitude toward Jewish tradition, in spite of variations in detail. Nonetheless, life itself led to the crystallization of Conservative Judaism, *which is dedicated to the conservation and development of traditional Judaism in the modern spirit.*

Its basic attitudes may be set forth under seven headings.

1. Jewish tradition, properly understood and intelligently interpreted, has sufficient vitality and capacity for growth to meet the needs of modern American Jews no less effectively than it served the great Jewish communities of the past, such as ancient Babylonia, medieval Spain, and Eastern and Central Europe in modern times.

2. The religious outlook and world-view of Judaism, with its faith in God and its concept of man, offer our distraught and confused generation a sane and courageous philosophy of life, second to none.

216

3. The Jewish way of life, embodied in the ritual and ethical *mitzvot* of Judaism, far from being outmoded, is indispensable, both for the survival of the Jewish people and for the happiness and dignity of the individual Jew. The observance of the *mitzvot*, the Sabbath and the Festivals, daily prayers, Kashrut and the home rituals are commandments, binding upon each Jew, male and female, young and old.

4. Jewish knowledge is the privilege and duty of every Jew, not merely of the rabbi and the scholar. A Hebrewless Judaism that has surrendered to ignorance and has ceased to create new cultural and spiritual values, is a contradiction in terms, and must perish of spiritual anemia. The regular study of Torah on whatever level is incumbent on every Jew, a supreme commandment second to none.

5. Jews the world over, for all their differences in outlook, political citizenship, and status, are members of the Jewish people, sharing a sense of kinship and a common history from the past, a common tradition and way of life in the present, and a common destiny and hope for the future.

6. The future of the Jewish people as a creative and self-respecting member of the human family is inconceivable without the rebuilding of security and peace in the Land of Israel, which has already brought home to its borders the scattered remnants of Oriental and European Jewry. Hence the support of the State of Israel and of its progress as a democratic Jewish commonwealth built upon the foundation of justice and equality, in which the body of the Jew will be safe and his spirit unshackled, is a cardinal *mitzvah* of Judaism in our day.

7. The sense of Jewish unity is thoroughly compatible with freedom of thought and difference of viewpoint. Whether one adheres to Orthodoxy, Reform, or Conservative Judaism, the noun is more important than the adjective. Conservative Judaism is grateful for the contributions that both Orthodoxy and Reform and many other movements have made to Jewish life, and seeks to encourage every manifestation of Jewish vitality and creative activity.

Basically we believe that Israel's race is not yet run and our task is not yet done. With mind and heart and hand, we must labor unceasingly to help fashion a world worthy of its Maker, in the creation of which we are the partners and co-workers of God.

NOTES FOR CHAPTER 7

1. In writing this chapter, the author utilized the quotations from Solomon Schechter cited by Myer S. Kripke in his highly useful paper, "Solomon Schechter's Philosophy of Judaism," which appeared in the *Reconstructionist* 3, nos. 12 and 13 (October 22 and November 5, 1937).

2. L. Ginzberg, *Students, Scholars and Saints* (Philadelphia, 1928), p. 209.

3. *Reconstructionist* 7, no. 13, p. 9.

4. Mordecai M. Kaplan, *Judaism as a Civilization*, p. 432.

5. Cf. Mordecai M. Kaplan's "Reply," in *Reconstructionist* 7, no. 18 (January 9, 1952).

6. Cf. the excellent study of the subject by Isaak Heinemann, *Ta'ame Hamitzvot Besafrut Yisrael* (Jerusalem, 1949), who traces the quest for a rational basis for the commandments in the Talmud and in Hellenistic and medieval literature.

7. See Dr. Simon Federbusch, "Mishpat Hahozer Le-Musar," in his *Hamusar Vehamishpat Beyisrael* (New York, 1943), chap. 7.

8. Contrast the principle "Saving a life sets aside the Sabbath prohibitions" (*Shabbat* 132a) with the doctrine "Nothing takes precedence over saving one's life, except the commandments forbidding idolatry, sexual immorality, and murder" (*Ketubbot* 19a).

NOTES FOR CHAPTER 9

1. Albert Einstein, "Some Thoughts Concerning Education," *School and Society*, November 7, 1936, p. 589.

2. Bernard Noskin, "Socialism and Faith," *Jewish Frontier*, January 1942, p. 2.

NOTES FOR CHAPTER 14

This paper was presented at the forty-fifth Annual Convention of the Rabbinical Assembly of America on June 27, 1945, as an introduction to the *Sabbath and Festival Prayer Book* issued by the Joint Prayer Book Commission of the Rabbinical Assembly and the United Synagogue in 1945. Since this pioneering effort, there has been a substantial output of liturgical material by Conservative Judaism. These include the *Daily Prayer Book* and the *High Holy Day Mahzor* edited by Rabbi Jules Harlow among others.

1. For Zunz's views on the Hamburg prayer book cf. I. Elbogen, *Der jüdische Gottesdienst in seiner geschlichtlichen Entwicklung* Leipzig, 1913, p. 415.

2. Ibid., p. 425.

3. Ibid., pp. 422 f.: "Es war eine Fortsetzung dieses Irrtums, wenn die Gemeinde von den politischen Verhältnissen Deutschlands ihren Ausgang nahm, sich auf die deutschen Glaubensgenossen beschränken wollte; der Gegensatz von religiöser und vaterländischer Gesinnung hatte keine innere Berechtigung, eine wirklich religiöse Reform musste fur alle Juden anwendbar sein. Und endlich war es eine Verkennung der Wirklichkeit, wenn die Gemeinde die Erfüllung des messianischen Berufes des Judentums für sich allein in Anspruch nahm; dieses Streben verfolgte die gesamte Judenheit, freilich auf dem Boden des geschichtlichen Judentums, nicht auf dem des freien Menschentums, wie die Wortführer der Genossenschaft verkundeten."

Cf. also pp. 390 and 405, where he wisely notes that political prejudices must be fought on political grounds, and that the belief in the Messiah was no real basis for denying political equality to Jews, as Macaulay had noted.

4. Cf. *Jewish Encyclopedia*, s.v. "Prayerbook," vol. 10, p. 178b; Elbogen, op. cit., p. 432.

5. Cf. the M. Levin revision of the Berlin prayer book (1885) and the prayer book edited by I. Elbogen.

6. In the Vilna edition of the Jers. Talmud, the citation reads: כל המשנה על המטבע שטבעו המטבע שטבעו חכמים לא יצא ידי חובתו.The omission of בברכות does not affect the meaning. The passage is cited in connection with the Mishnah dealing with the blessings over fruits and vegetables. Rabbi Solomon Serillio, ad loc., specifically notes this limitation in his commentary on this passage in the Yerushalmi: שטבעו חכמים בברכות — בברכות ההנייה דאי בתפלה האמר בפרק קמא דע"ז דאם בא לומר בתחפלתו מעין כל ברכה וברכה כסדר יום הכפורים יצא.

7. Thus Wise retains the traditional text (a) in מתי תמלוך בציון in the Kedushah, where Szold reads (b) in מתי תמלוך על כל העולם ובא לציון גואל which Szold deletes, (c) in ותחזינה, where Szold reads ומביא גואל (d) in בא"י שאותך לבדך בירא נעבוד, where Szold reads ומביא גאולה (e) צור ישראל where Szold omits: ופדה כנאמך יהודה וישראל.

8. On the prayer book see the valuable studies of Rabbi Moshe Davis, notably his Hebrew paper "Benjamin Szold and Marcus Jastrow," in the *Sefer Hashanah Liyehude Amerika*, 5702 (1942), pp. 427–39, and the comparative tables which appear only in the offprints of this paper. See now his book *The Emergence of Conservative Judaism* (New York, 1963).

9. Cf. his paper, "The Syntax of the Sentence in Hebrew," *Journal of Biblical Literature* 64 (March 1945): 1–13. The quotations are on pp. 2 and 3.

10. I. Abrahams, *Permanent Values in Judaism*, pp. 14, 23.

11. In his Commentary on *Orah Ḥayyim* 46:4, where he cites the Talmud, Tur, and Asheri. On the entire subject, cf. the commentaries *Tikkun Tefillah* and *Anaf Yoseph* in *Otsar Hatefillot* (Vilna, 1928), pp. 123 f., and Israel Abrahams, *Companion to the Authorized Daily Prayerbook* (London, 1931), pp. xvi f.

12. Cf. A. B. Ehrlich, *Randglossen zur Hebräischen Bibel*, ad loc., and the writer's study, "Some Hitherto Unrecognized Meanings of the Verb *Shub*," *Journal of Biblical Literature* 52 (1933): 153–61. It may be added that the above rendering construes רבבות אלפי ישראל as an *accusative loci*. It is quite possible that the phrase is in apposition with the divine name and is an epithet for God, who is identified with the myriads of Israel. Cf. Elisha's designation of Elijah as אבי אבי רכב ישראל ופרשיו (II Kings 2:12). On this identification of God and people, cf. Krochmal's famous study of גוים ואלהיו in *Moreh Nebukhe Hazeman*, chap. 7.

NOTES FOR CHAPTER 16

1. The use of the term "rabbi" in the New Testament, which describes actors and events in the decade before the destruction of the Temple, is probably an anachronism, reflecting the period of the authors rather than of the figures in the Gospel narratives. Its usage in the New Testament is parallel to its later use in rabbinic 'iterature as an honorific term employed by a pupil in addressing his teacher (Matthew 26:25; Mark 9:15, 11:21, 14:45; and John 1:38, etc.).

2. Babylonian Talmud, *Berakhot* 28a.

3. Babylonian Talmud, *Berakhot* 35b.

4. Babylonian Talmud, *Berakhot* 17b, *Yoma* 35b, *Ketubbot* 105a, *Baba Batra* 22a.

5. Nehemiah 8:8, 13.

6. J. Freudenthal, *Die Flavius Josephus Beigelegte Schrift über die Herrschaft der Vernunft* (Breslau, 1869).

7. Op. cit. p. 7, n. 3.

8. I. Maybaum, *Jüdische Homiletik* (Berlin, 1890), p. 12.

9. Babylonian Talmud, *Baba Batra* 22a.

10. Babylonian Talmud, *Nedarim* 37a, *Bekhorot* 29a.

11. Mishnah, *Abot* 2:2, 4:10, 5:23.

12. A. A. Neuman, *The Jews in Spain* (Philadelphia, 1942), vol. 2, pp. 80, 84 f., 90, 99 f., who indicates that the authors of fully half his rabbinic sources were physicians. A vast amount of information on the functions of the medieval rabbi is to be found in S. W. Baron, *The Jewish Community,* 3 vols. (Philadelphia, 1942); see Index, vol. 3, pp. 510b–512b.

13. *Commentary on the Mishnah,* Abot 4:5.

14. Neuman, op. cit., vol. 2, p. 91.

15. Maybaum, op. cit., p. 13.

16. Cf. the excellent study of medieval preachers by Israel Bettan, *Studies in Jewish Preaching* (Cincinnati, 1940).

17. Neuman, op. cit., vol. 2, pp. 97 ff.

18. Deuteronomy 28:32.

19. On the categories of natural, compulsory, and voluntary community, first proposed by the author, see his *The Jew Faces a New World* (New York, 1941), pp. 3–31, and *Judaism for the Modern Age* (New York, 1955), pp. 3–29.

20. Maybaum, op. cit., p. 182.

21. Ibid., p. 177.

BIBLIOGRAPHY FOR FURTHER READING

NOTE: It is of the essence of Conservative Judaism that it does not and cannot isolate itself from society and religion in general and from all other creative movements in Judaism in particular.

Accordingly, the appended Bibliography contains four types of material: (a) books offering an over-all exposition of Conservative Judaism as a movement from varying points of view, (b) seminal works that have exerted an important influence on Conservative life and thought, though the authors may not have been formally identified with the movement, (c) treatments of specific areas of Jewish and human concern from a Conservative perspective, and (d) interpretations by Conservative scholars of the content and relevance of religion in general and of Judaism in particular, both as a worldview and as a way of life that inevitably reflect their authors' distinctive orientation.

Because there is no hard-and-fast demarcation among these frequently overlapping categories, all the titles are subsumed under a single rubric. Only books have been included.

ADLER, Cyrus, *I Have Considered the Days,* New York: Burning Bush Press, 1941.

AGUS, Jacob Bernard, *Guideposts in Modern Judaism: An Analysis of Current Trends in Jewish Thought*. New York: Bloch, 1954.

AHAD HA-AM. *Al Parashat Derakhim,* Four volumes, Berlin, 1930.

———. *Selected Essays,* tr. Leon Simon. Philadelphia: The Jewish Publication Society of America, 1912.

———. *Ten Essays on Zionism and Judaism,* tr. Leon Simon. London: G. Routledge and Sons, 1922.

ALTMANN, Alexander. *Studies in Nineteenth-Century Jewish Intellectual History*. Cambridge, Mass.: Harvard University Press, 1964.

ARONSON, David. *The Jewish Way of Life*. New York: The National Academy for Adult Jewish Studies, 1957.

———. *Torah: The Life of the Jew*. New York: The National Academy for Adult Jewish Studies, Jewish Tract Series, 1964.

221

ARZT, Max. *Justice and Mercy: Commentary on the Liturgy of the New Year and Day of Atonement.* New York: Burning Bush Press, 1963.

BENTWICH, Norman. *Solomon Schechter: A Biography.* New York: Burning Bush Press, 1964.

BERGER, Milton, Geffen, Joel S., Hoffman, M. David. *Roads to Jewish Survival.* New York: Bloch, 1907.

BLAU, Joseph L. *Judaism in America: From Curiosity to Third Faith.* Chicago: University of Chicago Press, 1976.

———. *Modern Varieties of Judaism.* New York: Columbia University Press, 1966.

BOKSER, Ben Zion. *Jewish Law: A Conservative Approach.* New York: Jewish Tract Series of the Burning Bush Press, 1964-75.

———. *Jews, Judaism and the State of Israel.* New York: Herzl Press, 1973.

———. *Judaism: Profile of a Faith.* New York: Alfred A. Knopf, 1963.

———. *Judaism and Modern Man: Essays in Jewish Theology.* New York: Philosophical Library, 1957.

COHEN, Boaz. *Law and Tradition in Judaism.* New York: The Jewish Theological Seminary of America, 1959.

DAVIS, Moshe. *The Emergence of Conservative Judaism: The Historical School in Nineteenth Century America.* Philadelphia: The Jewish Publication Society of America, 1963.

DORFF, Elliot. *Conservative Judaism: Our Ancestors to our Descendants.* New York: United Synagogue Youth, 1977.

DRESNER, Samuel H. *The Jew in American Life.* New York: Crown Publishers, 1963.

———. *The Jewish Dietary Laws: Their Meaning For Our Time.* New York: Burning Bush Press, 1966.

———. *The Sabbath.* New York: Burning Bush Press, 1970.

EPSTEIN, Louis M. *Lishe elat Ha agunah.* New York: 1940.

———. *Sex Laws and Customs in Judaism,* intro. by Ari Kiev. New York: KTAV, 1968.

———. *Toldot Ha-k'tuvah be-yisrael.* New York: 1954.

FELDMAN, David M. *Marital Relations, Birth Control and Abortion in Jewish Law.* New York: Schocken, 1968.

FINKELSTEIN, Louis, ed. *The Jews: Their History, Culture and Religion,* fourth edition. Three vols. New York: Schocken Books, 1970-1.

———. *The Pharisees: The Sociological Background of Their Faith.* Philadelphia: The Jewish Publication Society of America, 1962.

———. "Tradition in the Making," reprinted in Mordecai Waxman, ed., *Tradition and Change.* New York: The Burning Bush Press, 1959.

FRIEDLAENDER, Israel. *Past and Present.* New York: The Burning Bush Press, 1961.

GINZBERG, Louis . *On Jewish Law and Lore*. Philadelphia: The Jewish Publication Society of America, 1955.

———. *Students, Scholars and Saints*. Philadelphia: The Jewish Publication Society of America, 1928.

GOLDMAN, Solomon. *Crisis and Decision*. New York: Harper, 1938.

———. *A Rabbi Takes Stock*. New York: Harper, 1931.

GOLDSTEIN, Israel. *Toward a Solution*. New York: G. P. Putnam's Sons, 1940.

GORDIS, Robert. *Conservative Judaism: An American Philosophy*. New York: Behrman House, 1945.

———. *A Faith for Moderns*. New York: Bloch, 1960.

———. *Judaism for the Modern Age*. New York: Farrar, Straus and Cudahy, 1955.

———. *Judaism in a Christian World*. New York: McGraw Hill, 1966.

———. *Leave a Little to God: Essays in Judaism*. New York: Bloch, 1967.

———. *Love and Sex: A Modern Jewish Perspective*. New York: Farrar, Straus & Giroux, 1978.

GREENBERG, Simon. *The Ethical in the Jewish and American Heritage*. New York: The Jewish Theological Seminary of America, 1977.

———. *Foundations of a Faith*. New York: The Burning Bush Press, 1967.

HELLER, Abraham Mayer. *Jewish Survival*. New York: Behrman House, 1939.

HERBERG, Will. *Judaism and Modern Man*. Philadelphia: The Jewish Publication Society of America, 1951.

HESCHEL, Abraham Joshua. *God in Search of Man: A Philosophy of Judaism*. Philadelphia: The Jewish Publication Society of America, 1966.

———. *The Insecurity of Freedom*. Philadelphia: The Jewish Publication Society of America, 1966.

———. *Man Is Not Alone: A Philosophy of Religion*. New York: Farrar, Straus and Young, 1951.

———. *Man's Quest for God: Studies in Prayer and Symbolism*. New York: Charles Scribner's Sons, 1954.

———. *The Sabbath: Its Meaning for Modern Man*. New York: Farrar, Straus and Young, 1951.

———. *Torah Min Ha-shamayim Ba-Aspaklaria shel Ha-dorot*, 2 volumes. London: Soncino Press, 1962-5.

JACOBS, Louis. *A Jewish Theology*. New York: Behrman House, 1973.

———. *Principles of the Jewish Faith: An Analytical Study*. New York: Basic Books, 1964.

———. *We Have Reason To Believe*. London: Vallentine, Mitchell, 1962.

224   BIBLIOGRAPHY

JOSEPH, Morris. *Judaism as Creed and Life*, fifth ed. New York: Bloch, 1925.

KADUSHIN, Max. *The Rabbinic Mind*, third ed. New York: Bloch, 1972.

———. *Worship and Ethics*. New York: Bloch, 1963.

KAPLAN, Mordecai M. *The Future of the American Jew*. New York: Macmillan, 1948.

———. *The Greater Judaism in the Making: A Study of the Modern Evolution of Judaism*. New York: The Reconstructionist Press, 1960.

———. *Judaism as a Civilization: Toward A Reconstruction of American-Jewish Life*. New York: Schocken Books, 1967.

———. *Judaism Without Supernaturalism: The Only Alternative to Orthodoxy and Secularism*. New York: The Reconstructionist Press, 1958.

———. *The Meaning of God in Modern Jewish Religion*. New York: Behrman House, 1937.

KLEIN, Isaac. *A Guide to Jewish Religious Practice*. New York: The Jewish Theological Seminary of America, 1978.

———. *Responsa and Halakhic Studies*. New York: KTAV, 1975.

KOHN, Jacob. *Evolution as Revelation*. New York: Philosophical Library, 1963.

———. *The Moral Life of Man, Its Philosophical Foundations*. New York: Philosophical Library, 1956.

LEVINTHAL, Israel H. *Judaism—An Analysis and An Interpretation*. New York: Funk and Wagnalls, 1935.

———. *The Message of Israel*. New York: Lex Printing Co., 1923.

———. *Point of View: An Analysis of American Judaism*. New York: Abelard-Schumann, 1958.

NEUSNER, Jacob. *History and Torah*. New York: Philosophical Library, 1965.

———. *The Way of Torah: An Introduction to Judaism*. Belmont, California: Dickenson Pub. Co., 1970.

NOVAK, David. *Law and Theology in Judaism*. New York: KTAV, 1974.

———. *Law and Theology in Judaism*. Second Series. New York: KTAV, 1976.

PARZEN, Herbert. *Architects of Conservative Judaism*. New York: Jonathan-David, 1964.

RABINOWITZ, Saul Phineas. *Rabbi Zechariah Frankel*. Warsaw: 1898.

ROSENTHAL, Gilbert S. *Four Paths to One God: The Jew and His Religion*. New York: Bloch, 1973.

ROTENSTREICH, Nathan. *Tradition and Reality*. New York: Random House, 1972.

ROUTTENBERG, Max J. *Decades of Decision*. New York: Bloch, 1973.

———. *Seedtime and Harvest*. New York: Bloch, 1969.

RUBENOVITZ, Herman, and Mignon L. *The Waking Heart.* Cambridge, Mass.: Nathaniel Dame, 1967.

SCHECHTER, Solomon. *Aspects of Rabbinic Theology.* New York: Schocken Books, 1961.

———. *Seminary Addresses and Other Papers.* New York: Burning Bush Press, 1959.

———. *Studies in Judaism.* First Series. Philadelphia: The Jewish Publication Society of America, 1896.

———. *Studies in Judaism.* Second Series. Philadelphia: The Jewish Publication Society of America, 1908.

———. *Studies in Judaism: A Selection.* New York: Meridian Books, 1962.

SIEGEL, Seymour, with Elliot Gertel, eds. *Conservative Judaism and Jewish Law.* New York: The Rabbinical Assembly, 1977.

SIGAL, Phillip. *New Dimensions in Judaism: A Creative Analysis of Rabbinic Concepts.* New York: Exposition Press, 1972.

———. *The Emergence of Modern Judaism.* Pittsburgh: Pickwick Press, 197

SKLARE, Marshall. *Conservative Judaism: An American Religious Movement.* (New aug. ed.). New York: Schocken Books, 1972.

STEINBERG, Milton. *Anatomy of Faith,* ed. Arthur A. Cohen. New York: Harcourt, Brace, 1966.

———. *Basic Judaism.* New York: Harcourt, Brace, 1947.

———. *A Believing Jew: The Selected Writings of Milton Steinberg,* ed. Edith A. Steinberg. New York: Harcourt, Brace, 1951.

———. *The Making of the Modern Jew: From the Second Temple to the State of Israel.* New York: Behrman House, 1952.

———. *A Partisan Guide to the Jewish Problem.* Indianapolis and New York: Bobbs-Merrill, 1945.

WAXMAN, Mordecai, ed. *Tradition and Change.* New York: Burning Bush Press, 1949.

INDICES

INDEX OF NAMES AND SUBJECTS

'abodah, "religious worship," 146
Abrahams, Israel, 148, 219
'Aggadah, the 171-2, 178
Agudat Israel, 95, 116, 124
'Agunah, "chained wife," 86-87, 102
Agus, Jacob B., 3
Ahad Ha-am, 22, 97, 122; cultural Zionism of, 98-103
'Aharonim, 36
Akiba, Rabbi, 26-7, 37, 55, 60, 69, 79, 170
Aliya, settling in Israel, and effect upon the Diaspora, 99-100
Amateur spirit, and the Jewish community, 208-15
Ambrose, 171
Amos, 207, 208
Amoz, Dan Ben, and Netivah ben Yehudah, Millon Olami Ivri Medubberet, 103
Angels, 30
Anti-Semitism, 93, 97, 133, 178
Arab-Israeli relations, 92, 104-5, 110, 126
Arama, Isaac, 174
Arzt, Max, 140
Asheri, 150, 219
Atonement, Day of (Yom Kippur), 71

Ba'al Shem Tov, 108
Balfour Declaration, 118
Bamberger, Bernard, 67
Bar Mitzvah, 27, 182

Baron, Salo W., 6, 220
Beard in Jewish law, 34
Begin, Menahem, 125
Ben Azzai, 13
Ben-Gurion, David, 99
Berger, Peter, 204
Berlin, Meyer, 119
Bettan, Israel, 220
Bialik, Hayyim Nahman, 164, 209; and oneg Shabbat, 102
Bill of Rights, United States, 38
Bokser, Ben Zion, 3, 119
Brandeis, Louis D., 214
Buber, Martin, 100, 105

"Canaanites" (Israeli organization), 103
Cassuto, Moshe David, 101
"Catholic Israel," concept of, 45-47, 53-57, 61, 78-79, 80, 141
Chaim of Volozhin, 80
Chmielnicki massacres, 4
"Chosen people," concept of, 136, 143-145, 154
Christianity, 96, 144, 164, 168, 178, 206; Paulinian, 50; Protestantism, 156, 158, 204; Roman Catholicism, 156, 158, 162, 204; the "secular city," and, 196
Chrysostom, John, 171
Church and state, separation of, 128-130
Circumcision, 50

227

INDEX OF SOURCES

THE HEBREW BIBLE